T0246181

DIGITAL MADNESS

ALSO BY NICHOLAS KARDARAS, Ph.D.

Glow Kids: How Screen Addiction Is Hijacking Our Kids—And How to Break the Trance

How Plato and Pythagoras Can Save Your Life: The Ancient Greek Prescription for Health and Happiness

DIGITAL MADNESS

How Social Media Is Driving
Our Mental Health Crisis—and
How to Restore Our Sanity

NICHOLAS KARDARAS, Ph.D.

ST. MARTIN'S PRESS
NEW YORK

First published in the United States by St. Martin's Press, an imprint of St. Martin's Publishing Group

www.stmartins.com

The Library of Congress Cataloging-in-Publication Data is available upon request.

ISBN 978-1-250-27849-4 (hardcover)
ISBN 978-1-250-27850-0 (ebook)

Our books may be purchased in bulk for promotional, educational, or business use. Please contact your local bookseller or the Macmillan Corporate and Premium Sales Department at 1-800-221-7945, extension 5442, or by email at MacmillanSpecialMarkets@macmillan.com.

First Edition: 2022

10 9 8 7 6 5 4 3 2 1

To the memory of my mother and father,
and to the life to still live with my wife, Luz,
and my sons, Ari and Alexi

CONTENTS

It is no measure of health to be well adjusted to a profoundly sick society.

—Krishnamurti

Introduction

It was the Before Times: late July 2019.

Just a few short months before the COVID pandemic would hit New York like a viral nuclear bomb in early 2020, I was talking to my father at his kitchen table in Woodside, Queens. He was dying from cancer, slowly and quite painfully; he only had a couple of months left and wouldn't live to see what COVID would soon do to our world during the most surreal of years.

Yet he was prescient about some of our troubling and toxic societal dynamics that COVID only helped to amplify. My dying Greek father, being of a different time and place, had an intuitive sense that something was profoundly wrong with the way that we lived.

During those last couple of months of his life, I would fly to New York every week from my home in Austin where I ran a mental health clinic, as we both did our best to savor our final times together. Once strong and proud, now that the cancer had spread to his bones, he was reduced to catheters and a wheelchair, where every movement—no matter how slight—led to a sharp grimace and a low moan of pain.

As a teenage boy, he'd survived the Nazis invading his village in northern Greece; lived through the bloodshed of a communist civil war; survived a transatlantic migration by sea to the Washington Heights section of New York during the 1960s; survived working three jobs, seven days a week, for decades to support his family and put my brother and me through college in the hopes that we'd have a better life. But he couldn't survive the onslaught of a relentless cancer.

It was heartbreaking to see his deterioration. Yet while every organ system in his body was rapidly beginning to fail him, at eighty-eight, his mind remained razor sharp—maybe too sharp—as he would often surprise me with his insights and clarity about things. We would talk politics, current events, scientific advancements, feuding relatives . . . anything, really.

In a world of Kardashian-esque frivolity and inane tweets, he was from an earlier time where people said what was on their minds and didn't mince their words; there was a clarity to his thinking, a moral and intellectual certitude uncluttered by the fads of the day.

But he had begun to feel like an anachronism, like a stranger in an increasingly strange land. As we would sit and talk about things that excited me in the rapidly changing world around us—everything from AI to social media and the evolving nature of identity—he would smile his knowing smile and say, "Ah, Niko . . . I'm glad I'm not going to live long enough to see the world that you describe."

He didn't understand a world dependent on technology—one where people didn't look each other in the eye, where they were stuck in front of a screen for hours on end and felt lost and empty. He hated what he saw as our tech obsession. A devoted lifelong gardener who also loved to cook for everyone as an expression of his love, he'd chide me as I kept checking my phone for work messages during my visits: "Niko, stop looking at that stupid thing and be *here* if you're going to be here." He had never heard the much-hyped word *mindfulness*; he had never read *Be Here Now* by Ram Dass . . . but he got it. Better than most.

He'd laugh when I'd tell him that parts of Greece were "Blue Zones," known for longevity; that maybe he would defy the doctors and have many more years left to live, like his father, who lived well into his nineties. "Niko, I don't know about Blue or Red Zones; I know I live *here* now. But I also know that we lived a simpler life then. A more human life. All this nonsense today . . . it's not the way people are supposed to live."

He had grown up in a tiny and remote mountain village in northern

Greece during the 1930s and '40s. There was no electricity, no indoor running water. It was a cold and spartan existence. Yet he would talk about his childhood (at least before the Nazi invasion) as a special time of peace, joy, and a profound love of nature. The trees he planted in his village as a boy still stand today as towering living examples of his symbiotic relationship with the natural world: he nurtured nature, and nature nurtured him. People did work hard, but there was a purposeful pace, not the frenetic and chaotic cacophony of modern city living. And the values were different; genuine relationships were more important than things like money or the right car.

I began to wonder—yes, while we often tend to idealize life in the past—if maybe there was some merit to what he said. After all, for the past decade, as both an author and a psychologist, I had written about the impacts of the modern age on our deteriorating mental health and run clinics around the country treating all manner of psychiatric and addictive distress—issues that only seemed to be getting worse.

And I had spent the last few years trying to better understand a simple conundrum: Why is our mental health deteriorating as we become a more technologically advanced society? After my dad died, I began to realize that his life may hold many of the answers to the "modern" problems I was trying to better understand: why we're so sick and getting sicker.

And make no mistake, we've become a very, very sick society.

While we lose ourselves in the digital masturbation of *Candy Crush*, Instagram, and YouTube kitty videos, we're dying in record numbers: more than two hundred thousand people, mostly young adults, died in the United States in 2019—*before* COVID—from psychologically driven "deaths of despair" (suicide, overdose, and alcoholism). Add the record rates of loneliness, anxiety, depression, extremism, political unrest, and mass shootings and you have the telltale signs of a society on the brink.

Post-COVID, those numbers and volatile dynamics have only gotten much worse.

What's happening?

The answer is that humans simply aren't genetically designed for technologically driven twenty-first-century living; we aren't meant to be sedentary, screen-staring, atomized, and meaning-devoid beings. The unfortunate reality is that modern life is antithetical to our hunter-gatherer psychological needs; we're hardwired for face-to-face community, genetically designed to be physically active, and psychologically primed to seek meaning.

But the digital age is kryptonite to those sanity-sustaining needs. We're all living in a world gone mad, driven insane by a digital rat race of overworked, under-slept, cubicle-confined, sensory-overloaded, lonely, meaning-devoid, overstressed people who are perpetually turned "on" and plugged in, yet never really allowed to recharge and be fully human.

And all of this doesn't include the digital holy grail of the metaverse that Mark Zuckerberg has said he wants us all to inhabit. His vision of our future is an "embodied internet," a holographic and augmented immersive "shared reality" in a virtual universe where we'd all live our lives. I guess Zuckerberg somehow missed *The Matrix* in film class . . . but more about Zuckerberg's metaverse later.

The problem is that *none* of this—none of it—is the way that humans were evolutionarily designed to live. And as our tech has outpaced our biology, it's literally driving us insane as we've become mad for our devices—even as our devices are driving us mad. Hooked and seduced by our wonderful tech, we've become psychologically *and* physically ill.

The surreal pandemic has only fanned the flames of our total tech immersion. Big Tech embraced the old maxim "Never let a crisis go to waste" as our new socially distanced reality *necessitated* a turbocharged dependence on digital connection—even though we long ago crossed the Rubicon of too much screen time and an unhealthy overreliance on tech.

The new COVID-normal was remote school, remote work, remote friends, and remote *lives*. Bye-bye to barbecues, in-person classrooms, handshakes, shopping malls, and life as we knew it. Hello to a hermetic new existence consisting of a veritable home multiplex of ubiquitous screens as we binge-watched Netflix, feasted on Facebook, Zoomed with Grandma, and were spoon-fed by Amazon—all as we felt increasingly more alone, empty, isolated, and depressed.

When I wrote *Glow Kids* in 2016, it was a pioneering work about tech *addiction*. At that time, the idea that digital devices were not only habit-forming—what I called "digital heroin"—was extremely controversial. Many in the media at the time pushed back, "Really? A digital drug?" I was asked on CNN, NPR, FOX, and *GMA*. But *Glow Kids* struck a nerve, and my "Digital Heroin" *New York Post* op-ed went viral with over seven million views, the most widely read article from that newspaper in 2016.

Fast-forward to today: it is now well accepted both in the clinical community and in the general population that screens *can* be habit-forming and are potentially harmful for our mental health, as ample research shows that they can increase depression, anxiety, ADHD, and thoughts of self-harm. And documentaries like *The Social Dilemma* show former tech execs that lay out their *addiction-by-design* playbook.

Internal emails showed that there was a discussion at Facebook about modifying their harmful algorithm, but that was firmly rejected by the decision-makers. The company's response to the data indicating that their product was killing teens? Cost of doing business. According to former Facebook staffer and whistleblower Frances Haugen's testimony before Congress, it was deemed not good for the bottom line to change the toxic algorithm because that was driving engagement—despite the fact that it also happened to increase self-loathing and suicidality. Facebook was apparently willing to accept that some teenage girls may have to die and be collateral damage in the quest for obscene profitability.

These internal Facebook documents were the equivalent to the smoking gun back in the day of Big Tobacco, where it was shown that cigarette manufacturers knew their products were carcinogenic—but chose to market Joe Camel to kids *anyway.* Indeed, during Haugen's Senate testimony, Connecticut senator Richard Blumenthal said that "Facebook and Big Tech are facing a Big Tobacco moment, a moment of reckoning."

It was a similar smoking gun and reckoning that Big Pharma and Purdue Pharmaceuticals faced. Their own internal emails showed they also knew that their ostensibly harmless painkiller, OxyContin, was highly addictive, even though they publicly denied its addictive potential—and from that original sin, an opioid epidemic that would kill tens of thousands was spawned.

Today, we know what some had long suspected about Big Tech: Yes, we had known that their products and platforms were *designed* to be addicting in order to increase engagement and, thus, profitability; but now we have proof that the toxic mental health effects that *resulted* from that intentional addiction to their products was a known—and *acceptable*—harm.

Indeed, research shows that the empty, sedentary, addicting, isolating, and self-loathing lifestyle created by Big Tech drives depression and hopelessness. Yet the more depressed and empty we feel, the more we're driven to escape those feelings with more of the digital drug that's driving the problem to begin with—a classic addiction catch-22. Round and round we go as Big Tech pockets the change every time we take a spin around our digital escapism.

How do we fix this mess? As I'll discuss in the book, the answer may not be as simple as a repeal of Section 230 of the Communications Decency Act, which grants Big Tech liability immunity for their content, or of antitrust legislation to break up Big Tech. Although both antitrust legislation and a repeal of Section 230 inevitably need to happen, they won't entirely solve our Big Tech problem and the social media toxin they emit. Nor may it be as simple as more governmental regulation and oversight. As many legal scholars have pointed out, that could lead to First Amendment issues and the equivalent of content censorship. And if that were the case, who would get to decide which content is problematic or "disinformation"? Mark Zuckerberg? Jack Dorsey? Elon Musk? The problems presented are complex and without any easy solutions.

Yet there is a simple antidote to combat what many consider is an onslaught of misinformation and its cousin—disinformation: the sword of critical thinking. The media and our politicians seem to be focusing all of their energies and efforts on the supply side of the misinformation equation (i.e., hysterical rants about the toxic effects of inaccurate or misleading news and information), yet very little attention gets paid to the demand side; that is, the viewer/listener/reader's ability to discern what may or may not be problematic content.

If people could use reason and critical thinking, they would be immunized from the never-ending flow of information—misinformation or otherwise. The person imbued with the powers of rational thought would be able to discern the factual from the fantastical. Unfortunately, the larger issue is that logic and critical thinking were either never taught to kids in school, or if they were, people's ability to think analytically and critically has melted away like spring snow under a constant social media torrent.

One of my guilty pleasures as a younger man who suffered from insomnia was to listen to Art Bell's syndicated overnight radio show. Art Bell had a wonderful and soothing radio voice along with an inquisitive mind and would have the most diverse range of guests imaginable; one night you might hear physicist Brian Greene discussing string theory, and the next you may have a time-traveling Big Foot hunter. Needless to say, some shows were highly informative, yet others were entertaining nonsense. But Art Bell trusted that the listener had the ability to decide, and so no one was ever censored or barred from his show.

Today, as debates rage about content censorship and misinformation, I think it's important to remember that—and to focus more on helping people to reclaim their innate abilities to use reason and to critically think. There's an old adage that a person can only change the things that are under their control—themselves. Thus part of the solution to the Big Tech/social media problem that I discuss later in the book is an embrace of classical thought in order to optimally fortify our individual ability to think clearly and analytically as we wade through murky digital water during turbulent times.

That is not to imply that there aren't regulatory and legislative initiatives that need to occur to stop Big Tech from *knowingly* harming their users. As mentioned, we need to address Big Tech and the corrosive social media that is driving our mental health crisis—not just by the abovementioned tech addiction and the empty depression that accompanies it, but also because their platforms are *compromising* our ability to think clearly.

The constant immersion in polarizing social media platforms has changed the architecture of our brains and the way that we process information in a way that's inherently pathological and unhealthy and undermines any potential for rational thinking. Indeed, as social media has swallowed up our world, we've developed a type of societal binary black-and-white thinking—which is the opposite of nuanced critical thinking; after all, it's hard to find nuance in 144 characters or in never-ending polarization echo chambers.

Unfortunately, not only has this polarizing binary thinking accelerated our current cultural clash and political divide, but Twitter, Facebook, Instagram, and now TikTok have had profound *clinical* implications as binary thinkers who can't see shades of gray are more reactive, less resilient, and primed toward increased impulsivity and fragility—all of which are ingredients and symptoms of a number of mental health disorders.

Facebook itself was born as a binary choice of "Hot or Not"—now it's "Like" or "Unlike," as these binary choices and other forms of extreme polarizing content are inextricably embedded into the platform's genome. In fact, in what's been called an "*extremification* loop," *all* social media platforms act as self-reinforcing sorting mechanisms that are binary in nature, sending algorithmically fueled, increasingly intensified content to the user, designed to excite the primal lizard brain based on perceived preferences. Lean left, and the algorithm-fueled echo chamber feeds the user ever-increasing left-leaning content. Lean right, and the same thing happens in the opposite direction, thus widening and deepening the polarity chasm.

This programming *prime directive* of the social media organism has evolved into the ultimate confirmation bias system, amplifying and inflaming an individual's already existing beliefs in pursuit of greater user engagement or "stickiness." Because at the end of the day, that's how all social media platforms are monetized. The unfortunate reality, however, is that this binary *extremification* loop acts as a mental health toxin for many of its users.

Shortly after I wrote *Glow Kids,* I started seeing some of these toxic mental health effects firsthand; in my mental health clinics, I noticed more and more young clients who saw things in absolutes and were unable to cope with the daily stressors of life. Many seemed highly reactive, angry, lonely, empty, lacking a core identity, easily manipulated, confused, suffered from a poor self-image, were depressed, self-medicating, and generally had difficulty thriving.

The common denominator was that almost all saw things in black or white. Indeed, I was seeing more and more young adult patients being referred who were struggling with more problematic *personality* disorders—a type of mental disorder featuring a rigid and unhealthy pattern of thinking, functioning, and behaving. And beyond my clinics' clients, in our society at large, I saw a significant increase in polarization, at a level that I had never seen before.

It seemed to reflect what Marshall McLuhan had famously said in the 1960s: "The medium is the message"; now, the medium (digital, binary, social media) is not only the message, it also *shapes* the brains of people receiving the message into limited and binary *dichotomous thinking* that lacks the breadth and complexity of what's known as *spectrum thinking*. And, unfortunately, this black-and-white dichotomous thinking also happens to be the diagnostic hallmark of borderline personality disorder, or BPD.

Where will this lead? It's unclear, but the prognosis for anyone—or any society—struggling with BPD without any intervention is extremely poor. COVID only made things worse. Like kerosene on an already raging fire, all the quarantines, social distancing, and virtual life led to a doubling of screen time and a tripling of depression, along with record spikes in overdoses and suicides.

My father was right—this was not the way that human beings were meant to live.

This high-tech, screen-staring modern lifestyle and its pronounced lack of physical movement isn't just toxic for our mental health but also directly leads to our record rates of cancer, heart disease, obesity, and diabetes—all the telltale signs of an unhealthy and sedentary society in distress. Sure, we may have some snazzy electronics and oh-so-smart devices, but, to paraphrase Al Pacino in *Dog Day Afternoon,* "We're dying here!"

Physically. Mentally. Emotionally. We're shot.

The sad reality is that most of us are too digitally sedated or distracted—dare I say *addicted*?—to notice our mental and physical deterioration. To paraphrase Pink Floyd, we're all too *comfortably numb* to know—or to care—and we're not even in the metaverse yet!

Who's curating and controlling this modern nightmare? Forget the bankers, the politicians, and the industrialists; the real power in the twenty-first century rests with a handful of tech billionaires. It was indeed the meek—with slide rules—who inherited the earth, tech geeks who would grow up to become megalomaniacs with names like Bezos, Gates, and Zuckerberg. This New Technocracy spawned from Big Tech not only rule the world but also data mine our lives and control what we see, how we think, how we vote, how we live—and even how we die.

Is their agenda simply greed or something more? As I researched this book, I discovered clues about what may be motivating the Big Tech oligarchs. Beyond the pedestrian hunger for greed and power, I discovered that they may have another more *interesting* motivation—one befitting the most powerful people who have ever lived on the face of the earth and who have developed grandiose God complexes . . . More about that later in the book.

Regardless of motivation, we've learned the Big Tech playbook from high-level defectors like Google's Tristan Harris and Facebook's Chamath Palihapitiya (among many others): create algorithmically fueled, habit-forming platforms and gadgets to maintain engagement and drive profit. Use the most lizard brain–activating content (political outrage, violent games) to maximize this engagement and create habituation. Then, as Harvard's Shoshana Zuboff explains, data mine and create a monetized "surveillance economy." Rinse and repeat.

Beyond the addicting and negative mental health effects, there's another troubling dynamic: depending on the whims of the Big Tech oligarchs, people's behavior can be algorithmically shaped to do more than just create more product engagement; algorithms can create a content-driven groupthink effect that can skew people's behavior, including their voting habits, their ideologies, as well as their perception of what may or may not be considered normative and nonnormative behavior.

In effect, our tech addiction—which leads to compromised mental health—can then also lead to digital brainwashing and behavior modification. Unlike prior dictatorships that were *only* able to physically imprison people or compel conformity out of fear, now, for the first time in human history, a handful of people can control our *thoughts*—once thought to be the hallowed ground of a free society. Even during the worst days of totalitarian oppression—from the gulags to concentration camps—tyrants could break the body, but the prisoner could remain free in their mind. Not so today. Today, the mind *is* the battleground—and Big Tech wants complete control.

And here's another news flash: not only have we become trapped in addicting and brainwashing digital cages, but in true Stockholm syndrome fashion, we've fallen in love with our captivity and with the captors who created the cage.

Welcome to the machine. Or the Matrix. Or Plato's cave. Or the digital dream. Whatever you choose to call it, like the roach motel—once you go in, you can never get out.

Or can you?

I've found that, yes, there is a way out of the Matrix, and, like Neo, there is a red pill that we can take to regain our individual and collective sanity in this modern digital madness.

The solution?

The cure to our modern high-tech lives rests firmly in the past. In fact, the antidote to the modern is ancient—as in *really* old-school. As I'll explain in the book, we have an ancient blueprint for healthy living with enhanced mental well-being and clarity that can help us get back into a healthier, saner, and more balanced realignment; we can once again reclaim our humanity and live in the way that people were genetically designed and evolved to live.

The harsh reality is that we're out of balance as a species. Technology can be a wonderful tool, but as Thoreau once said, "We've become the tools of our tools." To that, I would also add: today, not only are we the tools of our tools, we've also become the *broken* tools of the people who make our tools.

No longer. It's time to wake up from the dream-as-nightmare . . . it's time to break free from our honey-soaked digital cages and once again live as fully engaged and embodied humans.

We need that ancient cure *now* more than ever.

PART I

A WORLD GONE MAD

1

Addicted to the Matrix

A Butterfly Dreaming . . .

It was a picture of a cow.

Yes, a picture can be worth a thousand words—but this picture was so bizarre, so immediately jarring to the senses that all that I could think was that something had gone terribly, terribly wrong. Because this wasn't just a picture of any old cow—it was a picture of a cow wearing a virtual reality headset.

Real cow. Virtual headset. Reality optional.

Like a Salvador Dalí clock, at once familiar yet strangely disconcerting, it was science fiction meets the surreal in one singular image that made it clear that we're all in for a bumpy ride and we had better strap in—and that we also had better wake up *quickly*.

I had this cow-induced realization on a rainy and overcast afternoon in San Francisco on December 3, 2019. My father had just died a couple of months earlier, so the typical Bay Area weather reflected my mood as well. I'd been invited to be a presenter at the prestigious Commonwealth Club, a venerable and staid institution that's the oldest public affairs forum in the entire United States. It's hosted a variety of innovative thinkers and world leaders who make our world go round; it was where FDR delivered his iconic New Deal speech, and President Eisenhower, Soviet premier Nikita Khrushchev, Hillary Clinton, Al Gore, and several Nobel Prize winners have all graced its stage.

Rain or not, it's a special place to speak.

As a psychologist, professor, and author who explores how new technology is impacting our species, I'd been asked to make a presentation and then participate on a panel that was ominously titled: "Humanity at a Crossroads: New Insights into Technology's Risks for Humans and the Planet."

The topic was right up my alley.

I was still mourning my dad's death, but the event was too important and had been planned months in advance with speakers coming from around the world; so, after much thought, I decided not to cancel. In fact, I thought it might be a good way to honor my father's memory and make him proud.

The auditorium was standing room only as the panel of scientists and experts discussed all manner of impending doom and gloom; the common theme was human and planetary destruction by our own tech-intoxicated hand as the esteemed panel presented frightening research about 5G and cancer effects, discussions of sentient and nefarious AI, and neurological and clinical disorders as a by-product of our obsession with our shiny little gadgets.

It was admittedly all rather depressing fare—until the slide of that surreal cow popped up on the huge screen behind the stage. People in the audience initially chuckled at the absurd image, then became quiet as the more ominous implications of that picture settled in. According to the presenter, a respected scientist from the Netherlands, VR-living cows tricked into believing that they're in a better, greener pasture will produce more milk.

Forget Happy Wife, Happy Life—this was the more readily and synthetically achievable Happy Cow, More Milk. That reality-challenged bovine was in the Matrix—and, like Neo, had absolutely no idea quite how illusory its world was. The sense of unease that everybody in the auditorium began to feel was the realization that if we're beginning to put cows in VR headsets to trick them into believing that an illusion is real, then what—or who—would be next?

Worse yet, like glitching software, there are clues that we're already living in a digitally curated and contrived illusion; one that distorts our identities, our perceptions, our politics, our values, our sense of freedom and, indeed, our very existence.

At the time of this writing, as I had just completed writing about our virtual reality bovine friends, Mark Zuckerberg announced the rebranding of Facebook as Meta and his new metaverse vision for our not-so-Brave New World. As I'll describe more in part 2, the cows in VR glasses that I was using as a metaphor for our high-tech illusory world may not be metaphorical after all. If Zuckerberg gets his way and implements his new Grand Plan for a Meta-world, we'll all be wearing VR glasses and inhabiting a "spatial internet" and illusory virtual "shared reality" world—that he would control.[1]

According to his confidants, Zuckerberg is going all in on his new messianic vision for how we should all live—and how he'll curate that new reality for us. But surely enough people have seen science fiction, haven't they? We can't go quietly into the digital night—can we? Futurists and science fiction writers have long prophesized about the darker aspects of a tech-driven future; from Orwell to Aldous Huxley; from H. G. Wells to Robert Heinlein; and yes, in films like *The Matrix, The Terminator,* and *2001: A Space Odyssey,* all warned of potential future tech-induced dystopias . . . of enslaved humans . . . of sentient machines taking over.

Obviously, we've enjoyed amazing benefits as a result of our technological advances and have seen life drastically transformed over the last one hundred years. But wonderful innovations have always come at a price: morphine helped wounded soldiers, but led to an addiction epidemic; we discovered the mysteries of the atom, which led to abundant energy—and destructive nuclear bombs; even the original discovery of fire, which allowed early humans to survive, has also led to significant destruction.

It's what some theorists call the *promise* and the *peril* conundrum and the foundation of what scientists call the *Precautionary Principle*[2]—namely, if some scientists think a particular action or invention may be too risky or profoundly negative, then it's best not to proceed. Unfortunately, this principle is seldom applied. And, sure enough, if we look closely, many of the ideas and themes that futurists and science fiction writers have envisioned have, in some form or another, morphed from the page or the screen into our everyday realities—along with some of the *peril* of unintended consequences:

Fantastic smartphones that allow us to communicate with anyone on the planet and access unlimited information at our fingertips (but that are addicting and never allow us to truly be "unplugged"); completely automated factories (that render human workers obsolete);[3] driverless cars (that can glitch or be hacked);[4] globally connecting interactive social media (that are perpetually tracking us and data mining our lives while amplifying agenda-driven narratives);[5] human-sounding AI-powered "smart" home assistants designed to serve us and predict our needs (while also eavesdropping on us and enabling our physical and mental deterioration);[6] advancements in the sciences and medicine that have cured horrible diseases that have long-haunted humanity (while also *creating* strange new viruses, diseases, biohazards, and potential planetary destruction as the by-products of ethically questionable and reckless research).[7]

Some might say, "Hey, okay, some bad with the good—a necessary trade-off. We'll take it," because, after all, hasn't life in the Big Tech–driven twenty-first century just gotten so much easier? Smart homes that simplify our lives, and smartphones that keep us all nicely connected and informed. "These are good things," most people might say. "I like my iPhone, Alexa, and Netflix on demand . . . what's the problem?"

Alexa, music on, please—and two cubes of ice in the martini!

Indeed, many feel that we are living in a seemingly magical age of ease and comfort; certainly none of us has had to stare down the existential threat of AI in the form of a guns-blazing, humanity-destroying, "I'll be back"–spewing Arnold Schwarzenegger Terminator. So the feeling has been, "Hey, let's all lighten up and enjoy our new tech-massaged reality; let's all enjoy the tasty digital sausage without worrying so much about how it's made—or who's making it and why."

Then the pandemic of 2020 hit. What had felt like a world that had been made easier by our tech (albeit with some very clear red flags), now began to feel like a world where our lives had become more and more *dependent* on it. Like the two-martini-for-lunch drinker who now needed a fifth of vodka to get through the day and not get the shakes, our tolerance—and need—for our tech has skyrocketed.[8]

Like any addiction, we needed it . . . we needed it *real* bad.

The tech fix was in, and the screen habit sure became hard to break.

By some estimates, screen time doubled during the pandemic—as, not so coincidentally, depression rates tripled. The bold headline of a March 21, 2020, *New York Times* article written by formerly tech cautious writer Nellie Bowles declared: CORONAVIRUS ENDED THE SCREEN-TIME DEBATE. SCREENS WON.

She writes wistfully that before coronavirus, she used to worry about too much screen time and would try various "digital detoxes," but she'd invariably fall off the wagon and wind up "back on that smooth glowing glass." Now in the age of quarantines and social distancing, she's surrendered to the seemingly inevitable: "I have thrown off the shackles of screen time guilt. My television is on. My computer is open. My phone is unlocked, glittering. I want to be covered in screens. If I had a virtual reality headset nearby, I would strap it on."

Game. Set. Match. Screens win.

But if the screens have won, who's lost?

We have.

We've all rolled snake eyes (apologies for mixing tennis and dice metaphors). Well, at least most of our species has lost; a select few are obscenely winning by rigging the game as they run the equivalent of digital casinos; highly manipulative, desperate, and unnatural places where we've become trapped by habit-forming dopamine-spiking digital feel-goods as we spiral down the rabbit hole of *Tiger King* marathons, Reddit benders, social media triviality, and video game hate-my-real-life escapism.

In addition to our addiction, I also began to suspect that we were developing a tech-induced mass delusion, like the cows in the VR headsets; that we were all slipping too comfortably into the warm bath of a seductive digital dream. As we slipped further into that dream, we were becoming even weaker, sicker, more tech-dependent—and evermore vulnerable for further tech dependence.

To be sure, things weren't so hot for the human race pre-pandemic; sure, we had some material wealth, but we were depressed, obese, lonely, overdosing, addicted, committing suicide, getting cancer and heart disease at record levels. Post-pandemic, those numbers only got much worse.[9] As I've mentioned, the sad truth is that our hunter-gatherer genetics simply weren't designed for tech-driven, twenty-first-century living; we're not meant to be sedentary, screen-staring, atomized, and meaning-devoid beings stuck indoors and enslaved by our dependence to tech.

That's why as technology has progressed, humanity has regressed. Unlike the old Virginia Slims ad, we've *not* come a long way, baby! We're plugged in and tuned out; self-absorbed rather than self-reflective; bright-screened and dull-eyed; high-tech yet in poor health—and it's been our technology and our technologically driven lifestyles that are driving us crazy and making us weaker, sicker, and ultimately killing us.

But many of us are oblivious.

The Oblivious Frog

We might better understand this obliviousness to our own self-destruction by way of the old frog parable. Perhaps you know the story?

A frog sits in a pot of warm water.

Slowly, ever so slowly, the temperature gets warmer.

The frog doesn't move.

Eventually, the flame gets stronger and the water gets so hot that it reaches a boil. The frog still doesn't move. Lulled by the gradual progression, the frog dies as it's boiled alive and never makes an effort to save itself. Yet if a frog is tossed into water that's already boiling, it invariably jumps out to preserve its life.

Disclaimer: no actual frogs were hurt in the retelling of this popular story. And while the veracity of this parable has been hotly—no pun intended—debated, it remains a great metaphor for people's inability—or unwillingness—to perceive danger if it happens gradually.

In our digital age, things have gotten warmer very fast, as in the blink of an evolutionary eye we've gone from cave drawings to Instagram. But if things have reached a boil so quickly, then why haven't we jumped out of the water? Why are we allowing ourselves to be boiled alive—especially since we now better understand that we are getting *harmed* by our tech obsession?

Well, things did initially warm up gradually—almost three million years ago, we created primitive tools;[10] then the discovery of fire around one million years ago;[11] and the formation of tribes and what we call "civilization" . . . some farming advances . . . wars interspersed—we can't forget those. Millennia passed, and we still were essentially the same species: tribal, hunter-gatherer-turned-agricultural, and warlike. Then bang! The Industrial Revolution . . . and in the blink of an eye . . . computers, the information age—and Twitter.

In that sense, the water would seem to have been cold, cold, cold—then boiling hot! While it took eons to go from cave drawings to 144 characters, it was that last bit of human development—from the steam engine to the search engine—that was breathtaking in its rapidity.

Indeed, the world underwent a seismic shift with the advent of the first personal computer (the Altair) in 1974, to the first commercially successful PC in 1984 (Apple's Macintosh), to Steve Jobs's game-changing iPhone in 2007 and iPad in 2010.

For most people born after the year 2000, a highly digitized world is just the norm—there's no point of reference of life before PCs and smartphones. For these digital natives, like the fish that doesn't even realize that there's such a thing as water because that's what they were born in and the only thing that they've ever known, most younger millennials and Gen Zers just take our tech immersion for granted.

And for the over-thirty crowd (guilty as charged), well, even though our screen-based tech world may have been extremely rapid by evolutionary standards, by our own individual *personal* perception across our own life spans, the total self-destructive immersion into our technological screen orgy all happened rather gradually over the course of several decades.

I'll use my own life as an example (I'm fifty-seven at the time of this writing . . . cusp baby boomer and Gen Xer). In my lifetime, the screen and tech evolution looked like this: A rather enormous furniture-like color TV that was all wood paneling and a small and resolution-challenged screen that was the anchor of our living room in Queens,

New York, in the 1970s. As it aged, it required pliers to change the channels to enjoy its limited bounty of five stations.

That monolithic and gargantuan TV gave way to a sleeker Sony Trinitron in the '80s. Life and screens stayed pretty steady for the next twenty years or so; my writing was limited to an *electronic typewriter* in high school; that eventually gave way to something called a word processor in college. In my twenties, a rather clunky personal computer came into existence. I abstained, but my nerdier friends from Bronx Science and Cornell got one. Around this same time, a local rich kid got a large and bulky mobile telephone that didn't seem very mobile.

Ten years passed . . . gradual warming of the water . . . then my buddy got a cellular flip phone—it looked straight out of my favorite TV show as a kid—*Star Trek*. TVs went on a diet and got gradually slimmer . . . and slimmer. Until one became flat! And right around that time, my friend got something called an iPhone that was able to connect to the internet . . . It was crazy!

Eventually, I joined the party in my late thirties and got a smartphone and became really smitten with the way that I was able to hold in my hand a portal to all of the accumulated information on the planet. Forget the Library of Alexandria—I had a Samsung Galaxy!

I was in love.

But a funny thing happened on my way to my tech love affair. As my TV became flatter, my belly became, well, fatter. And I started getting attached to my little gadget. Like, really attached. My sleep suffered, my attention span waned, and my mood became increasingly sullen. They say smartphones make dumber people; for me, it seemed like my bright phone made me a darker and more depressed person.

As I seemed to move backward, my phone marched onward with ever-evolving iterations. Who could keep up with the little dickens? Answer: no one. Tech is designed to increasingly tickle our dopamine and leave us hungry for more—always more. And what we are primed to crave are the latest and greatest versions of our gadgets that we're promised will lead us to even higher highs of orgasmic digital ecstasy.

But like any addiction, there's never enough. That's the second reason why people aren't mad as hell and screaming, "We aren't going to take this any longer!"; it has to do with simple addiction dynamics. To wit, why doesn't any addict scream and complain about the alcohol industry or the tobacco industry or Big Pharma—or their local drug dealer? Answer: because they *need* them.

If nothing else, the digital age is all about addiction and our *need* for our now indispensable devices—made indispensable by algorithm-fueled platforms designed to increase "engagement" (a marketing term for creating a digital habit—a fix, by any other name) and dopamine-spiking rewards ("Yes! They 'liked' my photo!"). Forget two-for-one happy hour specials, this is marketing on a whole other level; sophisticated behavior modification developed by brilliant people and their even smarter AI-driven systems. The average person—much less a kid—doesn't stand a chance.

And all that information! The mind can only handle so much. Is it any wonder that we're going insane from the continuous and never-ending tweeting, beeping, flashing, and scrolling hyperlinks, YouTubes, texts, Instagrams, and news feeds?

The term *information overload* doesn't do it justice.

There are times that I've stared and stared at my computer screen, brain-numbed by all the blurry images and information, where I've wanted to scream out to the heavens, "Can I just have an hour to stare at a freaking tree and admire its leaves and branches . . . and the beautiful bluebird that just landed on it? Can I please, O all-knowing Algorithm God, who art in Sergey Brin's brain, can I please, *pretty please,* just have my life back?"

You know, the *real* one?

But the screen just keeps seductively staring back at me, omnisciently feeding me addicting content it thinks I want. Like most people in twenty-first-century America, I feel trapped, a prisoner of my own devices, leaving me to ask the question: who's the warden controlling our new virtual imprisonment?

The New Technocracy

We all know who they are; they're the small handful of billionaires that are the Lords of Technology . . . megalomaniacs with names like Bezos, Gates, Jobs, and Zuckerberg.

This New Technocracy not only rule the world (and if that weren't enough, are now competing with each other to conquer space), they're also data mining our lives as they control what we see, how we live, how we think, how we vote. For our Digital Overlords, we're just so much data for their algorithms and consumers for their multitude of products and platforms. Correction: as many tech industry defectors have suggested, it is *we* who are the product that they're monetizing—our data; our attention; our behavior. The devices aren't the product—they're just the bait that they use to catch us (and our data) with.[12]

This handful of once-idealistic, brilliant, but ego-driven tech geeks would grow up to become the masters of our universe; the kids who were tinkering with circuit boards in their garages would become the richest and most powerful people who have ever lived.

But in the process of growing their innovative tech companies, they would not only lose their idealism, they would also unleash a powerful beast onto the world—a beast that changes and morphs and breaks free from its creators . . . like a digital Frankenstein's monster.

Social Media Mind Shaping

The modern monster that's broken free from its creators is our unshackled social media.

For a socially hardwired species like ours, social media should have been a match made in heaven, like chocolate and peanut butter. What can go wrong? Now, well over a decade into the experiment, it's as if social media has morphed into a living, breathing sentient organism, fed by our most intense and vitriolic emotions—our primal id, writ small on a QWERTY keyboard.

We feed the beast, and then the beast feeds us—a toxic and polarizing echo chamber.

However, we need to ask ourselves, what type of personality or mindset develops when one's beliefs, interests, and ideas are constantly reflected back toward them in this amplification of confirmation bias—in this *extremification* loop—where our digital ecosystem is created in our own image? Narcissism, by any other name. A digital inhabitant doesn't *think* that the world revolves around them, it *does* revolve around them.

Thanks to data mining and predictive algorithms, a person who believes in a certain political ideology now inhabits a digital reality where that ideology is the religion of the realm; that same person may have searched on Google for running shoes and, miraculously, running shoe ads come pouring in from all ends of the datasphere. Like gods, we can think something and then that thought becomes manifest and shapes our digital world—which, in turn, not only reinforces our original beliefs in exaggerated confirmation bias fashion, but also creates an egocentric universe that can very easily morph into narcissism.

With their introspective need for self-realization, we had called boomers in the '70s the "Me Generation"; in the digital age, introspection has been distorted through the social media prism into navel-gazing self-absorption, as *TIME* magazine dubbed "entitled, narcissistic" millennials the "Me Me Me Generation" on a May 2013 cover story. Almost ten years later, things have only gotten worse, as we've now had an entire generation born into and raised in the algorithm-curated me-me-me-verse.

The clinical fallout from this social media contagion that breeds self-centeredness and polarized, binary thinking is spreading. Indeed, we're seeing that society at large and the body politic are getting sick and corrupted by this invasive digital virus that's sickened the entire host body. And, as we know, sick societies breed sick people; brutal cultures breed violent people; oppressed cultures breed despondent and depressed citizens. And our tech-addicted, impulsive, hypersensitive, egocentric, instant-gratification society with its polarizing social media echo chambers has bred an angry, intolerant, narcissistic, and borderline-like volatile population.

This extreme polarization in our current political and social landscape may be an inescapable reflection of the inherent DNA of the social media beast and the digital womb that it spawned from. Indeed, it's a metaphorical *and* literal reflection of the definition of "digital," where the 1s and 0s of binary polarity have now shaped our cultural and psychological landscape into non-nuanced, black-and-white extremes; in a world where you can only either be a "1" or a "0," there is no room for fractions or for the subtle gray area in between extremes.

Borderline personality disorder—typified by all-or-nothing black-and-white thinking—is now our cultural diagnosis, where hysterical ALL CAPS tweets and political extremism (on both ends of the spectrum) have replaced rational critical thinking and civil discourse.

Tech addiction. Mental illness. Polarization. A society on the brink. Many newly remorseful tech defectors lament that this had not been the plan; this was not the way things were supposed to be. Chamath Palihapitiya, former Facebook VP for user growth, has expressed "tremendous guilt" over their creation, as he says that social media are "tools that are ripping apart the social fabric of how society works," and added, "No civil discourse, no cooperation, misinformation, mistruth."[13] Ex-Twitter exec Jeff Seibert laments that this was all unintentional: "Nobody, I deeply believe, ever intended any of these consequences."[14]

But unleashing new technologies is an unpredictable game. The innovative researcher can discover something wonderful like penicillin—or blow up the entire lab with everyone in it. This high-wire balancing act between the potential benefit of new tech versus its downside has sometimes been phrased as *promise* vs. *peril.* But even if you don't blow up the lab, it's often impossible to predict the unintended consequences. Bailey Richardson, an executive from the early days of Instagram, describes this unpredictability vis-à-vis algorithms: "The algorithm has a mind of its own, so even though a person writes it, it's written in a way that you kind of build the machine, and then the machine changes itself."[15]

Once you let the genie out of the bottle . . .

Yet Sean Parker, Facebook's first president, colorfully portrayed by Justin Timberlake in the film *The Social Network,* paints a different picture. Parker, now a "conscientious objector" to social media, has claimed that all these consequences, including tech addiction and the dopamine-spiking, lizard brain content that drives the "battle of the eyeballs," was *indeed* intentional and by design—and not "unintended":

"It's exactly the kind of thing that a hacker like myself would come up with, because you're exploiting a vulnerability in human psychology," he said. "The inventors, creators—it's me, it's Mark [Zuckerberg], it's Kevin Systrom on Instagram, it's all of these people—understood this consciously. And we did it anyway."[16]

At the end of the day, whatever the intentions, the results were the same: an atomic bomb was dropped onto the sociocultural landscape. Yes, you can FaceTime Grandma, but as we shall see, a whole host of unanticipated damage has been unleashed. And that's the problem in a nutshell: Sean Parker may have just been looking to increase engagement with advanced behavior-modification techniques, but the monster grew beyond mere tech addiction into insanity-inducing platforms that have fundamentally changed our society and have driven our mental health crisis and linked to the record spike in suicides.[17]

For the New Technocracy, their motivations may have been benign in the early heady days of Silicon Valley, where childhood scientific curiosity had turned into young adult "we can change the world!" exuberance; then that inevitably morphed into an insatiable thirst for more money and more power. And they were also driven by myopic God complexes, as many inventors and scientists often are—and, unfortunately, they don't spend enough time reflecting with ethical discernment on what may happen when their IT lab monsters are born.

Or, for obscene amounts of money, they can stop caring.

Consider Google. Google founders Larry Page and Sergey Brin, filled with wide-eyed optimism as Stanford grad students, came up with the company motto of "Don't Be Evil" and had promised to never monetize their search engine.[18] *Now* look how that's turned out.

Once they realized how easy it was to generate money via the search engine itself through the sale of keywords to eager companies (rather than the clutter of selling ad space, like their competitors had been doing), it was game on! All high-minded lofty ideals fell by the wayside; they needed to make room for the money truck to back up. A euphoric Sergey and Larry even gleefully proclaimed on their website at the time: "You can make money without doing evil."

But after a few hundred billion dollars in monetization, accusations of spying on both their employees *and* users, cannibalizing over two hundred companies in pursuit of industry dominance and an obvious monopoly play, *and* accusations of rigging searches with an inherent bias and agenda, Google decided to ditch its now meaningless "Don't Be Evil" motto; it was removed completely from Google's corporate code of conduct in 2018.[19]

Evil was now permissible—of *course* it was.

And one may argue this is indeed the inevitable way of growth and power; as Lord Acton famously said, "Power corrupts and absolute power corrupts absolutely." So why wouldn't this apply to the tech industry and the people who created it? After all, we're talking about more wealth and real power than any human being has ever experienced. The question that we need to ask then is how would their perspectives—even their humanity itself—be warped by such power?

To be clear, none of this had been my original focus.

As a psychologist specializing in mental health and addiction, my entire focus over the past decade had been "screen addiction," not the larger context of the cultural and economic aspects of the problem. Having seen firsthand the increasingly adverse clinical effects of screen time, I'd become alarmed at how quickly these new magical devices were creating serious problems for people—especially younger ones.

I started writing about, researching, clinically treating, and generally raising awareness about the impacts of the screen invasion on our society and the attendant "tech addiction" that invariably came with it. My entire focus had been technology *addiction,* as I went on to develop treatment programs and protocols to address what was becoming a growing global epidemic.

I had even been contracted by the U.S. military to do trainings for the Department of Defense (DoD) mental health providers on how to assess and treat video game addiction. Gaming addiction is so severe in the military that there have been several documented and shocking cases of military babies dying in the crib from parental neglect as their fathers played marathon video game sessions. The problem became so significant that the DoD had to create a new cause of death for the infant death certificates: "Death due to Electronic Distraction."[20]

I began to realize that, like those neglectful video-game-playing military fathers, we were all, to some degree or another, "electronically distracted" not only from our lives but from the bigger picture as well. Yes, tech addiction—bad. But that VR cow helped me to realize that

I was pissing in the wind by myopically focusing on too much screen time as *the* problem, without understanding and addressing the larger societal dynamics that were occurring.

I had a nagging and growing sense that the problem was much deeper and direr than simple yet horrible "tech addiction"; habituation to our devices just happened to be a necessary mechanism for a more comprehensive agenda. The problem was indeed much more complex than "Johnny and Suzie like to be on their screens too much." There were major societal shifts happening; there were mental and medical impacts; there were sociopolitical and economic implications. Most importantly, our species was getting weaker and dying.

And as I researched this book, I discovered that this wasn't just about greed (although that's always a factor); greed alone is too pedestrian for the most powerful people who have ever lived. Greed is so *yesterday*. I'll discuss those other motives more in part 2 of the book.

Regardless of whether the motivation is greed or something more, the agenda is clearly more than merely tech *addiction*. Addiction as control is a necessary ingredient—as it *always* has been in power dynamics and oligarchies throughout the ages.

Because addiction traps a person; it crushes their free will and makes an individual a slave to their addictive impulses. Rational choice is gone, and what's left is an all-consuming craving or desire for more of whatever the person is addicted to—a craving that doesn't seem rational, as it often has adverse impacts on a person's life: the diabetic with such a severe sugar craving that they'll eat the entire gallon of ice cream, despite the potential for a diabetic coma. Or the smoker with lung cancer and emphysema who just can't give up their Marlboros.

The Dopamine Cage

On a human level, addiction can seem confounding. Why would an otherwise rational person act so irrationally in the furtherance or pursuit of their addiction? Yet on a neurophysiological level, addiction is fairly simple to understand, and it starts with the feel-good neurotransmitter dopamine and how it affects the brain's reward system.

When a person engages in a feel-good dopaminergic behavior

(think sex, drugs, Instagram), dopamine is released into the nucleus accumbens, a cluster of nerve cells beneath the cerebral hemispheres that are associated with pleasure and reward, also known as the brain's *pleasure center.*[21]

Then the fun begins. Engaging in a dopaminergic behavior increases dopamine levels so that the dopamine reward pathway is activated; this is a feel-good neurofeedback reward loop (also known as the *mesolimbic dopamine reward loop*) that tells the individual to repeat what he or she just did in order to get that same pleasurable dopamine reward again and again. And, depending on how dopaminergic (dopamine-activating) a substance or behavior is, that then correlates with the addictive potential of that substance or behavior.

One might ask, if that's the case . . . then why don't all of us just pursue pleasurable dopaminergic experiences *continuously* if our brains are wired that way? Why aren't we all compulsively addicted to something? Well, some might answer that, in a sense, many of us are; many of us do have compulsive guilty pleasures that we have difficulty managing.

The broader answer to that question is that the brain also has what we may consider a braking mechanism. If addiction is the gas pedal linked to our primal lizard brain, then our frontal lobe—which allows us to consequentially think—is our brain's braking system. Yes, we may get a dopamine-fueled impulse, but the frontal cortex allows us to do what's called "if . . . then" thinking: *if* I'm diabetic and I eat that gallon of ice cream, *then* I may fall into a diabetic coma. Or, a person may have a sexual urge, but that neural braking system allows the average person to think through the consequences of whatever the impulsive action may be.

If we put these neurobiological constructs into Freudian terms, we might say that the addictive urge is part of our id, and the voice in our head saying, "Not so fast!" would be our superego, otherwise known as our *conscience,* which is the internalized norms of our society, our parents, and other influences. So if the urge is to kick our desk over, run naked through the office, and pour hot coffee on our boss's head and tell them that they can take their job and shove it, the good old frontal cortex/superego tells us, "Well, hold on now—that may not be such a great idea; you've got rent to pay, a family to feed—and it wouldn't be the *right* thing to do."

Fair enough. Then the $64,000 question is why doesn't the brain of the person struggling with an addictive disorder just pump the brakes, as it were, and not allow them to feed the impulsive addictive behavior? Answer: for a person who's addicted, for a variety of reasons, the "rational" use of our braking system has been hijacked—or compromised.

To understand that, we first have to understand that the dopamine reward loop originally had an important evolutionary function (it wasn't always all about cocaine and Instagram). The original function of our dopamine reward response was to incentivize two critical life and species-sustaining biological functions: eating and procreation. Since eating and sex feel good because they increase dopamine, we seek out those activities to get the feel-good dopamine high—and stay alive as a species as a result.

Simple enough. But natural dopaminergic activities like sex for procreation and eating to survive usually occur after some level of effort and occur for relatively short periods of time—with apologies to Sting and any other tantric enthusiasts. Typically, although there are exceptions, we don't marathon binge-eat or marathon procreate, because once we satiate the dopamine craving, we tend to stop the behavior.

For people who are predisposed toward addiction, moderating feel-good behavior feels impossible; for a variety of etiological reasons, the addicted person just can't seem to stop once they light the fuse. And addictive drugs and dopaminergic behaviors like cocaine, gambling, or digital vices light the dopamine fuse. Indeed, dopaminergic drugs or digital platforms provide a shortcut to our dopamine reward system that can be repeatedly engaged in for *hours or even days* at a time. Using these substances or engaging in these experiences repeatedly and for prolonged periods also floods the nucleus accumbens with too much dopamine for extended periods of time, yet without serving any essential biological function.

Unfortunately, evolution hasn't given us a defense against this hijacked dopamine onslaught, so that when people become addicted, they experience a dopamine reduction or shutdown in order to give at least *some* relief to their overwhelmed receptor cells. With this reduced capacity to produce dopamine naturally, the addicted person then needs to ingest more of the addictive substance or engage in more of the addictive behavior—as in *more and more* time on social media, for example—just to maintain his or her baseline dopamine levels.

Then, in a classic addiction catch-22, chronic exposure to addictive substances or behaviors reduces the gray matter in the frontal cortex—the brain's decision-making "braking system" associated with impulse control—which, in turn, then compromises a person's ability to *not* engage in the addictive substance or behavior.

In essence, addiction breaks our brakes.[22] And then round and round the addiction merry-go-round goes as the addict tries to satiate a dopamine craving that can never be satiated, while lacking the impulse control to stop the vicious cycle.

The added addiction problem with the digital age (as opposed to substances, for example) is the ubiquity; we're awash with constantly arousing digital feel-goods that are perpetually spiking our dopamine and flooding our dopamine receptors.

Dr. Anna Lembke, Stanford University School of Medicine professor and author of *Dopamine Nation,* writes about this addictive trap of modernity: we have too many choices and too many things that can stimulate us, thus spiking our dopamine. We then develop an increased tolerance for dopaminergic activities and are bored by everyday activities and things.[23] You only have to look around at the faces of so many young people who seem entirely bored and apathetic with living and who only find a sense of sensation in arousing digital platforms—whether that's immersive hyperreal fantasy gaming, continuously dopamine-reinforcing social media, or increasingly explicit and extreme porn. For them, reading a book, a walk in the park, or kissing a romantic interest just doesn't cut it anymore.

That's the brain part of addiction. But there are also other factors, or what we may call *etiological theories,* as to what may also cause or contribute to a person being more vulnerable to addiction than another person.

For many, clinicians and researchers alike, truly understanding addiction is like a riddle wrapped in a mystery inside an enigma. Many have a hard time even categorizing it—is it a bad habit, a lack of will-power, a disease, a mental disorder, a maladaptive learning response, a moral failing, a genetic condition, a psychological condition? Etiological theories abound, from social learning theory to attachment theory, genetic theories, trauma-based theories, and so on.

Research *has* shown that people who are predisposed toward addiction have lower baseline levels of dopamine, as well as other neurotransmitters, such as endorphins and norepinephrine; thus, they're more likely to get hooked on any substance or behavior that increases dopamine because their brains crave it more than those of people who have normal baseline neurotransmitter levels.

That's also why so many people with addiction are comorbid—that is, that they also struggle with another mental health disorder. In fact, the vast majority of people struggling with addiction—over 85 percent—also have other mental health issues; whether they're diagnosed or not is another matter. The two big ones are depression and anxiety; the majority of folks who struggle with addiction will say that they also struggle with depression and/or anxiety and are *self-medicating* with the addiction. The problem is that addiction and mental health disorders are "bi-directional" forces that synergize and amplify one another.

An example of that would be the person who is depressed and then starts drinking excessively to numb the depression. Since alcohol is a depressant, it may temporarily numb some of the depressed feelings but ultimately drives the depression deeper by reducing serotonin levels. Same thing with technology; most of the clients that I treat will say, "Well, my excessive gaming or social media is how I escape my anxiety or depression." Again, the problem is that the more sedentary and screen-staring you remain, the more the depression deepens. And the less likely you are to do the things—like exercise and group socialization—that we know can help alleviate depression.

Having said that, we also know that there are certain substances or behaviors that affect dopamine more than others—and can be considered more addicting. For example, brain imaging research shows us that eating can raise dopamine levels by 50 percent, while sex can raise dopamine by 100 percent; snorting cocaine increases dopamine by 350 percent, and ingesting crystal meth creates a whopping 1,200 percent increase in dopamine.[24] That's why we'd say that crystal meth has the highest dopaminergic effect—and thus the highest addictive potential—among the substances just mentioned.

So how dopaminergic are virtual experiences? According to the brain imaging study mentioned above, video games increased dopamine as much as sex: about 100 percent. In essence, a person is getting the equivalent of a brain orgasm every time they play a video game. Is it any wonder, then, that we're so hooked on our devices?

With our complete societal immersion in our tech culture, almost all of us are, to varying degrees, too dependent on our gadgets. And that dependence gives an enormous amount of power and control to the people who create our devices and the platforms that we all use—because addiction has long been a useful tool for sedating the masses and maintaining control.

Digital Addiction as the Opiate of the Masses

There are certainly other methods beyond addiction to tame the masses. History books are filled with examples of powerful ruling classes controlling and oppressing people by a variety of techniques. The story of how the few control the many is as long as recorded history. Karl Marx colorfully described religion as "the opiate of the masses," a shared belief system that lulls the masses to keep them in non-rebelling check.

Or there's also subjugation by good old-fashioned military brute force, as seen in most dictatorships. When the men in the colorful uniforms take over, whether a junta, the colonels, the führer, supreme leader, or el generalissimo, it's usually time to run for the exits—otherwise, it's "All hail great leader!" for the next few years or decades.

But beyond religions and generals, addiction has proven to be an effective way to keep the masses nicely compliant. After all, addicts are a malleable bunch while in pursuit of their elixir. Any creature that feels trapped—mentally, physically, emotionally, economically, existentially—is much more likely to seek addictive and numbing escape; like the poor mice of the addiction experiments of the 1950s who were alone and trapped in Skinner cages, and then desperately and repeatedly hit the lever for the blissful escape of morphine—over food—until they invariably overdosed. We very clearly understand that the need to escape an untenable reality is one of the main drivers of addiction—and one researcher experimentally proved it.

Canadian professor and researcher Dr. Bruce Alexander proved in the 1970s, via his legendary Rat Park Experiments,[25] that it's really an unbearable reality or environment that drives addiction—*not* necessarily the addictive substance. In those early Skinner cage experiments of the 1950s, researchers assumed that they had proved the power of an addicting drug—that it was *so* tempting and addicting, the foolish rat would choose the drug over food and overdose rather quickly.

But Dr. Alexander had the idea that perhaps those experiments weren't measuring the addictiveness of the drug; instead, they were measuring the effect that being isolated and trapped has on a social creature—as rats and humans both are. To test his hypothesis, he devised "Rat Park": a veritable rat utopia where rats were free to roam and frolic and socialize with other rats. They had wheels to play with and to exercise in, cheese to eat, and partners to have sex with. And they also had free and unfettered access to drug water—the same high-octane water that the rats in the control group, alone in cages, also had access to.

Guess what happened?

None of the rats in Rat Park became hooked on the drug water, and none of them died. In fact, some sampled the drug water but didn't like it and avoided it thereafter. Who needs drug water? They had friends and open spaces to play in; it was heaven on Earth—for rats. As for the lonely rats trapped in cages? They all died from overdose. The critically important conclusion that Dr. Alexander drew was that escapist addiction resulted more from a toxic environment—including isolation and the lack of community—than from the substance itself.

Can these conclusions also apply to human beings?

According to Dr. Alexander, "People do not have to be put into cages to become addicted—but is there a sense in which people who become addicted actually feel 'caged'?" Indeed, every addict that I've ever worked with has described, in some form or another, their addiction as a cage, or a form of enslavement to the addictive substance or behavior.

But can we feel trapped and caged *before* we get addicted—and can that be one of the drivers of escapist addiction? Anyone can see how humans can be physically free, yet still feel trapped in a "cage" psychologically: the person who hates their job but can't quit for financial reasons; the person stuck in a bad marriage; the person without any job or housing opportunities; the person suffering from a debilitating physical or psychological condition. And as we will see, being in front of a glowing screen for hour after hour, every single day, is also a caged environment.

Dr. Alexander wanted to see if his rat results did indeed apply to people. Although ethics regarding human research precluded replicating Rat Park for humans, he was able to study the historical records of just such a "natural" experiment: the colonization of Native peoples and their subjugation onto reservations.

Dr. Alexander realized that the Native peoples of Canada and the United States had been put in their own Skinner cages: reservations that denied them their traditional cultural connections, practices, and social bonds. And what he found reflected his Rat Park conclusions: before the colonization (caging) of Native Americans, there were hardly any records of addiction. Yet after Native Americans were put on reservations? According to Alexander: "Once the native people were colonized, alcoholism became close to universal; there were entire reserves where virtually every teenager and adult was either an alcohol or drug addict or 'on the wagon.'"

Very tellingly, on reservations where alcohol was available but Native culture was preserved to some degree (typically on Canadian reservations), Native peoples were able to consume alcohol in a nonaddictive manner. Meanwhile, the reservations that stripped Native culture (typically on American reservations), saw rampant drug abuse and alcoholism.

Rat Park—and the colonization of Native peoples—has shown us that social beings put into physical, mental, or cultural isolation—"cages," if you will—are more susceptible to addiction, including behavioral addictions.

According to Alexander: "The view of addiction from Rat Park is that today's flood of addiction is occurring because our hyperindividualistic, hypercompetitive, frantic, crisis-ridden society makes most people feel socially and culturally isolated.... They find temporary relief in addiction to drugs or any of a thousand other habits and pursuits because addiction allows them to escape from their feelings, to deaden their senses, and to experience an addictive lifestyle as a substitute for a full life."[26]

The question that begs asking from Dr. Alexander's quote above: Does our current high-tech world *breed* the "hyperindividualistic, hypercompetitive, frantic, crisis-ridden society" that Alexander says is the driver of addiction?

I think any reasonable person would have to answer *yes.*

We can all understand how lonely people who feel trapped, lacking a strong sense of cultural identity or a supportive sense of community, who are then exposed to highly dopaminergic substances or experiences, can become prey to addictive escapism. People who feel trapped in their lot in life, like those rats in Skinner cages, are more likely to push the morphine lever—which then, in turn, perpetuates their caged and addicted disempowerment.

As I mentioned, Karl Marx called religion *the opiate of the masses;* he wrote it was the promise of an escape to a spiritual hereafter that made the daily grind and misery in a totalitarian state more tolerable (a more tolerable cage, as it were) and made the citizen more likely to accept their earthly fate and not revolt.

But now, instead of a metaphorical opiate, we have literal *opiates* of the masses such as fenatnyl—and we also have "digital heroin" as the *newest* opiate to exert social control, lulling and numbing people into a digital dreamworld.

They all serve the same common purpose: a sort of societal sedation-as-conformity. God-fearing churchgoers don't tend to incite rebellion; drug-addicted teens can't compete for jobs or social status—and lost-in-the-Matrix gamers typically don't leave Mom and Dad's basement.

In the digital age, we've all become tech-dependent, to some degree or completely. This tech dependence has primed us for addiction of all sorts—and transformed us into weakened, sick, and addicted *hungry ghosts,* pitiable creatures from Buddhist mythology with voracious-yet-insatiable appetites—because addictive hunger can *never* be satiated.

In our rapacious, digitally primed society, we've been conditioned to feed the bottomless hole and chase the next iPhone, the better car, the bigger house, the more attractive partner. Unfortunately, it's all fool's gold; the iPhone will never be good enough once the next model comes out; the house will never be big enough, nor the partner attractive enough if a person feels empty and is trying to fill the void with external rewards or validation. Feeding the senses is *never* the solution to existential emptiness.

Worse yet, we've not only been tricked into needing and loving our void-filling digital fix, but we've also fallen in love with the digital cages, to the point that we don't even realize that we're trapped in them. At least the rats in the addiction experiments *knew* that they were trapped in a cage; yet we've no concept that we're trapped by a global network of little screen prisons that have not only addicted and enslaved us, but that also have the capacity to monitor and brainwash us and inhibit our abilities to grow and flourish.

Blinded by our tech obsession, we understand that condition of helpless dependence is exactly the point.

The Metaverse

For maximum control, however, screens are too limiting. They are, after all, only *two-dimensional* cages; why settle for that, when fully immersive holographic VR cages are now possible? Hell, if we can reality-blur some poor cows with VR headsets—and get them to be more productive—why not try the same trick on humans? Better yet, why not create an entire altered "shared reality" virtual universe, a.k.a. *the metaverse,* and all accessible by VR glasses?

When I was at that conference in San Francisco at the Commonwealth Club in 2019 and saw the image of the VR cows, I didn't know what Mark Zuckerberg would announce only two short years later. All I knew is that I had a sick feeling in my stomach . . . because it felt like I was looking at *our* future. Enter Zuckerberg and his new cool Ray Ban–style VR glasses that he hopes will lead us all into *his* metaverse—and off the reality cliff.

It all began in September 2021, when Zuckerberg announced Facebook's latest product: a pair of Ray-Ban "smart glasses," which he had previously said were part of the company's push to, in fact, build a "metaverse company":

"The next product release will be the launch of our first smart glasses from Ray-Ban in partnership with EssilorLuxottica,"[27] Zuck told Facebook investors during an earnings call that year. "The glasses have their iconic form factor, and they let you do some pretty neat things. . . . These efforts are also part of a much larger goal: to help build the metaverse," Zuckerberg said in his distinctive humanoid monotone.

Cue the ominous music.

"I believe in the coming years, I expect people will transition from seeing us primarily as a social media company to seeing us as a metaverse company."[28]

Initially, the Big Tech playbook was addicting us to their platforms via various behavior modification techniques. Now, the goal is much more ambitious; by creating, controlling, and curating the metaverse and, thus, the realities that our minds will experience, we truly will be in the Matrix: "You can think about this as an embodied internet that you're inside of rather than just looking at," Zuckerberg gushed during an investors call in July 2021.

An "embodied internet"?

He went on to say: "The defining quality of the metaverse is *presence,* which is this feeling that you're really there with another person or in another place . . . this is going to lead to entirely new experiences and"—(wait for it)—"economic opportunities."

Funny thing, though: what Zuckerberg calls "presence" and "feeling that you're really there" via the metaverse, when in actuality you are *not* there—well, in graduate school, we were trained to call that a *hallucination.* But I suppose I'm getting hung up on semantics.

Let's hear more about this illusion—I mean, this *metaverse*—from Zuck: "Think about how many things that are in your life that don't actually need to be physical and could be easily replaced by a digital hologram in a world where you had glasses," he said at the 2021 VivaTech Conference in Paris. While Zuckerberg goes on to list things like art, clothing, and media that can all be virtual holograms, you can't help but think that our socially challenged Facebook CEO truly wants to say that we can also create virtual people—but he doesn't quite go there.

He does, however, show us his inner God complex as he riffs heavily on what he envisions as his new powers of creation: "I'll just be able to snap my fingers, and here's a hologram," said the thirty-seven-year-old Tech Oligarch. "It's going to be incredibly powerful."

I have no doubt.

I don't know about you, but I guess I'm old-fashioned—I like my reality straight up. I don't want anyone—or anyone's device—coming between me and my sensory perception of the *real* world. And by the real world, I mean the one that's *not* curated by the friendly team at Facebook, the folks who bought us disinformation, sold our personal data, and are driving the depression and suicide surge. No, thank you; I definitely do not want you filtering my perception of reality. Sure, as a younger person, I may have had my senses altered on occasion—but that mind-altering was not a "shared reality" controlled by Big Tech.

And like a good drug dealer who gives out free samples to get their customers hooked, Zuck is even willing to give his VR glasses away for free (now *that* should tell us something) in order to "encourage widespread adoption"—and immersion into his metaverse.

Resistance is futile.

But we *should* be resisting this "shared reality" from the folks who created a seismic change in our culture—and not for the better. But rather than crying out in protest, we swoon and allow the Tech Overlords to have their way with us, suffering from a form of societal Stockholm syndrome. We make people like Steve Jobs cultural icons, worship quirky tech moguls like Elon Musk, and deify the seemingly beneficent Bill Gates—even as we've unknowingly been enslaved by their algorithms.

Yet most people are blissfully unaware as they tweet and Instagram their lives away.

It's been said that the devil's greatest accomplishment (if there is such a creature) is convincing the world that he doesn't exist. The real trick in this digital dystopia, a despairing place that's inhabited by millions of hungry ghosts, is to convince the addicted and enslaved inhabitants that they're actually free—a necessary illusion—and that their lives aren't just that of futile gerbils going around in a never-ending spinning consumer wheel without any real purpose.

In totalitarian states like China, the bondage doesn't need to be seductive or sugarcoated. Why bother? The enslaved and oppressed in that society have no practical recourse to break their shackles; the hundreds of thousands of oppressed factory workers toiling for Foxconn in Shenzhen under hellish conditions to make our iPads only have suicide as a recourse (as we'll discuss more in part 2). They don't need to give their workers VR headsets or digital soma to make them feel better. The state doesn't care, because it doesn't fear revolt.

In "free" countries like the United States, the Matrix illusion needs to be maintained or else rebellion may break out. It's Orwell meets Huxley: techno-totalitarianism with a dose of soma to wash it all down and make it taste yummy. We are no different from the cows with the VR headsets; we think we're free range, while we're actually on digital lockdown. And now, if Facebook gets its way, we'll even have the VR headsets, too . . . maybe we can all "share reality" together, cows and humans, all lazily grazing in a nice peaceful pasture.

The illusion not only makes us better and happier workers, it also keeps us from breaking through the fence and escaping. Indeed, it's been said that the ideal workers of the future will be smart enough to maintain the machines, but not so smart (or awake enough) to see the big picture of their enslavement. And so Big Brother will keep the beer flowing and the video games on continuous play . . . but whatever you do, do *not* wake up! Just keep living in the virtual dreamworld like our poor bovine friends.

But unlike those VR cows, all we have to do is take off the seductive and reality-altering metaphorical glasses that we've been given (or Facebook's actual VR glasses), and open up our eyes to awaken from the dream-as-nightmare. We are humans, and we need to fight for our humanity and not go quietly into the virtual night.

Yes, there are other societal forces beyond Big Tech that are making us more vulnerable and more unwell: the $100-billion-a-year therapy-industrial complex, which pathologizes people, making them weaker and more dependent; helicopter parenting, which Bubble-Wraps young people and strips them of their ability to develop resilience and the psychological tools they'll need to learn to cope and live life on life's terms; true crises such as the pandemic, mass shootings, and the daily barrage of bad news and polarizing conflicts; and the loss of genuine purpose and meaning in our materialistic and empty pleasure-seeking Xbox world . . . all of these abovementioned dynamics have played a critical part in the weakening and subjugation of our species in the tech era.

But how *exactly* is our tech-dependent reality driving our mental health pandemic?

2

A World Gone Mad

Reflections on a Sick Patient

I was sitting at home one night not long after my father had died, scrolling through various depressing news stories.

This was just before the 2020 pandemic.

The house was quiet, my kids were in bed, and my office was dark—save for the cold blue light of my screen. I had an itch that I hadn't quite been able to scratch for several years. Actually, not so much an itch—but a dread.

A steadily creeping awareness that something is seriously, seriously wrong.

As a psychologist, I've clinically worked with more than two thousand patients during the past twenty years—from kids, to teens, to millennials, to middle-aged adults, to seniors. As a university professor, I've taught over one thousand graduate students and stayed on top of mental health trends to be a well-informed educator; and as an author who has written about the effects of technology on human beings, I've had to play the role of both sociologist and investigative reporter.

During that time, it had become slowly but increasingly obvious that the patient is very sick—and getting sicker. The patient is a macro-organism known as *Homo sapiens,* in the collective form. Let's refer to our patient as Homo Sapien—twenty-first-century edition. The clues have been there, hidden in plain sight; I, and many of my colleagues, have seen a shift in the mental health of our clients in our clinical practices—at the micro-level—over these past ten to fifteen years.

Now, as I sit in my office late at night reading various research journals, news stories, and items of the day, a clearer sense develops of the symptoms and, perhaps, the root causes of what's ailing the patient. Understanding all of that will be essential if we have any hope of restoring our suffering patient back to health.

Don't just take my word for it. Look up. Look around. Those with any sense of clarity can see that something has gone terribly wrong. Beyond the ugly and acrimonious political divide, there's a quickening of cultural and social tensions far surpassing that of previous decades.

There's a sense of dread and free-floating anxiety in the air. People feel uneasy and unsafe (as evidenced by the surge of in-home security systems and children's tracking devices and the spike in anxiety, depression, and pain medications prescribed). There's a sense of a ship—once big and beautiful—that's strangely adrift and veering into unchartered waters with an iceberg on the horizon. We don't quite see the iceberg just yet, but we can collectively *feel* it.

On a fundamental level, those who aren't distracted by the shiny baubles and digital distractions know that something has gone awry with our species—beyond the pandemic of 2020, although that has acted as an accelerant.

No, the patient is not well.

In fact, by every conceivable mental and physical health metric, we are getting sicker as a society: depression, anxiety, suicide, overdose, addiction, heart disease, obesity, and cancer rates are skyrocketing and at all-time record levels.[1]

Not only do we have the worst mental health on record, but our bodies aren't doing much better than our minds. We're obese, burdened by clogged arteries and diabetic insulin-starved blood.[2] And we have higher and higher rates of cancers, from the more common "hormonal" cancers of the prostate and breast, to increasingly rare brain gliomas.[3]

We're just not meant to be sedentary, screen-staring, and meaning-devoid creatures.

Yet like the folks who adhere to a Paleo diet because they understand that our genetics haven't caught up to our modern dietary habits, we are now beginning to understand that our genetics have also not caught up to our modern digital lifestyles.

And it's this pronounced lack of movement—of being overly sedentary in our screen-staring, tech-lubricated lives—that's toxic for *Homo sapiens,* directly leading to our epidemic rates of cancer, heart disease, obesity, and diabetes: all the telltale signs of an unhealthy society in distress.[4]

Sick and Dying in the Digital Age

According to the CDC, obesity has increased by 70 percent over the last thirty years for adults and a staggering 85 percent for children.[5] And obesity's deadly cousin, diabetes, has also been spiking; rates in adults have almost doubled over the last twenty years, and in teens and children under twenty, type 1 diabetes (the deadlier variety) has increased by an average of 2 percent each year from 2002 to 2012.[6]

It doesn't take a rocket scientist to figure out what's happening; sedentary screen-obsessed kids and junk-food diets don't mix well. But kids have been consuming fast food and sugary sodas for decades. What's changed has been the seismic shift in increased screen time—and its attendant decrease in physical activity; that's the new variable in the obese and diabetic child equation. It feels like so long ago, but some of us can remember a time when kids used to *actually* go outdoors to play—and they had never heard of Xbox or an iPad.

Good luck finding a kid climbing a tree today. Instead, they're usually indoors, tethered to their glowing devices and getting obese in record numbers. But both in our society and in popular culture, obese kids used to be rare. That's why Spanky from *The Little Rascals* circa the 1930s was so beloved: a portly kid was an outlier; today, in the e-sports era, thin kids are the rarity.

What did we expect? We have an entire generation of zombified kids staring at glowing screens for an average of eleven hours a day, mostly mind-numbing video games or inane texting or social media posts.[7] Or, in a perverse form of infinite regression, young people are watching YouTube videos of other young people gaming and watching YouTube videos, ad infinitum or ad nauseum, take your pick.

And in an obscene manipulation of the language of Orwellian proportion, it's the explosion of so-called e-sports that's largely driving the child obesity epidemic. The ironically named e-sports are not only the fastest-growing viewer "sport" in America but also the largest participant sport as well. Gone are the days when bowlers and billiards enthusiasts had to defend their games as true sports; now energy drink–guzzling kids stuck for days in their reclining chairs are telling Mom to back off—after all, they're "training"—as their insulin disappears and their weight soars.

Netflix is currently producing a seven-part series called *This Is e-Sports!* I was asked to participate in the episode that focused on the darker aspects of this new phenomenon—and shared with the producers the insanity of calling computer gaming a "sport" to help lull kids and parents into believing that this profoundly unhealthy recreation is somehow an actual physical sport.

The result of all this screen time? This new sedentary version of Homo Sapien—Homo Can't-Get-Off-the-Couch—has a soft, cushiony waistline expanding out like a freshly baked muffin top, even as our screens get flatter.

Starvation used to kill millions; now, it's the pendulum-swinging opposite—obesity, with its attendant heart attacks, diabetes, and high blood pressure—that's killing more people than hunger. The species that gave us the Spartan warrior, the Sistine Chapel, scientific innovation that allowed us to step on the moon and explore both the cosmos and the subatomic universe is now a fragile, brain-dulled, Weeble-like, poorly postured, no-eye-contact, couch potato species that considers the Kardashians high art.

The digital age has given us smarter phones but dumber people. Indeed, there are several studies that show how our memory, cognitive acuity, and physical health and fitness all suffer from a more sedentary and tech-enabled lifestyle. Beyond obesity and diabetes, we have skyrocketing rates of heart disease—also driven by sedentary lifestyles and unhealthy diets. Globally, 18.6 million people died of heart disease in 2016, with that number projected to grow to 23.6 million people by 2030.[8]

Unhealthy lifestyles can also drive cancer. Although we know that modern environmental factors like toxic household chemicals, pollution, food additives, and EMF radiation are endocrine disruptors that can be carcinogenic, we also know that stressful, sedentary, cortisol-spiking, and obesity-inducing modern high-tech lifestyles can also be cancer-causing as well.

To be clear, the cancer statistics can be a little misleading and complicated to interpret. Yes, the cancer death *rate* has fallen (from 171 per 100,000 people in 2010 to 151 per 100,000 in 2020), but more people are getting cancer—we just have more treatment to mitigate the fatalities. Yet despite that, *overall* cancer deaths continue to rise as more and more people are getting cancer: according to the CDC, in 2010 there were 575,000 cancer deaths in the U.S.; in 2020, that number grew significantly to 630,000 deaths.[9]

Some have attributed the increased cancer rates and deaths to an aging population, but that's misleading. Not only are more young people getting cancer, younger people are dying in greater numbers overall—and many of those youthful deaths, if they aren't cancer-related, are often lifestyle- and mental health–related by-products of modern twenty-first-century living.

Indeed, a record number of deaths among young people have been attributed to what have been dubbed "deaths of despair": drug overdoses, suicide, and chronic alcoholism, which, according to the CDC, took over 200,000 lives in pre-COVID 2019.[10]

It would seem that young people have been overwhelmed by our marvelous new postindustrial society. In fact, so many young people had died during the period between 2017 and 2019 that the average U.S. life expectancy had decreased for the first time in over a hundred years; not since the global devastation of the influenza pandemic of 1918—the much more lethal pandemic of yesteryear—had we seen average life span rates decrease in the U.S.

These "deaths of despair" are very much a "modern" phenomenon. Yes, some of the despair is economic and the by-product of hopelessness over lack of meaningful employment. But it also seems to be more than just those circumstances, as statistics show that millennials are suffering from a loneliness epidemic (one in five millennials have zero friends), and describe feeling lost and empty.[11]

Acedia: High on Digital Dopamine but Depressed with Everyday Life

Furthermore, many young people that I've worked with are in a profound state of ennui and boredom. It's theorized by people like Stanford University School of Medicine professor Dr. Anna Lembke (in her book, *Dopamine Nation*), among others, that our high-octane, dopamine-spiking screen experiences have primed young people (habituated them) to need higher and higher levels of intensity to get the same dopamine rush. They've developed a dopamine tolerance and need higher and higher doses to feel something—*anything*.

But the *real* world just doesn't work that way. In fact, by comparison, the humdrum real world seems extremely boring to a person perpetually overstimulated and awash in the constant stream of social media, gaming, and other dopamine-spiking digital platforms. The problem then becomes doing anything that doesn't involve the dopamine-spiking screens (i.e., sitting in a classroom, former hobbies, face-to-face relationships, a walk in nature, etc.) leaves a person feeling under-stimulated as they experience an inevitable dopamine crash . . . a depression, boredom, emptiness, and anhedonia, where experiencing pleasure can feel impossible.

In essence, we've created a generation of young people who are struggling with what the ancient Greeks called *acedia,* which was defined as a sort of apathy—a spiritual and mental sloth. It was an ancient term meant to describe a state of listlessness. In ancient Greece, *acedia* literally meant an "inert state without pain or care," while in modern times, literary figures have used it to describe a form of depression.

I think the term perfectly describes the modern dopamine-desensitized digital citizen: numbed, apathetic, and lacking any fire or passion. The concept of acedia, almost more than any modern clinical term, best captures the plight of digital-age modernity.

And, as I'll discuss later in the book, beyond apathy and ennui, we've also robbed young people of the ability to develop the skills of patience in our instant-gratification digital age. That's extremely toxic, not just because impulsivity also correlates highly with negative future outcomes like substance addiction but also because the things that typically give a person their most profound sense of purpose and meaning usually take time to earn or to achieve. Yet if a person is primed for impulsivity and impatience (as the research shows that those on high-octane screen diets are),[12] then they also miss out on finding those rewarding, special, and potentially life-defining meaningful accomplishments. Think academics, sports, art, music, relationships.

For many of our young people, all those things just take too much time and effort without an immediate reward—an immediate reward that they've grown conditioned to expect. We have to weigh all of that emotional, psychological, and neurological context of many young adults as we try to better understand why they feel so empty and hopeless and are committing suicide at record levels (over 47,000 suicides and 1.38 million suicide attempts in 2019).[13]

In fact, being sedentary, in and of itself, has been proven to be a significant driver of depression. Psychologists have known for decades that the best non-pharmaceutical antidepressant is physical activity—taking a walk, riding a bike, jogging, playing a sport. Anything that gets the body moving also increases serotonin levels and helps to oxygenate the brain.

But what's happened to physical movement in the digital age? Movement—what's that? As Dr. Stephen Ilardi, a neuroscientist and depression researcher from the University of Kansas, says: "Sitting has become the new smoking." And, further, with regard to our skyrocketing depression rates: "We were never designed for the sedentary, indoor, sleep-deprived, socially-isolated, fast-food-laden, frenetic pace of modern life."[14] It's also important to note that these "diseases of despair" and, indeed, even depression, which are all lifestyle-impacted ailments, are essentially nonexistent in nonindustrial and indigenous societies.

And we know that depression, while having a neurophysiological component, is a disease of lifestyle. If we look at the scientific depression research, it's clear that during the past twenty-year period of our exponential immersion in high-tech, sedentary, isolating, and screen-dependent lives, our mental health metrics have all significantly deteriorated. All the while, we've thrown the pharmaceutical kitchen sink at the problem: antidepressant prescriptions have tripled, opioid prescriptions have quadrupled, anxiety meds have doubled—yet we're still getting more and more depressed, anxious, and suicidal.

If we were to *entirely* embrace the chemical imbalance paradigm of mental illness, medications that address our neurochemistry *should* be fixing things. But they're not. So endogenous (biologically based) depression and mental illness theories can't be the entire story of our mental health crisis.

In fact, there was one pivotal researcher who helped us to best understand the difference between endogenous depression versus "reactive depression" (depression that arises after some sort of traumatic event), and that may best explain our current depression epidemic.

A Depressing State of Affairs

During World War II, George Brown was a teenager living in a London slum when he came down with an ear infection. He was in bad shape, and, due to the war, he didn't have access to antibiotics or medical help. Fortunately, his neighbor was a nurse and took care of him and was even able to get him antibiotics.

George became convinced that if it weren't for her, he wouldn't have survived. That's why he was so devastated to hear that the kindly nurse, only days after the war ended, walked to the Grand Union Canal and killed herself.

He couldn't get her out of his mind and wondered what had led this generous and caring human being to end her life. What hidden depths of despair could lead such a lovely, sweet, and seemingly happy woman to make the ultimate sacrifice?

George would eventually go on to get his sociology degree and write the seminal book *Social Origins of Depression,* becoming a depression researcher and thought leader who conducted one of the most important studies to explore the causes of depression.

At the time of his study in the late 1970s, the mental health field was divided regarding the etiology of depression, with one group espousing the "chemical imbalance" in the brain (endogenous depression) model, while the other embraced the "traumatic life event" (reactive depression) paradigm as the cause of depression.

Yet neither side had much empirical data.

Thus, George Brown set about developing an experiment to find out which explanation was best supported by the evidence as he and his team selected two groups of women in London to study. The first group consisted of 114 women from local psychiatric programs who had been diagnosed with depression by a psychiatrist. In-depth interviews were conducted with each of the women, and one of the main questions they were asked was what significant things (severe loss or adverse event) had happened in the year before they became depressed.

The other group consisted of 344 women who *weren't* diagnosed with depression and were chosen from the same income group and similar geographic suburb. They were asked the same questions as the first group, including asking them if any significant negative event had occurred in the year prior to the study. If the endogenous theory (biology) were true and depression was just a result of chemical imbalance, there should have been no difference between the two groups with regard to negative events in the preceding year.

Brown and his research team methodically collected an enormous amount of data by individually interviewing both groups of women.[15] They also collected data on what they called "difficulties," which were chronic situations such as living in substandard housing or being in a bad marriage. In addition to "difficulties," they also collected data about positive factors in the women's lives, called "stabilizers" (i.e., supports), such as the number of close friends, or whether they had a supportive family and were in a healthy marriage.

The results were telling: 20 percent of the women who *didn't* get depression had a significant adverse event in the previous year. Yet in the depressed group, a whopping 68 percent of the women indicated that they had a significant adverse event during the prior year—that represented a statistically significant 48 percent difference between the two groups.

The data was clear: experiencing something stressful in your life could trigger depression; thus, the evidence supported the "reactive depression" model rather than biology as the primary driver of depression. But there were other important differences as well.

Women who experienced long-term and chronic difficulties in

their lives were three times more likely to be diagnosed with depression when a significant adverse event occurred in the previous year than women who did not experience chronic stressors. It seemed that chronic stressors effectively tilled the soil and created the ripe conditions for depression that could be *triggered* or activated by a single bad life event in the preceding year.

Thus, George Brown had discovered that it wasn't just *one* negative event that would usually trigger depression; instead, it was much more likely to develop in someone who had chronic stress in their lives over a long period *before* the one acute event took place and acted as a tipping point.

And the other surprising result was that the more positive "stabilizing" factors the women had in their lives, the less likely they were to be diagnosed with depression—even if they had chronic long-term stress *and* an acute episode in the preceding year. Essentially, a healthy, supportive environment rich with "stabilizing" factors—such as a supportive friend, close family members, or a supportive partner—all worked to immunize the person from getting depression.

The short version of George Brown's seminal research was that a chronic challenging life with a lot of stress led to depression—but that a plethora of healthy supports trumped the adverse impacts of a difficult life. Environment matters—a lot.

The most unexpected findings of Brown's research were the cumulative effects. For example, if a woman had a chronic long-term stress profile, and no friends or support networks, and *then* an adverse event happened, she was 75 percent more likely to be diagnosed with depression. Each negative event that happened, along with each lack of a supportive factor, all *accumulated* to increase the likelihood of getting clinical depression.

A thousand little cuts.

Brown began to understand depression as the result of something that had gone seriously wrong in a person's life, rather than a neurochemical imbalance in the brain, saying that "rather than being an irrational response of the brain, depression was an understandable response to adversity." Long-term stressors over a lifetime wore people down and produced a "generalization of hopelessness."

In other words, depression was caused by a long-term toxic lifestyle—not, typically, a neurochemical imbalance. Yes, a chronically stressful life that led to depression would indeed alter a person's brain chemistry; it was the toxic lifestyle, however, that caused the neurochemical imbalance associated with depression.

And what would we call an empty and vapid lifestyle consumed by a never-ending flow of polarizing social media that increases depression and self-loathing? Would we call that toxic—and chronic?

Yes, I think so.

But does screen time, and its progeny of social media, actually increase depression?

Short answer: yes. We'll look at that dynamic in more detail in the ensuing chapters.

The Depression and Disconnection Connection

In the years *since* George Brown's 1978 study, there has been much additional research into the origins of depression. Much of this work focuses on various types of toxic lifestyle factors and looks at depression through the lens of connection—or, more specifically, looks at depression as a response to various forms of *disconnection* as a depression-causing toxin.

Now, to be clear, environment can impact biology—that is to say, something like trauma can change our neurochemistry. So when we say that most factors that impact depression are not neurochemical brain imbalances, we mean to say that the root cause is environmental or psychological in nature that then manifests as a neurochemical imbalance.

Researchers and authors, including Johann Hari, have identified seven separate types of human *disconnection* that can lead to depression:[16]

- **Disconnection from meaningful work.** If you're working at a dead-end job that you hate and that gives you little sense of purpose or passion—and that offers you little control or autonomy, that's a problem.
- **Disconnection from people.** This is a reflection of our loneliness

epidemic, where we don't share any meaningful experience with other people. Your cat doesn't count.

- **Disconnection from meaningful values.** Letting the shallow and materialistic so-called influencers and our popular culture shape the values of our society so that they're based on materialism and extrinsic rewards rather than intrinsic value.
- **Disconnection caused by childhood trauma.** Trauma does lead to mental health issues, and, as Dr. Brown's work indicated, the traumatic experience you go through as a child significantly increases the likelihood of a later diagnosis of depression.
- **Disconnection from respect.** The compromised self-concept and dignity of people in dehumanizing and oppressive systems can and do lead to depression.
- **Disconnection from the natural world.** As we'll discuss more in the next section, we profoundly need a connection to nature and the natural world and become very unwell when we are removed from contact with the natural world. Indeed, Native American warriors went literally insane when they were forced into captivity on reservations and lost their connection to nature, as do animals in zoos that experience what's called "Zoochosis," as they rock back and forth and often hurt themselves.
- **Disconnection from loss of hope for a better future.** When a person cannot clearly see a hopeful path forward in their lives, they can develop feelings of learned hopelessness and helplessness—and depression.

Why Aren't Cavemen Depressed?

Which leads us back to "the outside world" of our environment and lifestyle. As I've mentioned, human beings simply weren't genetically designed for twenty-first-century living—which adversely impacts almost all of the nine abovementioned "causes" of depression.

Think about it. In the blink of an evolutionary eye, we've gone from hunter-gatherer, sped past agrarian, and leapfrogged over the industrial age and landed smack-dab in the digital age. Yet our DNA and our psychological, social, and emotional needs are still genetically paleo. We need community, connection, physical activity, purpose, nature, hope—all of which have been diminished or for some people destroyed by Big Tech and our modern way of living.

Which is why the much-heralded longevity "Blue Zones" around the world tend to cluster in societies that share certain less modernized, pre-digital lifestyles. Extending on the demographic research conducted by Gianni Pes and Michel Poulain that was outlined in the journal *Experimental Gerontology*, *The Blue Zones* author Dan Buettner identified certain common characteristics of societies where people tended to live longer and had a significantly higher number of centenarians.[17]

Those healthy and seemingly life-extending characteristics included regular physical activity, a sense of life purpose, stress reduction, moderate caloric intake, engagement in a spiritual practice, and an engagement in a strong family and social life.

Now ask yourself this question: Do we think these characteristics are enhanced or dampened by the products and platforms made by our friends at Apple, Microsoft, Facebook, Twitter, Amazon, and Google? Not so shockingly, there were no ultramodern, high-tech Silicon Valley locales or any other urban-style communities that produced healthy, long-living humans in the Blue Zones.

Clearly, neither living in high-stress urban environments nor living a sedentary, screen-staring lifestyle lacking in meaningful community are the ingredients for the one-hundred-plus club. And without making any theological conclusions about the centenarian-rich societies, interestingly, they all had profound spiritual or faith-based communities.

Similarly, in separate research, Dr. Stephen Ilardi, the previously mentioned University of Kansas psychologist, researcher, and author of *The Depression Cure*, discovered that non-technological indigenous peoples were much healthier from a mental health standpoint; indeed, he discovered that there were so-called primitive cultures like the Kaluli in Papua New Guinea that had zero rates of depression. Imagine that—no iPhones, yet not a single member of the over two thousand locals who were studied showed signs of clinical depression.[18]

How is that possible? We all have the same basic genetic and neurological equipment, so how come these "primitives" seemed to be immune to the modern epidemic of depression? A mental health disorder that, according to the World Health Organization (WHO), is the number one chronic and debilitating illness in the world—and yet not one member of the Kaluli was depressed?

And keep in mind that they lived difficult, challenging lives where daily survival was a struggle. So how come none of them were depressed, yet we "moderns" have the highest rates of depression—even though we live in relative comfort and have increased the amounts of antidepressants that we've thrown at the problem by almost 400 percent over the last thirty years?[19]

According to Dr. Ilardi, our increased rates of depression (not to mention other mental health woes like anxiety and addiction) are a by-product of our modernized, industrialized, and urbanized lifestyles: "We've been engineering the activity out of our lives. The levels of bright-light exposure—time spent outdoors—have been declining. The average adult gets just over six and a half hours of sleep a night. It used to be nine hours a night. There's increasing isolation, fragmentation, the erosion of community." Thus, according to Ilardi, "we feel perpetually stressed. And the more we learn about depression neurologically, the more we learn that it represents the brain's runaway stress response."

Indeed, according to Dr. Ilardi, "Americans are 10 times more likely to have depressive illness than they were 60 years ago . . . and a recent study found the rate of depression has more than doubled in just the past decade."

Beyond just an American epidemic, depression has become a global pandemic. According to the WHO in 2020, almost three hundred million people worldwide suffered from depression.[20] For years, depression had been increasing and trending globally as the number one chronic and debilitating illness—COVID only accelerated that process.

Dr. Ilardi found that other low-tech societies like the American Amish also had almost nonexistent levels of depression. And the more he looked at the commonalities of these "depression-free" societies, the more he teased out certain common variables that he included in his groundbreaking research dubbed the Therapeutic Lifestyle Change project, where clinically depressed subjects were asked to incorporate several of these lifestyle changes into their lives for several weeks.

So what were these magical lifestyle changes, which have come to be known as Therapeutic Lifestyle Changes (TLC) (others call it "Caveman Therapy")? They were six things: getting regular daily exercise; being involved in some type of social activity where social connections were made; eating an omega-3-rich diet; getting plenty of natural sunlight; getting ample sleep every night; and participating in meaningful tasks that leave little time for negative thoughts—all things that our ancestors had in abundance.

Dr. Ilardi proved the benefit of this more "primitive" lifestyle when he conducted a study that had several hundred severely clinically depressed participants adopt the TLC of the depression-immune folks in New Guinea. And what he found shocked even him: if you take a depressed person and have them live a more back-to-basics type of lifestyle, their depression disappears.

Notice that the key three ingredients in the antidepression TLC protocols were physical activity, a sense of community, and meaningful tasks.

What can be considered a "meaningful" task?

Well, survival, for one. For the Kaluli, their days weren't spent photoshopping Instagram pics or going on Reddit benders; instead, they had to hunt and struggle just to stay alive. They didn't have time for the bored ennui of the entitled.

In fact, it seems that their resilience and strength flowed from their intense struggle; that's what my dad taught me, that's what the resilience research indicates, and that's what psychiatrist and author of the seminal *Man's Search for Meaning,* Viktor Frankl, discovered in an Auschwitz concentration camp: it is the struggle for survival that can hone and sharpen a sanity-sustaining sense of *purpose,* which we as humans *need.* Otherwise, we're adrift, like so much flotsam floating on the sea. More about Frankl and meaning later in part 3.

To underline the importance of meaning in our lives, there was a fascinating 2014 study conducted by social psychologists Christina Sagioglou and Tobias Greitemeyer, both at the University of Innsbruck in Austria.[21] They found that one of the primary reasons why people feel down after using social media or Facebook is because they felt that the time spent just wasn't *meaningful.* And, as we've just mentioned, having real, authentic, and genuine meaning in our lives is critically important; but the time-suck of social media, with all of its superficiality, vitriol, and lack of authentic connection, is antithetical to that.

Dr. Ilardi's research has shown us that a simpler and more naturalized lifestyle can immunize people from depression, and we also have a plethora of research that shows us the critical importance of nature in maintaining optimal mental health. For example, we know through the work of Edward O. Wilson at Harvard and his biophilia movement,[22] as well as from Richard Louv, who coined the term *nature deficit disorder,* that human beings are hardwired toward having a genuine connection with nature. According to Louv, the skyrocketing emotional and psychological problems are all related to the erosion of our connection with nature, which is caused in large part by our immersion in the digital world.[23]

An interdisciplinary Cornell research team reported in January 2020 that as little as *ten minutes* in a natural setting can help college students feel happier and lessen the effects of both physical and mental stress. "It doesn't take much time for the positive benefits to kick in—we're talking ten minutes outside in a space with nature," said lead author Gen Meredith, associate director of the Master of Public Health program.

Dr. Don Rakow, director of the Nature Rx program at Cornell, stated it even more clearly: "A wealth of evidence in recent years shows that being active in nature, just sitting outside in nature, or even looking at a picture of nature have benefits to your overall well-being."[24]

He believes that this is especially true with COVID: "Since the start of the pandemic, all of us have developed such a great dependence on technology, that time in nature takes a back seat," he said.

But the nature research is clear: "All people benefit from time outdoors in nature," he said, emphasizing, "Let me repeat: all people," adding that the psychological benefits include reduced stress, anxiety, and depression, and physiological benefits include improved concentration and cognitive function, pain control, and faster recovery time from injuries. In addition to psychological and physiological benefits, Rakow also included the "attitudinal" benefits of greater happiness, life satisfaction, reduced aggression, and better social connections.

There is a connective thread here between Dr. Ilardi's research, along with the work of Buettner, Poulain and Pes and their work with Blue Zones, Dr. Brown and his work with the adverse impacts of a toxic environment, Dr. Rakow's nature research at Cornell, and Johann Hari's insights into our "connections" deficit. They all indicate that the culprit in our mental health crisis is a toxic modern civilization.

The inconvenient truth is that we are simply not meant to live sedentary, overstimulated, more isolated and atomized, less communal, nature-disconnected, meaning-devoid, hyperkinetic, sleep-deprived, and overstressed twenty-first-century lives.

And, as we'll read in the next chapter, our social media–flooded, high-tech world is also driving us insane in another way as well: shaping our behavior by the "social contagion" effect. Social scientists had years ago identified what they had called *sociogenic,* or *social contagion,* effects—that is, behaviors, emotions, or disorders spread by social networks or groups of people. It's basic monkey-see, monkey-do "social learning theory" in application.

Things like smoking because your friends smoke; or all of a sudden you find yourself listening to country music and going to NASCAR races because you've moved to Nashville and have a new group of friends; or you're at a movie that you don't find particularly funny, but then start laughing—and finding the film funny—because everyone else in the theater is laughing; or you find yourself skinny-dipping at midnight because all your friends got into their birthday suits and took the plunge. These are all examples of fairly innocuous social contagion effects, which are modeling, peer pressure, and groupthink all rolled into one.

But social contagions can also be more nefarious than just skinny-dipping with friends. The Nazi movement was a social contagion. Cults and lynch mobs are social contagions. And, in the digital age, with the increased power, amplification, ubiquity, and reach of the new so-called social media, the social contagion effect has taken on an entirely new, troubling—and sometimes lethal—meaning.

3

The Social Contagion Effect

The Influencers: Fake Famous, Depressed Followers, and Toxic Values

HBO featured a fascinating and illuminating documentary in 2021, aptly called *Fake Famous,* that not only brilliantly deconstructs our obsession with so-called *influencers,* but pulls back the veil on the artificially curated and staged glamour and sheen of empty, vapid, and desperate people starved for life-validating attention. Their bottomless need to ravenously acquire the coin of the realm in the social media world—*followers*—is both fascinating and sickening.

The documentary was also a social experiment: What happens when producers pluck out three anonymous people and then use their bag of social media tricks to jet-fuel their Instagram notoriety? *Fake Famous* focused on the toll—both mentally and physically—that the quest for social media stardom takes on the so-called *influencer* (yes, there were tears and breakdowns).

But what effect does all this nonsense have on the millions and millions of *followers*? Forget the influencers, what about the *influenced*? How does this impact their mental health? How does this fool's gold of chasing followers impact the sense of self-worth of the follower who is shaped to see through a lens where one's entire value and self-worth are judged by the aggregation of ever-more followers or views on YouTube or TikTok, attracted to arguably counterfeit lives of glamour?

The late cultural icon and visual artist Andy Warhol had once said that "in the future, everyone will be famous for fifteen minutes." In a society where that Warhol line has become lived prophecy—on steroids—we have to explore the societal and psychological implications of such a fame-hungry culture.

But is that true? Does everyone just want to be famous—for fifteen minutes or otherwise? And, if so, *why*?

We know that schools are full of older guidance counselors who lament how the career goals of students have changed over the last twenty years. Where once you had students aspiring to be doctors, athletes, actors, musicians, and astronauts—some of whom may have found fame as a by-product of their career choice—the prospect of fame typically wasn't *the* primary reason for the career choice. Today, the most common response to the question of "What do you want to do after high school?" is some version of "I want to be famous" (here we can fill in influencer, YouTuber, TikTok star, etc.). Now fame is not the by-product but the goal.

Indeed, in a 2019 Harris Poll that surveyed three thousand kids from the United States, Great Britain, and China and asked what they wanted to be when they got older, the number one response from British and American kids was being a YouTube star. The top career goal for the kids from China? Being an astronaut.[1]

Ironically, the survey was conducted in honor of the fiftieth anniversary of the first manned moon landing by the Apollo 11 astronauts. The kids were given a choice among five professions to choose from: astronaut, musician, professional athlete, teacher, or vlogger/YouTuber. While 56 percent of kids in China said they wanted to be an astronaut, it was the last choice for the American kids, where fame seemed to trump merit or achievement. As professional YouTuber DeStorm Power told *Business Insider,* "Every time I go to schools, the most-said thing from 90 percent of kids is, 'I want to be a YouTuber.' They want to be social media stars."

So, what's wrong with that? I can hear the "Okay, boomer!" cries as I type these words . . . *C'mon, Dr. K . . . Stop being such a relic . . . What's wrong with being famous, getting attention, and having millions of followers?*

I get it. I really do. But the problem is when getting followers is the goal unto itself, it creates a shift in our values—in how we value both ourselves and everything else in our lives. Ours is an inherently shallow and vacuous value system; I think that's undeniable. We don't need to have the materialism discussion here; that ship sailed a long time ago—we are undeniably a consumer culture obsessed with the "stuff" of a materialistic society. All bling and no brains is what makes the influencer world go round and round—and creates a multibillion-dollar ecosystem.

Yes, we can say that there have *always* been social *influencers* in our society. Depending on how broadly we'd like to define that term, if we use the *Merriam-Webster* definition of *influencer,* where it's "a person who inspires or guides the actions of others," we can say that Martin Luther King, Jr., Gandhi, Cleopatra, Jesus Christ, and many others were profoundly influential during their time and beyond.

If we want to limit the term to the pop culture arena, we can easily go back to iconic stars and what used to be called "starlets" of the past century—people like Joe DiMaggio, Mae West, Muhammad Ali, Marilyn Monroe, Elvis Presley, and Jackie Kennedy. Most had talent; others had charisma and/or sex appeal.

If we'd like to narrow it even further, distilling it down to its current social media–based version, then, according to *Forbes,* "social media influencers are people who have large audiences of followers on their social media accounts, and they leverage this to influence or persuade this following to buy certain products or services." Think Kylie Jenner and her 278 million Instagram followers and her $700 million net worth (according to *Forbes,* back in 2019, she had even briefly touched the billion-dollar mark for net worth; since then, they've admitted the error and lowered the value of her personal empire to "only" $700 million).[2]

But what exactly is Kylie famous for? And where does all her wealth come from? Simply put, Kylie is famous for being famous—talent or achievement, optional. Kylie comes from the infamous Kardashian family tree of influencers, renowned for their fame based on the curation of a glamorized jet-set lifestyle of very conspicuous consumption—and not much else. They have become a cultural malignancy, spreading a "brand" that hundreds of millions of impressionable young kids live to emulate. And, in the process, they have taken the concept of celebrity worship to an entirely different level.

Even as a teenager, Kylie became incredibly wealthy by monetizing her social media fame: she was making $30 million a year for participating in her family's much-loathed and -loved reality show *Keeping Up with the Kardashians,* but most of her money has been a result of shrewdly leveraging her fame into successful clothing and cosmetic lines that her millions of adoring fans who want to emulate her purchase with reckless abandon.

Leveraging fame into a product line isn't necessarily new; Michael Jordan created a whole empire based on "Be Like Mike" and "Just Do It!" campaigns, where his fans were encouraged to buy everything from Gatorade to overpriced Air Jordan sneakers. That was an interesting shift—the extreme leveraging of celebrity by Madison Avenue. Sure, movie stars of yesteryear would shoot cigarette ads and encourage their fans to have a casual smoke, just like *they* did. Spencer Tracy did print ads shilling for Lucky Strike, while Bing Crosby, Ann Sheridan, Ed Sullivan, and even Ronald Reagan appeared in pitches for a nice relaxing Chesterfield cigarette.

But with the increased power and reach of the new visual media—television—and the evolving sophistication of marketing agencies, things went from the occasional celebrity endorsement to the creation of celebrity "brands." Michael Jordan became one of the first to fully embrace the power of branding and the marketing potential of having kids desperately doing whatever it took to "Be Like Mike." If this meant that poor kids with limited resources needed to do whatever they had to do to acquire the status symbol of wearing $100 Air Jordans to "Be Like Mike," then so be it.

It is important to point out that, while $100 sneakers may seem laughably cheap by today's bloated shoe industry standards, these were outrageously high prices for sneakers during their time. When the Air Jordan 1 came out in 1985, it was $65; by 1990, the Air Jordan V was retailing at $125. By comparison, before Air Jordans, the premier celebrity endorsed sneaker were Puma Clydes, named after New York

Knicks legend Walt Frazier's moniker, which the media had given him based on his stylized Bonnie and Clyde–like sartorial choices.

The blue suede Puma Clydes were an evolutionary leap over the basic canvas Converse Chuck Taylor All Stars of the day, which had retailed for about $12. But the stylish Puma Clydes cost a bank-breaking $25—a fortune for a sneaker in the 1970s. Regardless, many kids saved up to buy the Clyde, as Walt Frazier himself acknowledged: "You had to sacrifice like it was something special. If you got a pair of Clydes, you were taking the money out of your savings to get those shoes."[3] As a high school student in the Bronx, I was one of those kids; I saved my money from my part-time job to get my precious Puma Clydes. For me, at the time, it was less about status and more about the fact that I loved the Knicks and Walt "Clyde" Frazier and wanted to wear the shoe that he wore.

When the Air Jordans came out, there was a seismic shift. Kids *had* to have that shoe; it was as if their lives—or their sense of validation—depended on it. And some even got killed for their Air Jordans. In the '80s and '90s, thefts of Air Jordans spiked where teens would desperately do anything to get the status-endowing overpriced footwear. In 1990, *Sports Illustrated* ran a story about this phenomenon called "Senseless" describing the marketing exploitation of poor kids driven to crime—and even murder—just so that they could "Be Like Mike"—the OG of influencers.[4]

A prosecutor involved in one of the Air Jordan murders told reporter Rick Telander, "It's bad when we create an image of luxury about athletic gear that it forces people to kill over it."

Indeed, a rattled and teary-eyed Michael Jordan told Telander:

"I thought I'd be helping out others and everything would be positive. I thought people would try to emulate the good things I do, they'd try to achieve, to be better. Nothing bad. I never thought because of my endorsement of a shoe, or any product, that people would harm each other. Everyone likes to be admired, but when it comes to kids actually killing each other, then you have to reevaluate things."

Clearly, Michael Jordan hadn't anticipated the extremes that people would go to in our celebrity deification. Telander hit the nail on the head as he wrote: "Something is very wrong with a society that has created an underclass that is slipping into economic and moral oblivion, an underclass in which pieces of rubber and plastic held together by shoelaces are sometimes worth more than a human life. The shoe companies have played a direct role in this. With their million-dollar advertising campaigns, superstar spokesmen and over-designed, high-priced products aimed at impressionable young people, they are creating status from thin air to feed those who are starving for self-esteem."

Creating status from thin air to feed those who are starving for self-esteem.

Those words were written over thirty years ago, yet are even more appropriate for today's social media *influencer* obsession. I think it's fair to say that since 1990, the intersection of celebrity worship, product endorsements, and empty, lost young people seeking status by trying to emulate their famous role models has only gone nuclear—or should I say *viral*? All jet-fueled by today's sophisticated algorithms that target young people—and their insecurities—in an effort to drive engagement and juice product sales.

Unlike most of today's influencers, at least Michael Jordan had generational talent that his fans worshipped. And many of the other pre–social media stars who were influencers and celebrity-worshipped also had *talent* and often inspired their fans to push themselves to try to emulate their creative, athletic, or career success.

Unfortunately, the majority of today's social media influencers are talent-challenged and prey on lost, empty young people's obsession with luxury and status—all style with little substance. The value system has been turned upside down: achievement isn't what's being emulated; instead, a luxury lifestyle is—whether it's earned or not. So Kylie Jenner's fans want to ride in a private jet, just like they see her doing. But how can *they* do that? Well, the lesson learned from social media is to acquire millions and millions of followers—just like Kylie!

What could we have expected? If you have people who are feeling empty and numb—that sense of acedia that I mentioned earlier—and who also feel disempowered, they will inevitably gravitate toward those media idols who offer them inclusion into their rarefied circle—but only if they buy their (fill in the blank): sneaker, cosmetics, clothing line, fragrances . . . whatever.

University of Pennsylvania sociologist Elijah Anderson also addressed the issue of race and inequality as drivers of some of this phenomenon: "Inner-city kids don't have a sense of opportunity. They feel the system is closed off to them. And yet they're bombarded with the same cultural apparatus that the white middle class is. They don't have the means to attain the things offered, and yet they have the same desire. So they value these 'emblems,' these symbols of supposed success."

During the Michael Jordan–Nike controversy, Spike Lee, who had also starred in and directed some of the Jordan Nike commercials, had come under fire from a local New York columnist for his involvement in what was alleged to be exploitation of young Black kids and his role in the violence that accompanied the obsession for the celebrity-endorsed sneakers.

Lee angrily responded in *The National*: "The Nike commercials Michael Jordan and I do have never gotten anyone killed. . . . The deal is this: Let's try to effectively deal with the conditions that make a kid put so much importance on a pair of sneakers, a jacket and gold. These kids feel they have no options, no opportunities."

There's some truth to that. At the end of the day, the real problem isn't the "stuff" but the underlying factors causing so many young people to seek external validation through these materialistic "emblems" of success. I also think that the supercharged modern social media *influencer* culture is helping to create the conditions—the twisted values—that "make a kid put so much importance on a pair of sneakers, a jacket and gold"—or any other influencer-peddled status symbol.

Influencers don't need to be hawking products to be influential. Again, as we understand from social learning theory, influencers can shape the way that people behave, dress, think, or value themselves and the other people in their orbit simply by way of their modeled behavior. Jennifer Aniston made her *Friends*-era hairstyle a phenomenon; Billie Eilish created an army of baggy-clothed followers who emulated her no-body-shaming dress style, and Harry Styles's flamboyant and gender-blurring sartorial choices have impacted the fashion sensibilities of many of his followers.

And perhaps the most effective social media influencer of this generation is the forty-fifth president of the United States; a certain orange-hued personality whose unrestrained and unfiltered presence on social media profoundly (and perhaps irreversibly) influenced not only politics but the behavior of his followers (adversely or otherwise) and the entire media and news landscape like no other public figure before him. He remains a clear and powerful example of the impact that a charismatic person with an enormous social media following can have.

Where did all of these social media influencer dynamics begin? We can look back and say that perhaps the grande dame of the modern influencer movement—where people are famous only for being famous and where social media superstars are the new rock stars—was Paris Hilton. Her "stardom," just like that of her BFF and subsequent fellow influencer Kim Kardashian, started with a notorious sex tape in 2001, which then led to her own reality TV show (called *The Simple Life,* with fellow influencer Nicole Richie).

Reality TV was a sort of beta test of social media, a place where narcissistic, self-absorbed, and talent-challenged people found ego-fueling viewers. Today, we see that reality TV and social media influencers are almost interchangeable, as the top influencers usually also have their own reality shows to amplify their social media impact and vice versa—and all to our societal detriment as we get dumb and dumber.

But haven't we always had inane entertainment? Some might say, "How is this new generation of TikTok or YouTube buffoonery any different from slapstick comedians of yesteryear like the Three Stooges—didn't they also dumb down the society?" While I think that's a valid question, the issue is the power of the modern media to amplify messaging in more culturally pervasive and impactful ways than ever before, to the tune of *billions* of views; *that* is the difference. So their vapid videos are indeed dumbing us down as these videos are watched over and over again, hour after hour, day after day, month after month.

We have PewDiePie, the most popular YouTuber, with 110 million subscribers, or the most popular TikTok star of them all, teen Charli D'Amelio, with her 126 million followers. The content of their posts is some of the most inane and mindless nonsense one can imagine. Not everything needs to be high art, but the mind-numbing content is being consumed so repetitively and voraciously by so many young people that it is shaping and dumbing them down more than the occasional Three Stooges movie ever could—and at least the Stooges had comedic talent.

The giggly and cringeworthy Charli D'Amelio has no visible or discernible talent. And I tried to find some—I really did. But her TikTok videos are sheer, mind-numbing, fly-on-the wall snippets of the most mundane aspects of her life. You thought *Seinfeld* was a show about nothing? The torturous and boring-beyond-tears, eleven-minute TikTok video about Charli getting her wisdom teeth pulled—that I forced myself to watch—had been, incredibly, viewed over four million times at the time of this writing.

At least the formerly popular and yet oh-so-loathsome *Jersey Shore* crew had some train-wreck watchability and appeal. But I'd honestly rather watch C-SPAN multiple-hour filibusters or Connecticut grass grow than Charli D'Amelio TikTok videos. At least grass can be colorful. Yet I could reasonably argue that she has more impact on teenage girls than the president of the United States, Gloria Steinem, and Ruth Bader Ginsburg combined.

By the way, D'Amelio's four million views of her trip to the dentist is comparable to *The CBS Evening News* and their four million viewers—which at least happens to be well produced and interesting. Oh, where have you gone, Walter Cronkite and Edward R. Murrow? If there's an afterlife, for both of your sakes, I pray that you don't have the internet and TikTok.

Not to be outdone, the infamous "egg picture" on Instagram (literally a still photo of a light brown egg—and nothing else), has broken the previous likes record set by Kylie Jenner, which had eighteen million likes, and is currently a viral phenomenon at a whopping thirty million likes.

It's tough to predict what or when something will go viral. Like a windswept forest fire, these things spread faster than anyone can anticipate. I once had a newspaper article I wrote go viral with over seven million views and shares—it was, admittedly, a bit exhilarating.[5] And then the absurdity of it all sets in. Why did that particular piece catch fire while others didn't?

Luck and timing are two big factors in this equation. D'Amelio is thought to have shot to TikTok stardom mostly by chance—in 2019, on the relatively nascent TikTok platform, she started posting her dancing-in-my-room content that caught internet fire and shot her off into the influencer stratosphere. Now she has endorsement deals, her own merchandise line, and well-monetized content.

It is interesting to see how emotionally connected the influencers are with the number of followers that they have—not so much the actual followers themselves, mind you, rather their all-important aggregate follower count. Like the baseball player judged by his batting average, or the figure skater who lives and dies by the scores that the judges give them, the influencer is entirely defined—their entire sense of value—by the number of followers.

When Charli D'Amelio found out that she had lost a million followers, she became inconsolable on camera, crying as if Grandma had died—not to worry, she still has way over one hundred million followers, and that's all that *really* counts. But her pain was palpable, as you could see that these followers define her and validate her otherwise humdrum life.

As was mentioned, celebrity worship has always been a tricky thing. But at least our musicians and athletes excelled at their respective endeavors. Babe Ruth was able to hit home runs—a lot of them. He did something better than anybody else was able to, at least until Hank Aaron came along. The same can be said for our top musicians, writers, and actors—they're the best in the world at their craft.

Today, our most famous *influencers*—yes, you, Kardashian clan—seemingly have no talent other than cultivating their celebrity. And now, every kid who can upload a video wants in on the talent-challenged Olympics. Hey, I may not be able to hit a hanging curve or dance *The Nutcracker*—but I can post an inane TikTok video like it's nobody's business.

This pervasive emptiness changes us. I'll use my own kids as an example. They are fourteen-year-old twin boys who had a pretty balanced childhood: they played sports and music and were good students. Then COVID made a mess of things, as they were both impacted emotionally and educationally. Luckily, they made it through to the other side, but during COVID, they both became tuned in to YouTube and became obsessed with Mr. Beast and his "stunt philanthropy," as well as with Mark Rober and his science-themed videos.

I rationalized that at least Rober is an ex–NASA rocket scientist, and his videos are creative and inventive as he focuses on popular science and do-it-yourself gadgets as he generates over 580,000 viewers a day. Did I mention that CNN, according to the Nielsen folks, gets approximately 224,000 nightly viewers—less than half the people that watch Mark Rober every day? And let's not even get into the brown egg.

But I digress. As I was saying, my kids started getting into some of these YouTubers—and, perhaps most disconcerting, started obsessing over views—not just about YouTube but about *everything*. They started judging the quality of anything and everything by the views received. If we would fire up an old movie on YouTube, the first question would be "How many views does it have?" and a groan of disappointment would emanate if there were less than, say, two hundred thousand views, and squeals of joy if ten million people had seen what we were about to watch.

I would ask my sons, "What if it was the greatest movie in the world (*Citizen Kane* or *Avengers: Endgame,* take your generational pick), and it only had three views—would you enjoy it less?" Their honest answer? My one son said, "Yes. Because it would influence me and make me think it wasn't any good before I even watched it." Conversely, the worst film ever made would be perceived as wonderful if millions had watched it. And therein lies the problem: this influencer groupthink paradigm makes popularity—and not quality—the primary value.

The Zen koan version of this would be: if a tree falls in the forest and there's no one there to view, like, or share it, then who cares if it makes a sound? It doesn't *matter.* It only matters or has value if millions of people also saw or heard it. Emptiness perpetuates emptiness. The more we blast this habit-forming and inane content out there, the more we shape and create further emptiness. And round and round it goes.

A few decades ago, before social media, lost and empty people were at risk of joining cults to find a sense of belonging and purpose. But those lost, empty souls from yesteryear were a relatively small number; today, almost everyone feels a sense of emptiness (61 percent of Americans report feeling lonely; nearly half say they feel "left out"; and Gen Z are the loneliest of all, with 68 percent saying they feel that "no one really knows them.")[6]

I believe that our loneliness epidemic and these feelings of emptiness have been culturally and digitally amplified—and have also led us to join a modern-day cult: the Church of Big Tech. The very same people who have created our malaise . . . and now, we've become their loyal and devoted followers.

We've drunk the digital Kool-Aid and are entirely ready to follow our Big Tech High Priests—and their *influencers*—into the abyss—or is it the cloud?—with sometimes lethal consequences. Even worse, we now know that these "priests" know exactly what they are selling—and they will do anything to keep us hooked.

The Facebook "Whistleblower," Instagram Suicides, and Anorexia

Former Facebook employee Frances Haugen was having her moment. Within a two-week period in September of 2021, the incriminating "Facebook Files" she'd turned over to *The Wall Street Journal* were featured in an explosive exposé in that paper;[7] she appeared in a damning *60 Minutes* interview with Scott Pelley that was viewed by millions; she testified in front of the Senate's Committee on Finance about the dangers of Facebook and said that the company needs to declare "moral bankruptcy";[8] and she was one of the featured speakers at the annual Web Summit—the Super Bowl of the tech world—in Lisbon, Portugal, where she continued her one-woman scorched-earth campaign against her former employers.[9]

Haugen has painted a picture of a company that has an inherent conflict: what's good for Facebook isn't what's good for society—and vice versa. Her indictments against Instagram and its parent company, Facebook, were backed by thousands of internal emails and documents that she had surreptitiously copied.

But this wasn't the first time that Facebook internal research had caused a ruckus; in 2012, Facebook researchers used nearly seven hundred thousand Facebook users as guinea pigs, sending them happy or sad posts to test whether or not emotions can be contagious on social media. The results? Yes, the emotions shared via social media did indeed have a social contagion effect and were contagious.

When their findings were published in the *Proceedings of the National Academy of Sciences,* the blowback was loud and immediate, both from other social scientists' criticism of using participants without their knowledge and from the Facebook users themselves who felt used by unwittingly participating in this "research" where their emotions had been surreptitiously manipulated. In another example of after-the-fact remorse, one of the Facebook researchers issued an apology, saying, "In hindsight, the research benefits of the paper may not have justified all of this anxiety."[10]

In academic research, you could never do human research without going through a rigorous screening of an institutional review board (IRB), where methodology, consents, ethics, and all aspects of the research are closely reviewed. But not with Big Tech; they have repeatedly violated basic ethical principles of privacy and consent when it comes to their user base.

As for whistleblower Frances Haugen's allegations, they were manifold:

First of all, that the company had done internal research that had indicated that Instagram was harming teenage girls by increasing their thoughts of suicide and exacerbating eating disorders—and yet did nothing to change the algorithms that were causing the harmful imagery because it was thought that it would decrease engagement.

The second issue that Haugen exposed was the fact that Facebook would often selectively exempt high-profile users known as "xCheck" clients like celebrities, politicians, and journalists and would allow them to post content that violated Facebook's content policy against posts that contained harassment or that could incite violence—and as of 2020, there were 5.8 million designated xCheck users.

Third, Facebook made a conscious decision in 2018 to use an algorithm that they knew would increase anger among its users because they knew that anger was a more profitable emotion to elicit, as it increased platform engagement.

And, finally, Facebook allowed bad actors and foreign entities access to its platform by consistently understaffing its counterespionage information operations and counterterrorism teams, which Haugen considers a national security threat. While she was a Facebook employee from June 2019 to May 2021, she spent time working on the company's counterespionage team and saw China using Facebook to surveil Uighur dissidents and Iran using it for espionage.

Haugen confirmed what many had long suspected: while Facebook may present a façade of a benevolent company whose goal is to "connect people," their actual agenda is user engagement and profit—often at the expense of their users.

The Instagram research that showed the adverse effects on teen girls was particularly troubling. As academic research has already shown, social media can make people more depressed via the "social comparison" effect (more about that in a moment). Haugen's released Facebook Files confirm that, contrary to Facebook's public denials, they knew about these harmful effects—and still chose to do nothing.

The Facebook Files showed that for the past three years, Facebook had conducted internal studies into how Instagram was affecting its millions of young users, and the emails and reports recovered by Haugen were damning: "Thirty-two percent of teen girls said that when they felt bad about their bodies, Instagram made them feel worse," the researchers said in a March 2020 slide presentation posted to Facebook's internal message board that was reviewed by *The Wall Street Journal*. "Comparisons on Instagram can change how young women view and describe themselves."

Another slide from the researcher's 2019 presentation said: "We make body image issues worse for one in three teen girls," and "Teens blame Instagram for increases in the rate of anxiety and depression. This reaction was unprompted and consistent across all groups."

Perhaps most shocking of all, among teens who reported suicidal thoughts, 13 percent of British users and 6 percent of American users traced the desire to kill themselves to Instagram, another presentation slide showed—and yet they still refused to change the toxic algorithm.

In a truly despicable exploitation of their vulnerable users, Instagram "curates" images of anorexia to teen girls who have anorexia and other eating disorders by barraging them with photos and videos of other malnourished girls—a practice that experts say has been shown to worsen their eating disorders as it triggers their unhealthy compulsions.

They callously did this because it was good for business. Making anorexic girls sicker was good for the bottom line, as it kept the vulnerable girls more engaged on Instagram. So what if eating disorders have the highest mortality rate of any mental illness? Indeed, the mortality rate associated with anorexia is twelve times higher than the death rate of *all* causes of death for females fifteen to twenty-four years old. And a study by the National Association of Anorexia Nervosa and Associated Disorders reports that 5–10 percent of anorexics die within ten years after developing the disease; 18–20 percent of anorexics will be dead after twenty years, and only 30–40 percent ever fully recover.

In light of the above mortality statistics, think about the sheer greed and inhumanity to willfully contribute to the increase of that illness to increase revenue. It should sicken all of us. But that's what the Facebook vultures did. According to the recovered files, a team of Instagram researchers earlier this year created a test user that followed dieting and thinness-obsessed Instagram accounts, as well as hashtags like #skinny and #thin. Then Instagram's algorithm recommended more eating disorder–related content—including images of extremely thin female bodies and accounts with names like "skinandbones," and "applecoreanorexic," according to the disturbing internal study.

Teens who already have body image issues share them as "thinspo," images that "inspire" users to try to become impossibly thin, according to eating disorder experts. Yet, amazingly, there was total resistance to changing the algorithm that sent these images to these at-risk teens.

Things at rival social media site TikTok may have been even worse. According to another *Wall Street Journal* investigative report, a dozen fake automated accounts (bots) on TikTok were created by *The Journal* and registered as thirteen-year-old girls. Within weeks of joining, these twelve "thirteen-year-olds" were sent tens of thousands of weight loss videos by the video-sharing app's algorithm. Some videos included tips about three-hundred-calorie-a-day restrictive diets; others recommended consuming only water or taking laxatives, while others showed videos of emaciated girls with protruding bones, and shaming comments for those who wanted to reject these extreme diet ideas, like "You're disgusting, it's really embarrassing."[11]

TikTok's response to *The Wall Street Journal* report was that it will continue to remove videos that violate its rules. But what about changing the toxic algorithm that's designed as a heat-seeking missile to attack these girls' vulnerabilities? Removing videos after the fact misses the point that the platform is *designed* to send such emotionally resonant and hard-to-resist videos.

As for Facebook, they are apparently not willing to do anything that may hurt teen engagement, because Zuckerberg's Facebook mothership has steadily been losing users and has been looking for ways to increase its younger audience; that's why the success of its youth-based Instagram platform is so important—and why they had plans to create Instagram Kids, to cultivate a very young consumer to supplement their declining Facebook base.

Not unlike any good drug dealer, Facebook understand the notion of hooking their users while they're young. And Instagram is the preferred app of teens; according to slides reviewed by *The Wall Street Journal,* more than 40 percent of Instagram's users are twenty-two years old and younger, and about twenty-two million teens log onto Instagram in the U.S. each day, compared with only five million teens logging onto Facebook, where young users have been shrinking for a decade.

And, on average, teens in the U.S. spend 50 percent more time on Instagram than they do on Facebook. "Instagram is well positioned to resonate and win with young people," said one of the researcher's slides that was posted internally, while another read: "There is a path to growth if Instagram can continue their trajectory."

Thankfully, all the new whistleblower allegations, and the negative publicity surrounding those allegations, have led Instagram's chief, Adam Mosseri, to announce that they will "pause" the Instagram Kids initiative to—and this is rich—help build better parental supervision tools. Right. The parents. But what about the toxic algorithms?

In his September 27, 2021, press release announcing the "pause," Mosseri reaffirms his belief regarding the importance of developing

Instagram Kids, because, hey, you know, kids are going to be online anyway. Then he goes on to acknowledge the explosive *Wall Street Journal* exposé and the internal research about the adverse effects on teens: "Research . . . informs our work on issues like negative body image. We announced *last week* [italics are mine] that we're exploring two new ideas: encouraging people to look at other topics if they're dwelling on content that might contribute to negative social comparison, and a feature tentatively called 'Take a Break,' where people could put their account on pause and take a moment to consider whether the time they're spending is meaningful."

Last week, Adam? Really? You knew for three years that your algorithms were targeting vulnerable teens with toxic content that made them more unwell and potentially contributing to suicides, and then, coincidence of coincidences, right after *The Wall Street Journal* pulled back the curtain on your toxic product, you've decided to "explore" a new idea to encourage people to look at other topics if they're "dwelling on content that might contribute to negative social comparison"?

But encouraging "dwelling" on negative content has been your *entire* business model to increase engagement! *Now* you're going to "explore" encouraging people to look at other topics when they're doing what you've manipulated them to do in the first place—which is dwell on negative content. And this more responsible revelation coincidentally occurs only *after The Wall Street Journal* and Frances Haugen tag-teamed to expose your predatory and harmful tactics?

I'm sorry if it feels a bit like the serial philanderer who gets caught and swears that they'll never cheat again. There's a bit of a credibility issue with the timeliness of this new "initiative." And by the way, how exactly are you going to do all of this "encouraging" toward healthier content anyway?

Interestingly, it was later reported that it was Zuckerberg himself who insisted that Instagram Kids not be scrapped, as many within the company were pushing for in light of all the negative attention, and even as forty attorneys general called for plans for Instagram Kids to be scrapped. But Zuckerberg was adamant that the official wording released to the public by his underling Mosseri would be the abovementioned "pause" language. Let things blow over a bit and then full steam ahead with damaging the kids, teens, and young adults. Was the temptation for Zuckerberg to monetarily exploit a whole new vulnerable and highly susceptible market—kids—simply just too great.

The question really is: How can you trust a company that had heralded a change to its algorithm in 2018 that was allegedly designed to improve its platform, but that instead only served to make people angrier and more hostile—because anger is the sweet nectar of user engagement that makes the Facebook world go round?

Mark Zuckerberg had originally declared that his aim was to strengthen bonds between Facebook's users and improve their well-being by fostering interactions between friends and family. A regular Hallmark moment. Alas, those pesky Facebook Files that Haugen brought to light showed that, within the company, staffers warned the change was having the *opposite* effect—it was making Facebook, and those who used it, angrier.

But Zuckerberg refused to incorporate the fixes that his team had proposed because he worried that they would lead people to interact with Facebook *less*. And that's not good for Facebook—angry people are good for Facebook. Here exactly is the inherent conflict: Facebook only does well if we are unwell. Everyone emotionally triggered and staring at a screen for twenty-four hours a day would be the ultimate success for Facebook's bottom line—but wouldn't be so great for, you know, humanity.

* * *

WHILE FACEBOOK WAS doing its own research, academic research has long established the impact that screen time and social media were having on depression and mental health. One study showed that teens on a screen for more than five hours per day were 20 percent more likely to have "suicidal ideations and actions" than teens on a screen for less than an hour a day. In statistical terms, that's an enormous increase in self-harm.[12]

But why? What is it about staring at a screen that makes young people want to kill themselves? Is it the content? Is it the screen itself? Being sedentary more? Is it that the screen keeps you indoors and robs you of genuine "face time"? Is it the self-loathing that comes when comparing ourselves to the idealized lives of others? Yes, yes, and yes. Yes to all of the above.

Some more research: one of the largest studies on Facebook, published in 2017 in the *American Journal of Epidemiology,* followed the Facebook use of more than five thousand people over three years and found that higher use correlated with self-reported declines in physical health, mental health, and life satisfaction.[13]

Perhaps unsurprisingly, staring at Facebook doesn't seem to be good for people.

Another large, well-constructed research study at Case Western Reserve University School of Medicine back in 2010 looked at the social media habits of over four thousand high school students and focused on the outcomes of "hypernetworkers"—defined as students who were on social media for more than three hours per school day. The 11.5 percent of students who met that criterion had much higher rates of depression, substance abuse, poor sleep, stress, poor academic performance, and suicide.

"This should be a wake-up call for parents," warned the study's lead researcher, epidemiologist Scott Frank, in a Case Western press release, warning that parents should discourage "excessive use of the cell phone or social websites in general."[14]

But, as we all know, our screen usage over time has only increased. According to GlobalWebIndex, today, *most* teens would be considered "hypernetworkers," with average daily social media usage more than doubling over the last ten years.

Let's look at one reason *why* staring at Facebook may make a person more depressed.

In a 2014 study, researcher Mai-Ly Steers of the University of Houston and her colleagues found a similar depression-effect on Facebook users: the more time college students spent on Facebook, the more likely they were to experience depressive symptoms.[15]

They hypothesized that "Facebook depression" may occur because of the psychological phenomenon known as the "social comparison effect"—the dynamic whereby comparing ourselves to a continuous stream of *my life is great* content may make a person feel, *Hey, maybe my life isn't so hot after all.* That's why so-called *influencers* mainly influence people to feel bad about themselves—and it's why Instagram drives up suicidal thoughts and self-loathing.

Imagine a poor, lost teen without a strong sense of identity and lacking genuine social supports, staring at glam Kim Kardashian Instagram photos all day; or someone recently divorced and alone staring at their Facebook news feed and seeing a never-ending stream of one happy family vacation photo after another from all their friends? In both instances, we can see how the effect can exacerbate the feelings of emptiness and despair—of *my life is a failure.*

So being sedentary . . . more isolated . . . lacking the passion of acedia . . . and constantly comparing ourselves to idealized images of others—these are the ingredients of our modern madness, a madness fueled by social media that's driving our record spike in adverse mental health outcomes.

In addition to fueling the spike in suicide and anorexia, social media can be the carrier of a variety of other psychiatric or pathological "social contagions."

TikTok Tourette's Syndrome

TikTok Tourette's. It has a rather catchy ring to it. But instead of being a new jingle or a lyrical child's game, it's a strange new phenomenon that was first noticed by pediatricians all over the world during the COVID year of 2020: teenage girls who were on TikTok—and who followed certain very popular TikTok influencers who made videos about their tic disorder—started manifesting behaviors consistent with Tourette's syndrome.[16]

It was all rather odd and a strange bit of irony that a social media platform named TikTok was now being associated with a tic disorder. Tourette's is a nervous system disorder that causes people to make repetitive, involuntary movements or sounds, typically affects more boys than girls (by a rate of three to one), and tends to be diagnosed at a young age. And while the causes or etiology of Tourette's aren't fully understood, it does seem to be linked to various parts of the brain, including an area called the *basal ganglia,* which helps control body movements, and it also seems to have a genetic or hereditary component.

There is also a dopamine theory regarding the cause of Tourette's, as researchers have found evidence that indicates that there may either be too much stimulating dopamine being released in the brain of a Tourette's individual, or that their brain receptors that process dopamine may be overly sensitive to dopamine.[17]

While the exact cause remains murky, what is clear is that there are certain neurophysiological components involved along with certain gender-specific propensities (as mentioned, significantly more male than female) and clear behavioral markers that are the most common features in the disorder.

Unusually, the new cases that were flooding into pediatric hospitals in the U.S., Canada, the UK, and Australia were mostly teen girls instead of boys, and instead of the more common facial tics, most had exaggerated hand and arm movements and also what's known as *coprolalia,* the repetitive and involuntary use of obscene language—which is quite rare among those with genuine Tourette's syndrome.

Rare or not, the cases kept coming. At Texas Children's Hospital, the caseload for patients with tics had multiplied by several dozen since March 2020; at Johns Hopkins Tourette's Center, they went from a pre-pandemic rate of 2–3 percent of pediatric patients to a staggering 10–20 percent of their pediatric patients showing signs of a tic disorder. And at Rush University Medical Center in Chicago, their rate of patients reporting tics had doubled after 2020, with the vast majority of the new Tourette's patients being female.

Researchers and pediatricians were initially stumped until they began to notice a common denominator in all the new cases. According to several medical journal articles, including "TikTok Tics: A Pandemic Within a Pandemic," published in the *Journal of Movement Disorders,* the doctors who authored the study discovered that the girls they studied who were showing this adolescent-onset version of Tourette's had all been watching videos of TikTok influencers who claimed that they had Tourette's syndrome.

But they also made some other observations:

These so-called Tourette's "influencers" were extremely popular on TikTok—racking up over five billion views (!)—and causing the researchers to believe that it was these very same videos that were indeed causing the sharp rise in the (seemingly exaggerated) Tourette's-like symptoms in many of the teenage girls who viewed the videos. Indeed, some would even start speaking with the same British accent as one of the TikTok Tourette's influencers, or would even yelp out the same word that they had heard the influencer say on TikTok. For example, the word *bean* became a verbal tic that was originally said by one of the TikTok Tourette's influencers and was then repeated by many of the young female late-onset followers.

This clearly seemed like it was an example of sociogenic spread or the "social contagion effect" and reflected the basic principles of social learning theory: monkey see, monkey do. But the plot thickens; doctors who did a quantitative study of both the Tourette's influencers' TikTok videos as well as an examination of the adolescent-onset girls came to the conclusion that it was questionable whether *either* group genuinely had Tourette's syndrome. What remained unclear, however, was whether or not the girls were *consciously* aware that they were seemingly mimicking the tic disorder.

Some researchers and clinicians have developed the term "Munchausen by Internet."[18] Munchausen disorder, which has now been renamed Factitious Disorder, is a disorder wherein a person consciously feigns and reports symptoms of any number of psychiatric or medical disorders in order to receive attention and/or medical treatment. There isn't much current research on Munchausen by Internet, which has also been termed "Digital Factitious Disorder" (DFD), but we do know that up to 1 percent of all psychiatric referrals have a factitious disorder with the initial onset believed to be about 25 years of age.[19]

What remains unclear, at least to the best of my analysis, is whether these sociogenic psychiatric disorders are being consciously mimicked (or feigned), or are they unconsciously absorbed from their social model (the "influencer") and manifesting as authentic psychiatric phenomena.

Conscious or not, the predictors of developing a Factitious Disorder include anxiety, depression, stressful current life events, and past significant childhood trauma. Sure enough, the researchers of the Tik-Tok Tourette's phenomenon did find preexisting psychiatric common denominators as well: most of the teens had some level of a psychiatric history (depressed, anxious, etc.) and, interestingly, the Tourette's influencers themselves did not present with the types of tics that seasoned medical professionals have come to expect from a genuine tic disorder. It was as if the influencer was manifesting Factitious Disorder and acting or playing a part, which was, in turn, shaping the behavior of those who were watching the Tourette's influencer. But can this be possible? Can a video of someone presenting with a tic disorder lead to a viewer who repeatedly watches those videos to actually behave like they have a tic disorder?

It is certainly possible, as we've already seen, that certain disorders can be subconsciously mimicked, like people with pseudo-borderline personality disorder (which we'll discuss in the next chapter) or those with pseudo-seizures—for those people, whether they're sociogenic by-products of a social contagion effect or not, they certainly feel *real* to the person.

For doctors who've worked with some of these TikTok Tourette's disorder cases, they indicate that most of the teens were previously diagnosed with anxiety or depression that had either been brought on or exacerbated by the pandemic and that then seemingly made them more vulnerable to mimicking something like Tourette's syndrome—or any other type of witnessed disorder.

Indeed, according to Dr. Donald Gilbert, a neurologist at Cincinnati Children's Hospital Medical Center who specializes in pediatric movement disorders, physical symptoms of psychological stress often manifest in ways that patients have seen before in others. Dr. Gilbert specifically mentions having had patients who experienced psychogenic nonepileptic seizures (the previously mentioned *pseudo-seizures*), who, in most of the cases, had personally witnessed the seizures of their relatives who did have epilepsy.

Medical professionals also know that maladaptive psychiatric behaviors like cutting can also have a social contagion effect and can be broadly mimicked by other psychiatrically vulnerable young patients.

Can that same social mimicking of a disorder apply when the behavior is seen on a video—like TikTok—rather than in person?

Kayla Johnson was a seventeen-year-old from Sugarland, Texas, who had previously been diagnosed with ADHD and an anxiety disorder, but then developed a tic disorder. As she told *The Wall Street Journal,* she was referred to Texas Children's Hospital to address her newly emergent behaviors where she saw a movement-disorders specialist who asked about her social media use.

She told him that during remote schooling during COVID, she had a hard time staying organized and started watching YouTube to find videos of other students with ADHD to see how they were coping with remote schooling, screen time, and their attentional issues. That, in turn, led to TikTok videos of teens with ADHD or anxiety who also had tics. Soon thereafter, Kayla developed her own tic disorder and described what role social media may have played: "I do think my tics may have been triggered by these videos and that it spiraled into its own beast."

Doctors are now pointing a finger squarely at social media as the spreader of this contagion. According to a recent paper by Drs. Mariam Hull and Mered Parnes, child neurologists at Texas Children's Hospital who specialize in pediatric movement disorders, social media appears to be providing a new way for psychological disorders to spread quickly around the world.[20]

And, as a social media platform grows, so, too, does the potential to spread a whole host of mental disorders via the social contagion effect. And TikTok certainly is growing. As a video-based social media platform, it had grown exponentially since 2018: between January 2018 and August 2020, its number of monthly active users grew by 800 percent to a total of one hundred million in the United States and seven hundred million globally.

As the social media beast grew, so did the spread of the digital Tourette's contagion. Within a three-week period in March of 2021, views of videos with the keywords #tourettes and #tic had an astonishing 5.8 billion views—almost as many people as there are on the planet.

We have to understand that, while digital social media–driven contagions are a new phenomenon, previous social contagion effects have been well documented, with unsettling examples going back years and even centuries; as we'll read below, these have included everything from sudden suicide clusters to a well-documented case of uncontrollable mass dancing.

Before anyone snickers as they visualize an out-of-control Kevin Bacon in *Footloose,* this seemingly involuntary mass dancing outbreak was so severe and intense that several people reportedly died from exhaustion during their dancing craze.

So it would seem that even though TikTok may be a more recent social contagion effect that relies on digital platforms to spread, our profoundly social and highly impressionable species is no stranger to some rather odd—and destructive—socially influenced behavior.

The uncontrollable mass dancing episode is an example of a quickly spreading social contagion that comes to us from before the time of TikTok, before the internet—before any type of electronic media, for that matter. In fact, it's an episode of a mass social contagion from a period shortly after the Gutenberg press was invented, yet remains a powerful example of how powerfully contagious certain human behavior can be for an inherently social species.

The Dancing Plague of 1518

One morning in July of 1518, a woman named Frau Troffea walked into the middle of the street in the city of Strasbourg, Alsace (in what is now France), and silently began to twist, twirl, and shake. She kept manically dancing like that for nearly a week, by which time three dozen other people, mostly women, joined in. By August, this dancing epidemic had as many as four hundred people inexplicably gyrating and dancing.[21]

Historical documents from physician notes at the time, local and regional chronicles, and even notes by the Strasbourg city council all document this social contagion of a dancing mass hysteria. The inexplicable dancing lasted for such a long time that doctors eventually intervened, putting some of the dancers in the local hospital.

Some of the physicians blamed the "dancing fever" on "hot blood" and recommended that the afflicted might be able to dance and gyrate the fever away. To assist them in this dance-more cure, a stage was constructed, and professional dancers were brought in along with a band to encourage *more* dancing. What can we say? This was also the period where medicine relied on leeches and bloodletting.

Unfortunately, as the maniacal dancing continued, many dancers collapsed from exhaustion, and some even died from strokes and heart attacks. This was no *Footloose*. The odd episode didn't end until early September, when the dancing outbreak began to subside after nearly two months.

What could have led people to dance themselves to death? Some historians believe that the stress and horror of disease and famine that were ravaging Europe and Strasbourg may have triggered a stress-induced hysteria that led to the bizarre dancing outbreak.

Yet others theorize it may have been the work of a religious cult—they're always convenient to blame.

One final theory with some merit speculates that the dancers may have accidentally ingested ergot, a toxic mold that grows on damp or moldy rye and produces spasms and hallucinations. Interestingly, the hallucinogenic drug LSD is derived from an ergot alkaloid.

The ergot theory has also been suggested as the cause of the Salem witch trials episode. As the theory goes, women who ingested ergot started tripping, gyrating, and foaming at the mouth and were suspected of being possessed by the devil. The rest, as they say, is history.

It's unclear if the dancing plague of 1518 was a genuine social contagion effect or an ergot-induced episode. But if it were the former, then clearly, we would have another powerful example of a social contagion effect.

Beyond dancing plagues, social media tic disorders, and influencer toxic values, as mentioned, social contagions can often have lethal variants. In the next chapter, we'll look at some of these more closely.

4

Viral Violence

The Werther Effect and the Wales Suicides

In January of 2007, a strange thing started occurring in Bridgend, South Wales—young people started hanging themselves. By December of 2008, a total of twenty-six—mostly teenagers—had taken their own lives in the traditional Welsh community. Speculation ran rampant as to what was causing this suicide epidemic: Was it a suicide cult? Some sort of internet effect? Or just depressed teens feeling trapped in a gray and economically depressed former mining town?

Although rare, suicide "clusters" are not unheard of and are considered a classic social contagion effect. This type of suicide social contagion has also been called the "Werther effect," named after Goethe's novel *The Sorrows of Young Werther.*[1]

That novel, published in 1774, narrated the story of a young, sensitive, and passionate artist named Werther. Werther falls in love with a woman named Charlotte, who is engaged to an older man, Albert, whom she eventually marries. Charlotte does share strong feelings for Werther, but knows that their attraction cannot move forward and asks him to limit his visits. Werther is tortured by his unrequited love of Charlotte and has also been ridiculed during a brief foray into noble society, where he's rejected there as well. Convinced that his only option in this love triangle is the death of one of the three of them, he eventually realizes that he must take his own life because the idea of murder is unpalatable to him. So Werther borrows two pistols from his love rival, Albert, and shoots himself in the head.

The novel became an instant sensation and established the twenty-four-year-old Goethe as a literary genius. But it had one other significant—and lethal—effect: young men throughout Europe started to dress like Werther and would then kill themselves in what also came to be known as "Werther fever." They apparently found a deep resonance with his pain and alienation and were inspired and emboldened by this fictitious character to take their own lives. The problem became so severe that the book was banned in both Italy and Denmark in an effort to stop the spread of this suicide contagion that was seemingly caused by this provocative book.

Werther fever was a classic social contagion effect. With suicides, the thinking goes something like this: when one person does something extreme, it lowers the threshold and makes it more permissible for the next person to do it. And the same for the next person and each subsequent person thereafter. And thus with each successive suicide, it becomes more and more *normative* and acceptable for the next person to do it. Recall my earlier skinny-dipping example—it's hardest for the first person to strip and jump in the water; by the tenth person, it's now the normal practice of the group, and the forces of peer pressure drive action.

With Werther fever, young men were being influenced to end their lives—by a book. And a fictitious character, no less. Imagine the power of social media and real-life suicide *influencers*—now *that's* digital madness.

In Bridgend (perhaps not so coincidentally, the town's name is derived from the old Welsh for "Bridge's End"), the suicides remained rather mysterious. Some blamed the publicity that the suicides received for the apparent copycat effect. Also odd was the number of female teens who were hanging themselves. Hanging—like suicide by gunshot—is traditionally a male method of suicide, while women tend to overdose or slit their wrists. Some psychologists theorize suicide has gender differences: the violence of shooting and hanging drawing more men, while women may be temperamentally predisposed to choose less violent methods.

As mentioned, there was also speculation about an internet suicide cult. After some of the hangings, the person's friends would put up a memorial page dedicated to him or her on Bebo, a popular social networking site. In a couple of the cases, friends who wrote eulogies on the site were found hanging a short time later. This inevitably led to the memorial pages being taken down.

There are indeed instances of internet-influenced suicide cults, specifically in Japan, where there was an epidemic of people taking their own lives by inhaling gas made out of household chemicals—in most cases, hydrogen sulfide—in cars, closets, or other enclosed spaces. Also known as "detergent suicide," over two thousand Japanese suicides occurred during a two-year period between 2009 and 2011, inspired by websites that carried recipes for the chemical mix, as well as detailed instructions on how to use it.[2]

But the suicide cluster in Wales didn't seem to fit that category. It may have been as simple as a social contagion that started out with the usual suspects as the causes of the initial one or two suicides: boredom, anhedonia, and feeling trapped in a bleak, gray town. As one Bridgend girl told the *Telegraph,* "Suicide is just what people do here because there is nothing else to do." Another said, "I really do feel sometimes like I will never get out of here."

Or, as Loren Coleman, the author of *Suicide Clusters,* wrote: it "is probably merely being pushed along by the copycat effect, in which the model for suicide among impulsive, action-driven, forlorn youth has now been placed in front of them in an area that has turned grim in a downward economy reinforced in the nearly perpetual damp mists that shroud Bridgend in the long winter months. The darkness of despair can run deep. One need not blame cults, pacts, video games, the Internet, or even the media. The gloom is like the fog surrounding one at night in Bridgend, and for many, the modeling of past suicides shout out from those Welsh nights."[3]

People can sometimes want to kill themselves in bleak places where they feel trapped. But the large number of suicides in Bridgend that year was particularly unusual. That part—the twenty-six total suicides—speaks to more than just "damp mists" and "long winter months" and the occasional random suicide. It speaks to the power of social groups to influence one another as a social contagion and create a group effect where people can feel normalized to do the most unspeakable of acts.

However, in the digital age of social media, we now have new variants of the Werther effect that aren't limited to eighteenth-century books as the source of the contagion; these new digital variants are especially malignant and virulent and can lead the young and the lost into feeling a misguided sense of purpose and community as they commit horrific acts in the furtherance of their social media–inspired goals.

The Incel Movement

The incel movement is a perfect case study of what can happen when an initially innocent group of lonely people looking for kinship and support get twisted and perverted through the amplification and *extremification* of digital media.

I've said earlier that social media has become a seemingly sentient organism that feeds off our primal id and then regurgitates those baser impulses back to us in high-octane form, not only intensified but veiled by the normalcy of "community"—*Hey, look, others feel this way, too!* Today, on the so-called dark web, there are all sorts of groups catering to the once socially outcast; entire virtual communities devoted to everything from bondage enthusiasts, to cannibalism, to pedophile groups, to all manner of fetishes and/or deviancies.

Some might say, "Hey, it's not such a bad thing to have certain fetish enthusiasts come out of the shame, isolation, and darkness of their innermost and socially unacceptable impulses and come up into the warm bathing light of fellow peers who feel the same way. After all, our need to find community and a like-minded tribe is embedded in our psychological DNA." And that may be true for all sorts of fetishes, as many fetish groups are fairly innocuous, and, according to the values of our laissez-faire society, we *should* embrace a live-and-let-live, no-harm-no-foul approach.

The problem is that some fetish groups can cross the line of "no harm, no foul" into full-blown illegality or violence. Complicating things even further when it comes to fetish sites are the distinctions between fantasy and reality; for example, in the infamous "Cannibal Cop" case in New York, where an NYPD officer who was a member of an online cannibal chat group and had been arrested for conspiracy to commit murder, lawyers (successfully) argued that their client's lurid internet activities (including instructions on how to cook specific real-life people) fell under the category of fantasy and First Amendment–protected free speech.[4]

In that particular case, it did appear that the disgraced officer and his chat room buddies were, indeed, merely engaging in fantasy—a form of disturbing and perverse internet cannibal cosplay. Yet there are many other examples where such sordid internet fantasies that are shared on various chat sites do indeed turn into the real thing, with often deadly outcomes—from abductions to actual cannibalism. Unfortunately, in our modern digital landscape, it becomes exceedingly difficult for even trained mental health professionals to discern between those who may be living out a fantasy online and those who may be pouring kerosene on an already simmering fire of insanity and hatred and who may be pushed over the edge toward real-life violence by the *extremification* of their digital immersion.

The other confounding issue with some of the more troubling online groups is that some may start off as one thing—usually benign and harmless—then mutate into something quite different and potentially more lethal. That's exactly what happened with the incel movement, which had started out as a support group for the lonely and awkward of all genders, but has morphed into a subculture of misogynistic and angry young men, some of whom have committed mass murder in the name of their mutated and misguided "cause."

There are a couple of different versions regarding the origin story and creation of the incel movement, yet both describe a very different entity from the one that it's evolved into today. The first version is that a single, shy, introverted, and lonely teenager from the West Coast in the late '90s dipped his toe into the embryonic internet hoping to find community and connection in the early days of chat forums; community and connection that he was too shy to find in the real world. Sure enough, he discovered that there were many others like him who also felt awkward in real life, especially when it came to sex and dating.

These lovable yet romantically challenged souls eventually became a community and began calling their issues "involuntary celibacy," and later adopted the shorthand of "incels" to describe themselves. According to the founding member—that original teen, who is now a grown man using the handle "Reformedincel"—the incel world of the 1990s and early 2000s was a friendly place where awkward men *and* women would talk to one another about relationship support and advice.[5]

The other incel origin story attributes the founding of the incel movement to a female Canadian university student known only by her first name, Alana, who in 1993 created a website to discuss her lack of sexual activity called "Alana's Involuntary Celibacy Project." Her website and her later mailing list were intended for "anybody of any gender who was lonely, had never had sex or who hadn't had a relationship in a long time."[6]

Alana stopped participating in her online incel project in the year 2000 when she passed the baton to somebody else, but was saddened to see what her creation has become: "It definitely wasn't a bunch of guys blaming women for their problems. That's a pretty sad version of this phenomenon that's happening today. Things have changed in the last twenty years."

Unfortunately, things in the modern incel world have gone way beyond just blaming women. With technology and the internet acting as a hatred accelerant, sexual frustration has turned to hatred, and hatred has spilled over into full-blown premeditated acts of violence and murder against women—and the men that they love. Indeed, since 2014, at least eight mass murders with sixty-one fatalities have been attributed to men who either self-identified as incels or who had incel-related writings on the internet.

Today, incel chat rooms, rather than being support groups for the lonely, have become breeding grounds for the angry. When stray dogs in a shelter are given love and positive attention, they develop caring and loving dispositions; but if they're put together with other aggressive dogs, each dog's aggression amplifies the pack's aggression and creates the climate that shapes an aggressive temperament. Similarly, these incel chat rooms and all the other online hate groups create a pack mentality that inflames their members as they breed hatred and aggression. Technology then greases the tracks of this dynamic by rewarding the most vitriolic and hateful content in the never-ending battle for online attention.

Beyond creating an aggressive pack or mob mentality, the incel movement is also a Werther effect–style of social contagion, where one glorified individual acts as an inspiration and role model for a cultlike movement. And that pivotal alpha incel—the much-copied Werther of his day—was the sick and misguided Elliot Rodger. On May 23, 2014, Elliot Rodger went on a shooting, stabbing, and vehicular rampage where he killed six and injured fourteen near the UC–Santa Barbara campus.[7] A child of privilege, Rodger was the son of Hollywood filmmaker Peter Rodger, a director of *The Hunger Games,* and a Chinese mother, Li Chen, who worked in films as well.

Entitled and with the grandiosity of a true narcissist, Rodger bared his troubled mind and soul in his 141-page manifesto, describing his thirst for revenge against the women who had rejected him and a hatred for the men who they had given their hearts and affection toward. In that document, he proclaimed himself "the closest thing to a living God" and described himself as the "ideal magnificent gentleman," who couldn't understand why, at the age of twenty-two, not only was he still a virgin but he had yet to even kiss a girl. Yet, as many narcissists do, he veiled himself in a cloak of victimhood and angrily blamed others for his unhappiness and lonely plight.

It's unsettling and eerie to watch his smug, arrogant, and villainish laughter on the "retribution" video that he made the day before the murders, as he expresses his hatred for the women who denied him "love and sex," and for the "obnoxious brutes" who received the affection that he so dearly craved. Not to exclude anyone, he also expressed a hatred for *all* of humanity, which he called a "wretched and depraved species," saying he would "slaughter and annihilate everyone" if he could—and be a god in the process.

Throughout the repetitive video, like a true self-centered narcissist, he keeps referencing the "suffering" that he's been "forced to endure" as he sits behind the wheel of his BMW, and his manifesto is filled with his delusional rants as he declares: "I am the true victim in all of this. I am the good guy."

His perceived rejection drove his decision on whom and where to murder: he chose to attack the Alpha Phi sorority because they were the "hottest" at his college and "the kind of girls I've always wanted but was never able to have" and said he had "no choice but to exact revenge on the society" that had created these untenable—to him at least—conditions. After all the carnage was over, he took the path of the fictional Werther and shot himself in the head.

The amazing part of this story is how, like the fictional Werther and his unrequited love, Elliot Rodger became a role model and modern-day hero for all the other lost and misguided incels who viewed him as a martyr. Virtually canonized by his online fans, where mass violence by incels is regularly referred to as "going E.R." and, in true digital social contagion fashion, he's been referenced as the inspiration by the other incel mass murderers.

Rodger even had a short film trailer made in his honor called *The Supreme Gentleman,* comprising excerpts from his YouTube clips. In short, Elliot Rodger was the original *social influencer* for the misguided incel movement—which, let's not forget, had started as a well-intentioned inclusive online support group for the lonely and awkward.

While there are several other high-profile incel mass murderers in addition to Elliot Rodger, perhaps the other most notorious incel was Alek Minassian, who used a Ryder truck to murder ten and injure another sixteen in Toronto on April 23, 2018.[8] Shortly before his attack, he'd posted a military-style post on Facebook, citing the "incel rebellion" and giving kudos to Elliot Rodger: "Private (recruit) Minassian, infantry unit 00010, wishing to speak to Sgt 4Chan please. C23249161. The Incel Rebellion has already begun! We will overthrow all the Chads and Stacys! All hail the Supreme Gentleman Elliot Rodger!"

The "movement" was spreading and gaining followers. One incel follower posted after Minassian's attack: "I hope this guy wrote a manifesto because he could be our next new saint!" Police said that Minassian had been radicalized by online incel communities, and in a police interrogation video, he tells the officers that he's a virgin motivated by a hatred of "Chads and Staceys," the term incels use to describe sexually active men and women. The video also showed Minassian saying that he hoped the attack would "inspire future masses to join me" in committing acts of violence as a part of the incel "uprising."

Meanwhile, Alana, the alleged founder of the incel movement, was repulsed to learn what the incel subculture had become and tried to distance herself from her errant creation, like a remorseful Robert Oppenheimer, whose invention had been used for such great devastation: "Like a scientist who invented something that ended up being a weapon of war, I can't uninvent this word, nor restrict it to the nicer people who need it."

She expressed regret that her vision of an "inclusive community" for people of all genders who were sexually deprived due to "social awkwardness, Marginalization, or mental illness" had turned into an internet-fueled hate group that was inspiring mass murders.

But that's the nature of the beast. It needs and breeds hatred.

Over the past twenty years, the incel community, which, by some estimates, numbers in the tens of thousands of followers, has morphed from an inclusive support group into a virulent and misogynistic social contagion that spreads an ideology that has come to be called "the blackpill." According to journalist and incel researcher Zack Beauchamp, the blackpill (a play on *The Matrix*'s blue pill / red pill reality paradigm) is "a profoundly sexist ideology that . . . amounts to a fundamental rejection of women's sexual emancipation, labeling women shallow, cruel creatures who will choose only the most attractive men if given the choice. Taken to its logical extreme, the blackpill can lead to violence."

The incel movement is a classic social contagion, taking vile, hateful, and repressed impulses found within our society and then using technology and digital media to amplify those tendencies. As Beauchamp describes it, "Incels are not merely an isolated subculture, disconnected from the outside world. They are a dark reflection of a set of social values about women that is common, if not dominant, in broader Western society. The intersection between this age-old misogyny and new information technologies is reshaping our politics and culture in a way we may only dimly understand—and may not be prepared to confront."[9]

School Shootings

The incel contagion is also very closely paralleled by the school shooting contagion, where we've seen a rapid spread of mass shootings as social media has given yet another group of lost and empty young men a blueprint by which to express their rage. And beyond just creating a blueprint to mimic, the digital age has created the dynamics of emptiness and the need for attention that are fueling the school shooter phenomenon.

A uniquely American phenomenon (although the mostly firearm-free country of China has experienced a rash of school mass stabbings in recent years),[10] there have been an incredible 1,316 school shootings in the U.S. since 1970. However, that number is somewhat misleading, as it represents all instances of gun violence on school grounds and not just the much-publicized crazed-loner "mass shootings" that we've come to associate with school shootings.

According to research by experts, school gun violence falls into two broad categories: First, the significantly larger number of gun incidents resulting in death occur at schools with a disproportionate number of students of color and impact Black students the most. These incidents tend to be related to conflicts between students that reflect the socioeconomic realities of communities that are ravaged by crime, drugs, and gang activity.[11]

The second category is the abovementioned mass shooter phenomenon and disproportionately affects suburban white schools, where we've seen significant spikes in mass shootings after both Columbine in 1999 and the Sandy Hook shootings in 2012—Werther-style copycats on full display and fueled by digital media.

While these loner-type of mass shootings are rare, they've had a greater impact on the national psyche and in the nightmares of both students and parents alike. And, while all gun violence is horrific and a societal scourge, for the purposes of our exploration of Werther-style social contagion effects, I have chosen to focus on the school mass-shooting phenomenon, as those attacks are more reflective of a Werther copycat phenomenon that's shaped and disseminated by modern digital media and the attendant dynamics thereof.

While most consider Columbine in 1999 the beginning of the school mass shooting phenomenon—and, in many ways, the murderous actions of Eric Harris and Dylan Klebold on that fateful Tuesday morning on April 20 are indeed the beginning of a spiraling trend that continues to this day—they were *not* the first school shooters in the United States. That ignominious claim goes back to 1966 and belongs to Charles Joseph Whitman, the crazed University of Texas gunman, in what has come to be known as the Texas Tower shooting.

On a sweltering August day, the former All-American kid and ex-Marine climbed to the top of the University Tower in Austin with a sawed-off shotgun along with an assortment of other weapons and began shooting. His ninety-six-minute reign of terror killed fourteen people on campus, injured over thirty others, and only ended when he was killed by Austin police.[12] It is critical to point out that before Whitman, such an attack was unprecedented—and for decades later, shootings targeting innocent students were extremely rare occurrences.

Until Columbine.

When Klebold and Harris committed their school assault in 1999, we had an entirely different media landscape, one where there were twenty-four-hour cable news channels that would cover—and repeat—the horrific story around the clock. Klebold and Harris, lonely gamers who had been bullied into a vengeful rage, had originally intended to blow up their school, but eventually settled on a mass-shooting retaliatory strike against the kids whom they felt had mistreated them.[13] Their story was endlessly broadcast and amplified, and, unsurprisingly, there would be young people who not only identified with the alienation that Klebold and Harris felt but also the rage that led them to emulate their violent coup de grâce.

Even Whitman, the UT Tower shooter, had a copycat way back in the prehistoric media era of the nightly news and Walter Cronkite. In November of 1966, just a few short months after Whitman's carnage, an eighteen-year-old young man named Bob Smith would take seven hostages at Rose-Mar College of Beauty in Mesa, Arizona, shooting all seven and killing five, later telling police that he was inspired by Whitman.

Before Whitman, the U.S. had never had a school shooting; after his media-grabbing attack, we had two in less than six months. That is the nature of social contagions: they spread under the right conditions within a social environment. And in the modern media age—with social media as the ultimate carrier of social viruses—that effect is exponentially amplified.

We need look no further than the school mass-shooting trajectory since Columbine in order to see just how *viral* school shootings have become in the digital age. Since then, we've had to witness a steady stream of these seemingly senseless attacks—from the Virginia Tech shootings of 2007 (thirty-three dead and, at the time, the largest mass shooting in American history); to Newtown, Connecticut, in 2014 and the murder of twenty first graders and six adults; to Parkland, Florida, and Stoneman Douglas High School in 2017, where seventeen people were murdered; to Santa Fe High School in 2018, where ten were killed . . . on and on, there are so many more of these heartbreaking shootings.

The shooter profile is often similar: some underlying mental illness like depression; often very socially awkward and isolated; many have been bullied; all have been gamers; and several have explicitly written or stated that they were inspired by previous shooters, or left social media comments or manifestos in order to gain maximum attention for their actions.

Eerily similar to incel hero Elliot Rodger, the Virginia Tech shooter Seung-Hui Cho filmed a video manifesto and even mailed a media package to NBC News before his rampage. That in itself is telling. And, like Rodger, he expressed a hatred for popular kids and their "debauchery," and assumed a victim narrative blaming his victims and the world: "You caused me to do this."[14]

With the Columbine shooters, it was discovered that they had planned the attack for over a year and, as mentioned, had initially wanted to blow up the school, like the Oklahoma City bombing of 1995. We so often focus on the gun debate after these shootings, which is a valid one, but don't tend to focus on the main issue: the mental state of these shooters and what leads them to kill.

The Columbine shooters, albeit outcasts, had two very different personality types. According to investigative journalist Dave Cullen, author of the 2009 book *Columbine,* Harris was "the callously brutal mastermind," while Klebold was a "quivering depressive who journaled obsessively about love and attended the Columbine prom three days before opening fire."[15] So Klebold sounds more Werther, while Harris sounds more narcissist/sociopath.

While these shooters are outliers and extremely rare, they do represent a sort of canary in the coal mine of what the conditions in the proverbial mine are like. As discussed throughout this book, the modern digital age has created the conditions for emptiness, reactivity, anger, self-centered narcissism, and desensitization.

The predictive algorithms of our digital echo chamber make the user the center of the universe (narcissism), while addicting them to highly arousing and, ultimately, numbing content. Add to that a stripping away any sense of intrinsic meaning and purpose, and what do you have? Well, you have most teens and young adults today: young, numb, and looking to feel something, a jolt of *anything*—caffeine, a digital dopamine hit, a drink, a blow job, a gut punch, a razor across the forearm—*something* just to feel alive. Or to escape their emptiness.

At the extreme end of that bell curve, a razor or blow job just aren't enough. At the outlier end of the curve, you've got young, empty, and angry men who are actually ghosts. Like any ghost, they lack corporeal substance, and they also lack a soul or an identity; they are transparent apparitions that are merely the illusory shadow of a fully formed human.

And like the metaphorical *hungry* ghost of addiction, they have a bottomless and insatiable appetite; in this case, their desperate need is to feel *something*—anything—to feel what our limited language may call *sensation*. To misquote Descartes . . . it's "I feel, therefore I am." But how does an empty ghost feel *anything*? At the highest possible intensity, balls-to-the-wall violence. Have you ever seen a bored sociopath put out a cigarette on their skin? They smile and shrug . . . the pain gives them momentary corporeal existence and identity.

But cigarette burns get old fast. They lose their pop. What's needed next requires a higher octane. Or should we say *caliber*? A ghost with an automatic weapon in a crowded gathering place is looking for (a) their fifteen minutes to validate that they existed, (b) a rush to feel alive, (c) the power and control that the impotent feel when hurting others, (d) a delusional sense of accomplishing some misguided "mission" where for once in their emptiness, they feel a sense of purpose. Usually, it's (e): all of the above.

As mentioned, in 1966, we had the first mass shooting at the University of Texas. In 2018, we had a school shooting every eight days. A pandemic of school shootings by lost and misguided misfits at a rate that we've never seen before; mass shootings are now ho-hum, keep-moving, nothing-to-see-here mundane affairs.

The once horrifically rare is now commonplace.

These empty ghosts are created in our dehumanizing and numbing digital laboratory, and then they perpetuate themselves, Werther-style, via the digital contagion, as they find community and resonance with the other outliers in the modern *public square*: social media sites and chat rooms.

In a sickening twist, the worst of these shooters are immortalized in their preferred desensitizing media: first-person shooter violent video games. Incredibly, there has been a game created called *Super Columbine Massacre RPG!,* whereby the "player" assumes the role of Klebold or Harris and shoots figures based on the actual victims at Columbine. The Virginia Tech shooter was similarly immortalized in a game called *V-Tech Rampage.*[16]

Condemned by the press, some in the gaming world actually praised these games for their creativity and innovation. It is hard to imagine how someone can design such a sickening game and, worse yet, how some can praise those efforts. When the *V-Tech* designer was pressured to take his "game" down, pathetically, he requested a sort of ransom: he would remove the game from its hosted platform if he received $2,000 in donations—and for an additional $1,000, he would apologize.[17]

Not humanity's finest moment.

There are those who think even discussing the impact of violent media on unstable kids is just so much "Okay, boomer!" fearmongering and moral panic. However, that position shows a total lack of understanding of the impact of media on a social species that learns by modeling and mimicking behavior—and of the qualitatively different and more impactful effect of our new media.

Beyond Werther effects in the incel movement and in our epidemic of school shootings, there are other examples from our current culture that illustrate how technology has eroded our basic humanity.

iPhone Bad Samaritans

It was a shocking news story: On October 13, 2021, a woman is raped by a homeless man on the SEPTA commuter train in Philadelphia shortly before 10:00 P.M. The rape was a slow-moving event with multiple passengers witnessing portions of the attack. Initially, the attacker had approached the woman and started verbally harassing her; then he started touching her sexually. Finally, after forty-five minutes of her protests and his increasingly aggressive behavior, he raped her. The rape itself lasted for six minutes—about the time it takes water to boil. All told, the harassment and the horrible assault took place over the course of almost an hour.

And what did these witnesses do? Did they intervene to help stop this assault that was occurring right in front of them? No, not a single person helped the poor woman except for an off-duty SEPTA worker who did eventually call the police. But what of all the other witnesses? Perhaps they were too frightened to personally intervene or help; then they certainly must at least have been able to call the police; after all, almost everyone has a phone these days . . . and this woman was getting terrorized for close to an hour.

The SEPTA surveillance video does show that a couple of the passengers on that commuter SEPTA train that evening did indeed reach for their phones—but they didn't call 9-1-1. Instead, at least two of the passengers caught on that surveillance video were shown holding their smartphones toward the attack and *filming* it. In a disgusting show of human depravity, our inhumanity was on full display that horrible evening.

The local police superintendent, Timothy Bernhardt, told the national media that the attack could have been prevented if only someone had gotten involved. He went on to say: "I'm appalled by those who did nothing to help this woman. Anyone who was on that train has to look in the mirror and ask why they didn't intervene or why they didn't do something."[18]

What's happened to us? We used to be a caring, nice species, didn't we?

A week after the incident, the district attorney handling the case, Jack Stollsteimer, held a press conference to push back on the claims his fellow Philadelphians failed to act—and, worse, went so far as to film the attack: "People in this region are not, in my experience, so inhuman and callous . . . that they're going to sit there and just watch this happen and videotape it—as one journalist said today—for their own private enjoyment."

Stollsteimer said people were getting on and off the train continuously, and he speculated that no one person sat and watched the entire encounter and realized what was happening. But that was sheer speculation and an assumption by the prosecutor; he can't know whether the bystanders realized what was happening or not. Perhaps he was unwilling to believe that such callousness could exist among the people that he represents, but his comments are refuted by the actual evidence, as there is indeed an actual phone video made by at least one passenger that was in the possession of the district attorney's investigators, and the SEPTA surveillance video shows at least two passengers holding their phones toward the attack.

The SEPTA case in Philadelphia had some parallels with another "bad Samaritan" case from decades earlier in New York: the infamous rape and murder of Kitty Genovese. In that 1964 case, a twenty-eight-year-old waitress named Kitty Genovese was returning home to her apartment in Queens after her shift, when she was followed by a man into her vestibule. What made it a national story at the time was the apathy of the multiple neighbors who heard her desperate cries for help as she was stabbed, raped, and murdered over the course of an hour. Many of her neighbors later told police, yes, they were awoken by her screams . . . but they didn't call the police because most felt that someone else would. So why get involved? Turn the light off, get back to bed, and try to get back to sleep as the life of a young woman slowly gets extinguished.

Initial news reports had indicated that thirty-eight eyewitnesses had failed to act as Kitty Genovese was murdered. Later news accounts dispute the number of actual eyewitnesses, while conceding that perhaps even more people heard the bloodcurdling cries as Kitty Genovese was murdered. Also omitted in the original reports was the fact that there was indeed one woman, a neighbor by the name of Sophia Farrar, who did indeed run toward the screams and tried to help. Unfortunately, she got there too late, but was able to hold Kitty as she died.[19]

Yet as horrible as the Kitty Genovese case was—and there are some obvious parallels to the Philadelphia train rape of 2021—at least Kitty Genovese's neighbors who saw or heard the attack didn't reach for their home-movie cameras to *film* it.

We have to ask ourselves—what is that about? If you want to be a wretched bad Samaritan and not help a woman getting attacked—whether out of fear or apathy—while despicable, I think most can understand that "don't get involved" tendency.

But what is the filming about? Why reach for a phone to document the horrible event? What's going on there? Of course, we can only speculate, as there aren't any interviews with the witnesses involved, but a couple of theories come to mind.

In earlier chapters I had talked about the ancient Greek concept of acedia, which was defined as a sort of apathy—a spiritual and mental sloth, and I suggested that in our modern dopamine-saturated and humanity-desensitized world, many people are just numb and apathetic as they suffer from acedia. We can also look at it from a neurological standpoint, where we know that technology—and our love affair with it—has compromised the development of our "mirror neurons," which are critical for the development of *empathy.*

So those things may explain the apathy; Kitty Genovese's neighbors were apathetic, too—and that was 1964. But what explains the *filming* in 2021? A colleague of mine suggested an interesting explanation. In twenty-first-century America, our phones are our crutch . . . our security blankets. We reach for them reflexively whenever we're bored, anxious, or . . . scared? Is it possible that the people on that train just did the only thing that they were conditioned to do when under duress—reach for their phones?

And, let's face it: We've also become obsessed with memorializing everything—and I mean *everything* with a photo to post for posterity on Facebook or Instagram: our dinner, our view from our window, countless kid pictures—and the rape on the commuter train. In our reality TV world, sort of like Jim Carrey's *The Truman Show,* every aspect of our lives, the good, the bad, and the ugly, seemingly needs to get filmed, because in our overly-digitized lives, it's as if something doesn't exist unless there's an electronic record of it.

Finally, it may just be as basic and simple as we've become so desensitized by the constant flood of violent imagery in our lives that we now just view everyday pain and violence as just so much entertainment . . . a sort of feeding-the-Christians-to-the-lions sort of thing. We've lost our moral compass while we've also ratcheted up the intensity of our voyeuristic entertainment. Case in point, a TV exec friend of mine wondered out loud when we would start broadcasting live executions. This used to be the realm of dystopian sci-fi novels, but I think we're just about there now.

And a final thought about that filmed rape: we've always rubbernecked car accidents; stopped to watch a street fight. In fact, high school kids are notorious for getting excited when a fight breaks out and quickly form a gleeful and bloodthirsty egg-'em-on circle screaming, "Fight! Fight!" at the combatants. Unfortunately, it's the basest part of our human nature.

We used to raise our children to grow past that adrenaline-fueled barbaric id stage; now, I'm afraid, with the phenomenon of perpetual adolescence for most of our males via infantile video games that keep our young men developmentally stuck in a state of slack-jawed prepubescence, we have very immature young adults. And I suspect that the people filming on that train were not the *female* commuters . . . I suspect that it was our childish male brutes; numb and desensitized and conditioned to film and post anything that can generate a nice little dopamine hit. For them, that suffering woman may have just been a dehumanized avatar for a video to post.

RIP, *Homo sapiens*. You had a decent run.

Digital Extremism

Beyond our desensitized filming of brutal crimes, there are also other signs of our societal decay—and the role that technology has played in that decay.

Today, we have mass shootings (beyond just the school shooting phenomenon), protests, and bloodshed as part of the worst civil unrest in over half a century. The social issues driving this unrest are real, but the unrest is often exacerbated and amplified by polarizing social media echo chambers—on either extreme of the political spectrum. These digital echo chambers disproportionately influence and shape impressionable, psychologically fragile, and malleable young people who, in their search for meaning and a sense of belonging, are susceptible to extremism and indoctrination.

Forget about social media influencers and TikTok Tourette's: now we have digitally fueled extremism swallowing up some of our most vulnerable young people, especially young men. The lost, alienated, and empty young man looking for a team or tribe to belong is the prized low-hanging fruit for opportunistic extremist groups.

We have to keep in mind that many of these young men are desperately searching for a real sense of purpose and meaning in their lives, but they haven't yet developed a sense of their own core identity—or the resilience and critical thinking to forge their own independent sense of self. Meanwhile, they're continuously fed a steady stream of ideologically extreme content by hungry social media algorithms looking to feed and amplify whatever their initial political inclination may be.

Lean right, and the digital echo chamber brainwashes toward the right; lean left, and the algorithms will feed you a steady and increasingly virulent diet of left-leaning brainwashing content, always with the goal of increased viewership and attention—what's been called "the battle for the eyeballs."

Big Tech understands that there is no profit in the land of political moderation. The lizard brain needs to be activated. As old newsies used to say, "If it bleeds, it leads," understanding the human propensity toward morbid curiosity and our need to rubberneck the carnage of a car wreck. Now in the digital age, it's beyond "If it bleeds, it leads";

now it's "If it inflames the emotions, it creates viewer devotion." The fiscal reality is that there's simply no money or digital habituation in moderate content.

The task of AI on platforms like YouTube is to develop algorithms to recommend and autoplay videos that optimally encourage users to watch video after video after video. Initially, it was thought that algorithms should be designed to show videos that were similar to the ones that the user had already watched. But this led to users getting bored. To get past this, Google expended an enormous amount of resources on its AI research division to apply neuroscience, neuroeconomics, cognitive and behavioral psychology, moral reasoning, and deep thinking to their coding. In the process, developers embedded an *extremification* loop in the algorithm.

Because users are drawn to content that evokes emotional responses, the algorithm steers the user toward more and more extreme content to keep them engaged. After all, it's all about *stickiness* to the screen, and divisive political content is great for eyeball time.

The New Technocracy—and their behavioral experts—also have a deep understanding of human psychology (not just neurophysiology, where we know that the brain tends to chase "exciting" dopamine and adrenaline-activating experiences). They know that young people are psychologically hardwired to want to experience a "call to adventure," often found in the archetypal Hero's Journey that legendary psychologist Carl Jung and mythologist Joseph Campbell so richly described in their writings.

Young people *need* to feel the sense of purpose associated with what they interpret as a noble cause or quest; it quenches a real and important psychological thirst. The tech lords understand this, and that's why almost every video game is the classic Hero's Journey—an initiatory journey overcoming obstacles on the path toward empowerment. That's what makes them especially compelling and seductive for drifting, alienated, and disempowered teens; they can easily lose themselves in their avatar and live an albeit synthetic life of meaning on their game platform—or in the immersion into political ideology via various digital platforms or chat rooms like 4chan.

Essentially, all these kids are just looking for a team to belong to—aren't we all?

Without an intrinsic sense of identity with genuine core values, the empty-self teen being shaped by their extrinsic digital world is at risk for losing themselves in their synthetic world or, worse, at risk of digital brainwashing—with oftentimes tragic results. We can see an extreme example of this with a case that I worked on later in this chapter (see "Snapshots from the Dystopia: YouTube, Extremism, and Murder in Palm Beach").

The days of being politically informed by reading a couple of newspapers or watching the evening news are over. Today, we live in the information age (which should *never* be confused with the wisdom age), wherein we are flooded and drowning in a sea of digital content; millions of blogs, news stories, social media posts, tweets, images, YouTube clips . . . the assault on our senses and on our psyches never ends.

It also doesn't help that the New Technocracy have a monopoly as information gatekeepers and control every aspect of what we see and what we read in ways that William Randolph Hearst could never have dreamed of; forget Rosebud, AI-driven algorithms intended to hook the viewer are what the New Technocracy dream about—and what our nightmares are made of.

In the next section, you'll read about the dark side of what can happen when an empty young man gets lost in an algorithm-fueled digital echo chamber.

Snapshots from the Dystopia: YouTube, Extremism, and Murder in Palm Beach

The click-clack of the lawyer's heels on the hard tiles echoed as she escorted me through the cold steel doors of the maximum-security prison. She'd been late, so I'd been left waiting for a painfully long thirty minutes in an empty visitor area. The wait and silence gave my already anxious thoughts an unhealthy amount of room to dance and anticipate my task ahead.

I had flown to Florida from my home in Austin to interview a young man named Corey Johnson, accused of capital murder. His lawyers had reached out to me weeks earlier, asking that I be an expert witness for his trial. They were pursuing an insanity defense based on the premise that his homicidal episode was a direct result of being brainwashed by his constant immersion into YouTube. More specifically, his lawyers believed that his horrific crimes were the by-product of a lost suburban teen who'd been radicalized by watching thousands of hours of ISIS recruitment and propaganda videos, and desensitized and driven to violence by watching thousands of hours more of gruesomest ISIS decapitation videos—videos that shook even the most hardened investigators that I spoke to. All courtesy of YouTube and its parent company, Google.

It's unsettling to hear that steel door slam shut behind you as you're escorted inside a prison filled with the most violent criminals in South Florida; it's even more unsettling as you feel the intimidating stares of those same hardened inmates looking at you as you walk past.

It also didn't help my discomfort when I was brought into the smallest conference room that I'd ever been in and sat inches away from an admitted murderer who was involved in a vicious and grisly killing of a thirteen-year-old boy—on the boy's birthday, no less—as well as the attempted murder of his best friend's mother and thirteen-year-old brother. All had been repeatedly hacked and stabbed, with the murdered boy's head almost entirely severed.[20]

Most unsettling of all was his appearance and his demeanor. I had read the police report and had seen the nauseating crime photos, so I was expecting a steely-eyed sociopath or a wild-eyed madman. But I encountered neither. Instead, he looked like the boy next door; he looked like any kid that you might see at a skate park or someone that you'd trust to babysit your kids—not decapitate them. It was spine-chilling how normal, polite, and soft-spoken he was. Rather than Charles Manson, he looked like Doogie Howser in an orange jumpsuit. None of this computed, and my brain was having a difficult time processing it all.

Over several hours, he slowly and quietly told me the story of both his life and the crime. Left without a father at a young age, he often felt lost and rudderless; feeling like an outsider at school and not part of the popular kids' clique, he developed what psychologists call a *reaction formation* to the behaviors of those same "cool kids." Deep down, he wanted to do what they did—go out on dates, drink booze, and have sex. Yet because he was denied access to those experiences, he formed an intense hatred of those behaviors and of the people engaged in them. He thus developed a mindset that sought what he felt was "purity," and subsequently sought out any ideology that he felt embraced such purity.

Via YouTube, he first explored what he perceived were "pure" ideologies; first, the precepts of Nazi Germany, then other white supremacist movements that he discovered on alt-right online communities like Stormfront and 4chan. He was bright and quite informed in the most intricate details of the various sects and branches of the respective movements. He eventually became disillusioned with those ideologies because their leaders were not really being pure (they drank and had sex). That's when he discovered Islam through a video about Bashar al-Assad in Syria; this led to admiration for Hezbollah and Hamas, and sparked an interest in Islam.

He researched the differences between Sunni and Shia denominations and, while watching videos about Sunni Islam on YouTube, a Vice mini-documentary about life under ISIS was recommended and autoplayed. The Vice video piqued his interest. Next, YouTube suggested an ISIS propaganda video called "No Respite" that Corey watched over and over, as it deeply resonated with him.

This led to a plethora of ISIS propaganda videos, which were very appealing to a lost youth looking for a cause, as they portrayed ISIS to be a movement for social good with very slick and high-end production values. These idealized ISIS-as-utopia videos were interspersed with decapitation videos that would become the step-by-step manual for the events that transpired on the night of the stabbings.

When I asked the seemingly gentle and soft-spoken Corey how he was able to watch these gruesome and graphic decapitations, he calmly explained that, while initially repulsed, he viewed them as a sort of essential training and toughening up—not unlike boot camp—in order to become an ISIS warrior. He also added that, over time, the violence became normalized. This would be akin to the way medical students become accustomed to cadaver work—initially, they typically get nauseous, but then a couple of dozen cadavers later and they're having their lunch in the mortuary.

And what about his mother while all this gruesome YouTube watching was happening? Initially, she just thought he might be going through a phase, a bit of a religious exploration that she didn't discourage. But there were red flags; during the period that Corey was immersing himself deeper and deeper into Islam and ISIS, his mother told investigators that she did notice that he was watching videos nonstop, sometimes forgetting to eat, and that he would be in a trancelike state for weeks. While this may have been four-alarm time for many parents, the attorneys made it clear to me that his mother had her own issues that she was struggling with.

In the meantime, Corey's mind was getting more and more brainwashed. The sophisticated ISIS propaganda wing is called Al-Hayat and produces content strategically, as they use certain keywords in the title or certain types of images in thumbnails to appeal to the YouTube algorithm. As far back as 2014, an average of three videos and more than fifteen photo reports were blasted out into cyberspace each day in multiple languages, including Arabic, Turkish, Kurdish, English, French, and Russian.

And to give the impression that ISIS is a dynamic and growing organization, they engaged extensively in real-time outreach, such as being very active on Twitter. Indeed, there are somewhere between 46,000 and 70,000 ISIS-related accounts on Twitter, each tweeting an average of 7.3 times per day. In French alone, there are about 14,000 pro-ISIS tweets daily.

For an empty and vulnerable soul like Corey, this flood of social media propaganda was just too much of a digital tidal wave . . . Eventually, he was swept away. After watching thousands upon thousands of hours of propaganda and decapitation videos via his YouTube "recommended feed," it was only a matter of time before his full-blown indoctrination would be complete. Once indoctrinated into such a violent extremist ideology, the inevitable happened.

His crime was as bloody and as heinous as can be imagined.

As he described the sequence of gruesome events to me in soft-spoken detail (I often had to lean in to hear him clearly), he explained how the evening of the crimes had started innocently enough. On March 11, 2018, Jovanni Sierra was celebrating his thirteenth birthday a day early. The celebration started with paintball with friends, then dinner at an Italian restaurant where he connected with another close friend—thirteen-year-old Dane Bancroft and his seventeen-year-old brother, Kyle. Kyle Bancroft had been Corey's best friend since preschool, and Kyle had invited Corey to the Italian restaurant to engage in some healthy socialization, which he felt Corey desperately needed.

As Corey described the evening, they were all having fun, and he felt more "normal" than he had felt in a long time; indeed, the boys talked about music and pop culture and wanted to continue the good times at Dane and Kyle's house during an impromptu sleepover.

Jovanni's mother, Karen Abreu, was reticent; she had never met Corey before, and, after all, it was her son's birthday the next day. She'd told *The Palm Beach Post* that she had urged her son, "Please come home. It's your birthday tomorrow. I want to give you a hug and a kiss." She said he told her, "Mommy, I love you. I want to hang out with my friends."

She reluctantly agreed to let him go.

The boys continued to have fun that evening at Dane and Kyle's house—even vaping as they talked about things normal teens talk about. But as Corey would tell me, at some point during the sleepover, he felt the strong urge to kill himself because he could "never really be normal" like his friends Kyle and Dane and the birthday boy, Jovanni. But in his twisted mind, Islam forbade suicide; instead, he decided that he would need to kill "infidels" and be shot by the police in a bid for death-by-cop suicide.

Kyle went to bed first at about 1:00 A.M. The younger boys, Jovanni and Dane, had planned on staying up all night, talking as excited young teens are prone to do. But Dane fell asleep around 3:30 A.M., and Jovanni watched the earth-and-the-galaxy video on his phone at 4:43 A.M. Sometime between watching that video and 5:30

A.M., Corey had crept through the quiet house, stood over a sleeping Jovanni with a large kitchen knife, and viciously and methodically started attacking him, just as he had seen during endless hours of ISIS instructional decapitation videos. But Jovanni woke up and struggled; he wasn't dying as easily as Corey had thought—the videos made murder look sterile and easy; the real thing was messy and difficult and took many slashes of the knife in the horrific attack that almost decapitated alive the fighting and kicking Jovanni on the morning of his birthday.

At about 5:45 A.M., Elaine Simon, Kyle and Dane's mother, heard a commotion upstairs in the boys' rooms and headed up to see what was happening. Corey greeted her at the top of the stairs and yelled, "Go back into your room! Go to sleep! Don't worry. I'll take care of them. Everyone will be going back to sleep." She went back downstairs but kept hearing moaning coming from upstairs. When she ran up a second time, Corey lunged at her with the knife. He stabbed her over and over again, a total of twelve times, as she kept asking him, "Why are you doing this?" After all, she had known Corey since he was in preschool.

Eventually, her son Dane heard his mother's screams and ran to help her. Corey then attacked Dane, stabbing him an unbelievable thirty-two times. Elaine Simon was able to get away and ran, bleeding profusely, for help at a shocked neighbor's house, where she called 911 as her other son, Kyle, jumped out of their second-story window to escape the bloodbath.

The police arrived, and Corey described how he first hid in a closet before eventually surrendering. I asked him, still taken aback by the horrific details but trying to maintain my professional composure, "But, Corey, help me to understand . . . Jovanni's murder, the attempted murders of Dane and his mother . . . they were all done because you just told me you had a death wish that night and your whole plan was to have the police shoot you. So why did you hide and then surrender?"

He looked at me with a meek, almost embarrassed expression: "I . . . I was afraid that if I got shot, I would scream out in pain and wouldn't be able to say, 'Allahu Akbar' . . . which need to be the words on my lips as I die for me to go to heaven."

* * *

EIGHTEEN MONTHS REMOVED from the crime—and also removed from the toxic digital brainwashing that led to his atrocities—he was able to speak to me with the somewhat detached and resigned clarity of someone who is aware that they had touched the edges of insanity. He was profoundly aware—and remorseful—for the life that he took and for the lives of the people whom his actions have forever destroyed—including his own.

He understood that there are no mulligans in life and that what happened wasn't just a bad dream that he can wake from or live differently. That knowledge has led to two suicide attempts while he's been in jail.

Corey Johnson was a lost and empty young man who found connection and purpose in a slick ideological con game, manufactured with the specific intent to recruit rudderless boys like him who were looking for a team to belong to. Corey is the victim of a digital Frankenstein's monster, delivered via the internet and YouTube, and deposited directly into his fragile psyche. He is the hollow man filled with obscenities and distortions that are made more muscular and invasive by the digital age.

Twenty years ago, he may have just found *Dungeons & Dragons* and been done with it. Sure, it's possible that he could have been radicalized in an earlier pre-digital age by reading a tattered copy of *Mein Kampf* or *The Turner Diaries*. But that type of old-school brainwashing was the static experience of a book living on a shelf that would be intermittently read—and usually also needed a real-life charismatic cult leader to activate the brainwashing.

If you were to see, as I did, the vividness of the searing imagery and the constant stream of slick and seductive recruitment videos that landed like thousands of raindrops watering his barren mind, feeding and fueling their message deep into that part of him that was longing for an ideology to crystalize his empty and broken life into one of purpose and meaning; if you could begin to imagine what nonstop imagery does to the brain of a lost kid, then you can begin to understand and make sense out of the seemingly senseless. To us, his actions were insane. To him, they were totally in accordance with his digital programming in the age of the rarely filtered YouTube algorithm.

Cold, calculating, and amoral, the YouTube algorithm is programmed to increase engagement in the never-ending battle of the eyeballs. It doesn't care if the searched video is a kitty playing with a puppy, or of a religious extremist gruesomely and vividly sawing the head off a kneeling "infidel." The algorithm makes no value judgments. It just feeds the viewer an increasingly escalating stream of content to keep those eyeballs locked on the screen—ideally without sleep or breaks. Sure enough, Corey would position his computer sideways next to his bed so that he could keep watching the nonstop images that had been "recommended" for him in a steady stream of gift-wrapped horror. Although You Tube does attempt to remove these horrific videos once it becomes aware of them, by that time the damage has already been done to the person who just viewed the video.

Mein Kampf sat on the shelf. This modern version of toxic ideology drills its way into your imagination with balls-to-the-walls immersive imagery. This isn't your dad's radicalization; this is mind-fucking 2.0. Kids like Corey don't stand a chance.

Welcome to a very sick, algorithm-fueled neighborhood within the new digital dystopia.

Footnote: over a year after first meeting and assessing Corey Johnson, I would take the stand as an expert witness during his murder trial, which had been pushed back to November 2021 due to COVID. He was older and taller, his hair cut short. Everyone in the tense courtroom wore masks as the details of the horrible case were told—and shown—to the jury, as Corey sat expressionless. I gave my testimony about insanity and digital brainwashing over several hours and had a heated cross-examination with the prosecutor.

Corey Johnson's capable and kind defense attorneys did not anticipate an acquittal; they merely wanted to present the best possible defense—and explanation—of his incomprehensible crimes. He was found guilty of all counts. His guilt is beyond dispute, and the verdict is just. But what influenced him, and the digital delivery of that influence, remains unindicted—and that is *not* just.

5

Social Media and the Binary Trap

Too Much and Not Enough

"Life, well . . . it just seems like, y'know, it usually feels like it's not enough, y'know? But, at the same time . . . it's . . . it's way *too* fucking much for me . . . too much for me to handle."

That's what "Tommy," a young man sitting to my left in group, said when asked to best describe the reason why he was in treatment.

I was powerfully struck by his words.

Tommy had facial hair that aspired to be a beard, and the worn clothes of a guy who'd bounced around a few too many treatment programs—which he had. He also had two prior suicide attempts that he'd been hospitalized for, one via overdosing intentionally on pills, the other when he deeply cut his wrist. Like so many borderline personality clients, he was a "cutter," so he had a geometric array of scars on his forearms that blended in with his colorful tattoos and flannel shirt. Most cutters aren't suicidal, but some, like Tommy, have a death wish.

He looked like the other ten people in my group: young, in their twenties, who had seen too much, yet still seemed like kids—in spite of the track marks, piercings, and tattoos. I asked him to repeat what he'd said, because it was both poignant and powerful. And I knew the rest of the group resonated, because there was vigorous nodding as he spoke.

"Like I said . . . life feels empty, like it's not enough . . . and yet at the same time, it's way too much for me . . . and I find myself overwhelmed and just needing to check out and escape."

This *too much, yet not enough* paradoxical feeling was the rallying cry of more and more young people that I was treating. So many of my clients talk about being overwhelmed by life, of feeling lost, numb, and unfulfilled. Overwhelmed and empty—all at once.

What was causing such a spike in this phenomenon?

The Binary Trap

My client Tommy was suffering from the borderline paradox, otherwise known as the *binary trap*: The feeling of extreme, often paradoxical and binary emotions at the same time, such as "Go away—but don't leave me!"; "I love you—I can't stand you!"; to the ultimate binary choice: "To live, or to die?" These are all thought prisons—the prison of two opposite ideas—the prison of binary thinking. The binary inmate doesn't see the middle ground; between the ambivalence of love/hate, there is a gray area—the special realm of nuance.

That prison of two opposing ideas—of binary thinking—is the prison of many borderline personality disorder (BPD) clients, who may fluctuate between one extreme to the other at any given moment. The borderline paradox is when the BPD client can embrace both polarities *simultaneously.* In our societal version of BPD, we typically don't see that (a progressive doesn't tend to fluctuate between supporting Bernie Sanders to Trumpism; and they certainly don't embrace both simultaneously). But what our society has devolved into is indeed the binary trap: it's either Coke or Pepsi, red or blue—and there *cannot* be any middle ground.

That is the prison of two ideas.

Interestingly, there's another borderline paradox that's been identified: the borderline *pain* paradox. Individuals with a diagnosis of BPD often report experiencing high levels of physical pain as a result of long-term health problems; yet, when it comes to short-term visceral pain, such as from acts of self-harm, it apparently isn't felt at all.[1] In fact, when BPD patients were put under an electroencephalogram (EEG) and subjected to intense short-term pain, scientists were shocked to discover that BPD brains quickly start producing theta currents, the brain waves of sleep, trance, and deep relaxation.

We know that when the body is injured, pain-killing endorphins are released to help temporarily numb the pain. And dissociation, the experience of feeling out of your body during intense stress or trauma, also inhibits pain as, on a neurological level, the brain temporarily shuts down all but the most basic functions. That's why for BPD clients, visceral pain is often under-experienced, while they are also quite sensitive to long-term chronic pain.

This phenomenon also explains why cutting, burning, or other forms of self-harm often don't hurt the BPD client but are dangerously addictive—they're an endorphin rush and, like dopamine, a person can get habituated to chasing that endorphin rush. On a psychological level, many BPD clients talk about cutting themselves in an effort to feel *something,* where otherwise there is no immediate sensation other than numbness.

Borderline Personality Disorder

The term *borderline* has its roots in the 1930s, when it was used to refer to the border state between neurosis and psychosis—that Twilight Zone–like "borderline" realm between the two worlds of emotional disorder, dangling between being able to function and not function in daily life. In its more modern usage, borderline personality disorder (BPD) was first coined in 1980, along with a cluster of other personality disorders, in the *DSM-III* (the diagnostic bible of psychiatric disorders).[2]

According to the personality disorder training manual put out by legendary psychologist Dr. Gregory Lester, BPD is typified by certain characteristics and behaviors: instability, chronic feelings of emptiness, volatility, vulnerability, overreaction, verbal outbursts, exaggeration, self-harm behaviors or thoughts, thin-skinned, and spiteful. In addition, BPD clients tend to engage in what's called "splitting" (seeing others as "all good" or "all bad") and, indeed, seeing *everything* through an extreme black-and-white binary lens (also known as *dichotomous thinking*).

To be officially diagnosed with BPD, a person needs to meet at least five of the following diagnostic criteria listed in the latest *DSM-5*:

> A personality disorder characterized by a long-standing pattern of instability in mood, interpersonal relationships, and self-image that is severe enough to cause extreme distress or interfere with social and occupational functioning. Among the manifestations of this disorder are (a) self-damaging behavior (e.g., gambling, overeating, substance use); (b) intense but unstable relationships; (c) uncontrollable temper outbursts; (d) uncertainty about self-image, gender, goals, and loyalties; (e) shifting moods; (f) self-defeating behavior, such as fights, suicidal gestures, or self-mutilation; and (g) chronic feelings of emptiness and boredom.[3]

It's an extremely challenging—and lethal—disorder as BPD clients commit suicide at *fifty* times (yes, that's *not* a typo) the normal rate and are comorbid for addiction 70 percent of the time. They are also very reactive, struggle with relationships, and generally have extremely challenging long-term outcomes.[4]

The three dominant theories about the causes of BPD are the aversive childhood theory (bad childhood), the genetic theory (bad genes), and the biopsychosocial theory (bad environment). Today, there seems to be a consensus that all three of the above factor into the BPD equation, perhaps in different proportion in each respective BPD client. And, there is the additional clinical consensus that the genetic component needs to be present, and that borderline personality disorder is likely a combination of genetic predisposition combined with early childhood environmental factors and neurobiological dysfunction.

Let's look at BPD etiology a bit more closely.

As mentioned, borderline personality disorder is what's known as "multifactorial" in etiology—that is to say, there are several potential causes contributing to the disorder. There is a genetic predisposition, which has been shown by twin studies that indicate that BPD has over 50 percent heritability—which means that you can "inherit" BPD at even higher rates than major depression, which is thought to be highly inheritable.

Environmental factors that have been identified as contributing to the development of borderline personality disorder include childhood maltreatment (either physical or sexual abuse, or neglect), which was found in the histories of up to 70 percent of people with BPD, as well as maternal separation (which would explain the pronounced fear of abandonment—perceived or real), poor maternal attachment, inappropriate family boundaries, parental substance abuse, and serious parental mental illness.

There are also some psychological theories. According to the "mentalizing" model (*mentalizing* is the fundamental human capacity to understand our behavior in relation to *mental* states, such as thoughts and feelings), BPD is the result of a lack of resilience against psychological stressors. This idea, and a subsequent treatment model, was put forth by psychotherapists Peter Fonagy and Anthony Bateman.[5]

In this context, Fonagy and Bateman define resilience as the ability to generate "adaptive re-appraisal" of negative events or stressors; therefore, patients with impaired reappraisal accumulate negative experiences and fail to learn from good experiences. BPD patients accumulate negative narratives and interpretations of the events or stressors in their lives and ignore the good experiences that can counter that narrative.

In the biosocial model popularized by Dr. Marsha Linehan, genetic vulnerability interacts with a "chronically invalidating environment" to produce the cluster of BPD symptoms. According to Linehan, "an invalidating environment is one in which communication of private experiences is met by erratic, inappropriate, and extreme responses," and an environment in which inner experiences or feelings are dismissed or punished, instead of being validated.[6]

Yet another etiological theory by psychoanalyst Otto Kernberg theorized that an infant experiences their mother in a binary way: a loving and nurturing parent who provides for the child and then also a punishing, hateful mother who deprives the child. This seemingly inherent contradiction causes intense anxiety and, if it isn't integrated into a more unified "both can be true" understanding, can ultimately lead to the development of splitting, the defense mechanism in which the patient cannot form a realistic view of another person—and also drives binary dichotomous thinking.

However, this model recalls a similar-yet-dated and rejected explanatory model for schizophrenia, the so-called schizophrenogenic mother theory, first proposed in 1948 by psychiatrist Frieda Fromm-

Reichmann (and still embraced until the 1970s). In this model, it was thought that the mother essentially "caused" schizophrenia by her confusing (and schizophrenia-inducing) mixed messaging of overprotection and rejection.[7]

Besides all these psychological models, several neuroimaging studies have identified differences in the amygdala and hippocampus of the medial temporal lobes in patients with BPD. Neurobiological studies have also suggested that impaired serotonin functioning may be present in patients with BPD—yet BPD clients do not seem to respond effectively to medication-based treatment, SSRI (serotonin specific reuptake inhibitors) or otherwise.

So what can make the symptoms of a client with BPD *worse*?

Separations, disagreements, and rejections—real or perceived—are the most common triggers for symptoms. A person with BPD is highly sensitive to being abandoned and left alone, which then emotionally floods the BPD client with intense feelings of anger, fear, suicidal thoughts, and self-harm and often leads to extremely reactive and impulsive decisions. In addition, a lack of consistent nurturing, structure, and boundaries can be viewed as inflaming or causing the volatile dynamic.

There has been a rise in the clinical diagnosis of BPD, and it is much more common than many people may think. A recent study on the prevalence of mental health disorders in the U.S. found that about 1.6 percent of the population has BPD (and 20 percent of the psychiatric inpatient population). That means that there are more than four million people *diagnosed* with BPD in the U.S. alone, although often BPD goes undiagnosed or misdiagnosed, an error that can sometimes fall along gender lines.

That's because there is a large difference in the prevalence of BPD in women versus men (about 75 percent of those diagnosed with BPD in the U.S. are women). *However,* it's not known whether women are more prone to develop BPD or whether this is due to gender biases in the diagnosis of BPD. For example, it may be that men with the symptoms of BPD are just more likely to be misdiagnosed with other conditions like PTSD or major depressive disorder.

And when it comes to BPD, misdiagnosis can be a serious problem, as no medications have been approved by the Food and Drug Administration (FDA) for BPD, and medications for bipolar disorder are ineffective in treating BPD.

While bipolar disorder and borderline personality disorder may share some symptoms, they are very different diseases. Bipolar disorder can cause severe depression or mood swings, but in between episodes, those with this condition are able to function normally. Those with BPD have a more chronic condition that can cause self-harming behaviors or suicidal tendencies.

It is true that when a bipolar patient is rapidly cycling, they can exhibit some of the same destructive or harmful behaviors that are similar to BPD—and that's why misdiagnosis is extremely common during these phases. Another fact that makes defining the two more difficult is that some people can have both disorders, as about 20 percent of people with BPD have been found to have bipolar disorder as well.

Another significant reason why many clinicians believe that BPD gets underdiagnosed is because many people struggling with BPD refuse to seek treatment. Whether they feel they don't need help or that treatment will be useless, many people go without therapy and struggle with BPD on their own.

Yet another barrier to proper BPD diagnosis is the fact that 70 percent of folks with BPD are comorbid with a substance disorder. And the diagnostic recommendations are that a person be substance free for several months in order to be able to get a truly accurate clinical diagnosis that isn't skewed or caused by the substance use. But getting a person with BPD who has a substance issue clean and sober is no easy task.

Finally, there is the issue of stigma and the reticence of some clinicians to diagnose a person with such a serious illness. BPD clients can be so challenging in treatment settings because of their behaviors (which are often corrosive to other clients) that many mental health programs will either refuse to accept them or will refer them elsewhere, citing disruptive and unmanageable behaviors (lest cries of discriminatory practices ring out). Because of that common treatment bias, some clinicians will avoid diagnosing BPD under the misguided assumption that they're helping the client maintain more treatment options if they don't have the scarlet letters of *BPD* on their charts. The irony is that they are potentially seriously *harming* their clients if they don't properly diagnose this disorder, given the high rates of self-harm and suicide if proper treatment isn't received.

With these issues in mind, it is likely that the number of people with borderline personality disorder is much higher than 1.6 percent.

Whether it's misdiagnosed or underdiagnosed, the diagnosis rates of BPD are rising—and, anecdotally, clinicians and medical professionals are seeing more and more people who present with this difficult-to-treat personality disorder.

It's been suggested, and I've seen clinical evidence supporting this, that there may be cases of what we may call "pseudo-BPD"—that is to say, clients who present with some or many of the diagnostic criteria of BPD, yet don't have the actual clinical disorder with its genetic antecedents. These clients, for a lack of a better way of saying it, have absorbed or been shaped into BPD types of behavior by their environment.

This type of assimilation of psychiatric features or behaviors from the society or the peer group is another example of the previously mentioned *social contagion* model (borrowed from *social learning theory*, where it's "monkey see, monkey do"), and are also known as *sociogenic*. According to this model, young people can present with various psychiatric or behavioral issues that they have seen in their friends or in popular media—or in social media, which can also be considered a form of the previously mentioned Factitious Disorder or, when social media inspired, in what's been called "Digital Factitious Disorder" (DFD).[8]

As we've already discussed, social and peer contagion are established constructs that have been associated with a number of mental health concerns and risky behaviors among young adults and adolescents. A simple behavioral example is that young people are more likely to start smoking if they hang out with other peers who smoke. Similarly, if a person constantly sees a behavior or disorder on social media, they can often begin to, consciously or unconsciously, mimic that behavior.

For the pseudo-BPD clients that I've worked with in my clinics, the real test is how they respond to being in a safe, structured therapeutic environment *absent* the negative peer or social models. Indeed, the pseudo-BPD clients get better almost immediately. In contrast, the people with genuine BPD have an extremely long and difficult road of intensive treatment, usually involving consistent dialectical behavioral therapy (DBT), and even then can have challenging outcomes.

In addition to external social contagion or sociogenic effects, there are also entire medical texts that have been written about various forms of psychosomatic or "psychogenic" conditions that present as various physical disorders, but that are a direct result of intrapsychic distress (rather than external influences) and psychological in nature.

One such common phenomenon that was mentioned earlier is that of "pseudo seizures," now more commonly known as *psychogenic nonepileptic seizures* (PNES). These closely resemble epileptic seizures, but have a psychological or psychiatric origin, and usually with anxiety, abuse, or stress as their cause.[9]

So we can clearly see how the mind can help the body mimic certain disorders—whether as a psychogenic phenomenon or as a by-product of a social contagion or sociogenic effect—the former being caused by the mind, while the latter is created by a group effect.

The question that started haunting me was whether we were seeing another social media–fueled social contagion effect similar to what we saw with TikTok and Tourette's. Only now, instead of TikTok, it was ubiquitous and polarizing social media that was creating a mental toxin by amplifying reactivity and black-and-white thinking into something that not only affected individuals but began to shape our entire society in what increasingly looked like large-scale, societal pseudo-BPD.

The Borderline Effect

As I worked in my clinic in Austin, it dawned on me that it wasn't only my clients in my treatment programs who were showing all the behaviors and symptoms of BPD; rather, it was the entire society manifesting the same symptomology and behaviors on a macro level. The streets were on fire with extreme levels of volatility and polarization, psychiatric medication prescriptions were on the rise, suicides were at an all-time high, and reactivity, vitriol, and civil unrest were all at record levels.

Was there a social contagion effect driving this seemingly pathological behavior? Were we perhaps seeing social media–driven pseudo-BPD? My theory is that is exactly what's happening. As digital media has swallowed up our world via technology and all its social media variants, I believe that the evidence is clear that social media is shaping the architecture and framework of how our brains think, function, and process information into inherently limiting binary sorting machines.

Neuroscientists know that the way that we process information—either by reading, or via visual media, or nonverbal cues—shapes the way our brains "think" and function.

Anthropologists Edward Sapir and Benjamin Lee Whorf, in their eponymously named Sapir-Whorf theory of linguistic determinism, went further. They believed that words and language shaped our thoughts and the way that we experience the world (and not the other way around); that if we didn't have the word for an abstract concept like *alienation,* we literally couldn't think it. Indeed, they believed that people from different cultures who had different languages actually *thought* differently.[10]

Not only does language shape thinking—now we're also learning that technology and the internet are impacting language and thus, also, the way that we think. Linguist Gretchen McCulloch, author of the *New York Times* bestselling *Because Internet,* argues that teens are learning to think through the lens of texting, so that they're now writing and punctuating differently—and that punctuation reflects their new way of thinking.

This shaping of language via text platforms further indicates that social media changes the way young people think. It's a reflection of what Marshall McLuhan famously said in the 1960s: "The medium is the message"; except now the medium (digital, binary, social media) is not only the message but also *shapes* the person receiving the message. The medium impacts the way that our brains think, sorting our perspectives into limiting binary thought buckets that lack the breadth and complexity of what's known as *spectrum thinking.*

Unfortunately, this social media–amplified polarity of binary thinking is extremely unhealthy; in fact, it's inherently mentally ill. Black-and-white binary thinking—what psychologists also call *dichotomous thinking*—is a hallmark of several personality disorders, including BPD.

In this case, we would say that the diagnosis applies not only to a growing number of technology and social media–shaped young people but also to the larger collective society. That is not a good thing. As noted earlier, BPD clients have a fifty times greater risk of committing suicide than the general population, are comorbid for drug abuse 70 percent of the time, are explosive, are reactive, struggle with relationships, and generally have challenging lives.

If BPD is indeed what's happening on a societal level, it represents an existential threat to our species and our civilization. If we merely glance at the news, there's no denying that we're experiencing extreme social unrest and upheaval. Where will this lead? The prognosis for anyone—or any group—struggling with BPD without any intervention is poor.

The good news is that we *know* how to treat unhealthy binary thinking and BPD: by using dialectical behavioral therapy, one of the most powerful and impactful clinical interventions in therapeutic use today. DBT incorporates the ancient notion of the dialectic and helps train patients to use *spectrum thinking* (the opposite of binary thinking), as well as the ability to appreciate "nuance," so they learn that things aren't "always" or "never"—that there exists a reality between those polarities.

In addition, building and cultivating resilience is also taught, as BPD clients are shown techniques to increase their "distress tolerance," and how to better control their "emotional regulation" via mindfulness techniques, acceptance, and even in finding meaning in their distress. DBT clients are encouraged to get off polarizing social media and work on developing an "observing ego" (also known as "the witness": a thirty-thousand-foot view of oneself without judgment, reactivity, or affect). Finally, the DBT client is taught to develop a "walk in the other person's shoes" empathy, and shift out of spiraling self-absorption.

Tech and social media–fueled binary thinking—and the mentally unhealthy polarization that stems from it—is an insidious social plague that's been growing and making both our young people and our society sick. It is the societal diagnosis that best fits our macro-patient: Homo Sapien: Twenty-First-Century Edition.

As a thought experiment, I tried to apply the *DSM* BPD criteria to some societal metrics:

(a) self-damaging behavior (e.g., gambling, overeating, substance use): We're at record levels of addiction, with a record number of over one hundred thousand overdoses last year, and we're at an all-time high with self-harm, with over forty-seven thousand suicides the prior year.

(b) intense but unstable relationships: Let's look at domestic abuse and divorce rates as an imperfect metric of societal "intense but unstable relationships." Divorce rates have doubled over the last twenty years—and went up another 34 percent during the pandemic. And domestic abuse or "intimate partner violence" has been steadily rising, and increased 20 percent during the pandemic.

(c) uncontrollable temper outbursts: This is difficult to measure, but speaks to volatility. I think that it's fair to say that there seems to be more volatility nationally in the form of civil unrest, and episodes of highly reactive and "triggered" college students during combustive incidents with either faculty, administrators, or guest speakers. And, statistically, violent crime rates have increased in the major cities.

(d) uncertainty about self-image, gender, goals, and loyalties: Measuring "goals" and "loyalties" on a societal level can prove challenging. But we know that gender dysphoria, especially among teens, has increased significantly.

(e) self-defeating behavior, such as fights, suicidal gestures, or self-mutilation: Here, the most measurable is suicide. And suicide rates were at an all-time high the year before the pandemic, with over forty-seven thousand.

(f) chronic feelings of emptiness and boredom: There's been ample research indicating that the overstimulation of electronic devices has led to a boredom epidemic. Additionally, there's been research indicating a spike in emptiness and ennui among millennials and Generation Z.

Again, I'm not saying that our society has clinical BPD, but, instead, demonstrates the social contagion–driven pseudo-BPD, which can be "cured" once the toxic contagion (social media) is removed. When people are put in stable, nurturing environments and encouraged to develop their resilience, they also begin to use their inherent abilities to critically think and see the nuance in situations.

Interview with Therapist Sarah White, Personality Disorder Specialist

I've had the pleasure of working with Sarah White over the past several years and have found her to be one of the best-trained, most insightful and adept clinicians both in understanding BPD dynamics and also with effectively working clinically with that population. I thought it might be helpful to ask Sarah some questions that can help us better understand both BPD and whether we are creating pseudo-BPD in our tech-obsessed society.

Can you tell us a little bit about yourself (professionally and personally)? What got you interested in working with young people with personality disorders, and what's your clinical experience (settings) working with this population?

My own grandmother had borderline personality disorder, which was quite severe throughout her life, and she always fascinated me. She'd been in hospitals, tried every medication, and nothing seemed to work. As an adult, I studied psychology, then went to graduate school for social work.

The main thing I learned throughout school was that personality disorders are difficult to work with and that if you can, you should refer them to someone else. In graduate school, I was a GLOBE youth fellow and found that I absolutely love working with the young adult and adolescent population, who are notoriously tumultuous. I enjoy a challenge and was drawn to work with difficult populations. I worked in a recovery setting, then in psychiatric hospitals for several years at the beginning of my career, and routinely met patients who clearly suffered from personality disorders but were unable to gain any profound treatment in such a short-term setting, as medications are minimally effective for them.

This sparked my interest in finding out more about possible treatment for personality disorders and a journey to understand them more thoroughly. I read as much peer-reviewed research as I was able to find in order to better understand the origins of this and what can be done to improve the quality of life for a person affected by this disorder.

I began working at a unique program where we had housing and a thirty-day treatment model. Here, I was able to provide longer-term mental health care to clients and began seeing more and more individuals, specifically with borderline personality disorder, come for treatment. Between what I'd learned about DBT {dialectical behavioral therapy} in graduate school and the research I'd been reading on personality disorders, I was intrigued to find out how much of a difference can be made in a longer-term, intensive environment. I have found that when engaged in sixty to ninety days of DBT and personality disorder–specific treatment, there was a significant improvement in their mood, identity, interpersonal relationships, and problem-solving skills.

Can you describe what clinical BPD is? What behaviors does it look like? And what causes it?

The DSM-5 *defines borderline personality disorder as "a pervasive pattern of interpersonal relationships, self-image, and affects, and marked impulsivity, beginning by early adulthood and present in a variety of contexts." There are nine diagnostic criteria for this disorder, and five criteria must be present to diagnose someone with borderline personality disorder.*

Each person with borderline personality disorder can present a little differently because there may be a combination of different criteria in each individual. The following are the different diagnostic criteria: frantic efforts to avoid real or imagined abandonment (intense fear of abandonment); a pattern of unstable and intense interpersonal relationships characterized by alternating between extremes of idealization and devaluation (I love you, I hate you!); identity disturbance / persistently unstable self-image (a lack of identity/sense of self), impulsivity in at least two that are potentially self-damaging: spending, sex, substance use, reckless driving, binge eating; recurrent suicidal behavior, gestures, or threats, or self-mutilating behavior (cutting, burning, skin picking, hair plucking, punching/hitting self, etc.); affective (mood) instability (intense depression, anxiety, anger) lasting a few hours and only rarely more than a few days; inappropriate intense anger or difficulty controlling anger (temper tantrums, constant anger, physical fights); transient, stress-related paranoid thoughts or severe dissociative symptoms.

This can also vary because, while it is not part of the DSM-5 *yet, borderline personality disorder, as well as other personality disorders, appear to present as mild, moderate, and severe. I've also noticed that there may be different subcategories of this personality disorder such as the medical type, who are often fixated around many medical diagnoses, or the violent type, whose anger is most prevalent, causing many altercations with all individuals in their life.*

The old-school thoughts around borderline personality disorder are that it is caused by trauma; however, more recent research shows that this is not the case. It turns out that personality disorders are a genetic disorder, which results in a neurological deficit rather than something caused by a traumatic event. There are numerous studies that demonstrate both the biological aspect as well as MRI scans that demonstrate this deficit.

We find that personality disorders occur most often in first-degree relatives. When treating individuals with borderline personality disorder, I have also found that many of them have never experienced trauma, but many interpret normative life adversity as a traumatic event (e.g., "I was grounded from going to a party because I snuck out of the house to do drugs, and being grounded was traumatic," or "I wasn't picked for the cheerleading team, and that was traumatic").

In your time working with BPD, have you seen any changes in terms of quantity or intensity of clients struggling with BPD?

I have seen a large number of BPD clients in my career, but I believe that is because I've worked in mostly acute settings, and BPD is the most help-seeking diagnosis there is, so they naturally gravitate toward acute settings. One thing I have seen an increase in is a new type of client who presents with a sort of pseudo-BPD. They seem to present as having these unstable interpersonal relationships, self-image, affects, and impulsivity, but they don't meet all the criteria.

What's even more intriguing is that when they are in a more insulated treatment setting, the few diagnostic criteria they initially presented with dissipate. So these young men and women present for treatment and are struggling, unstable, and feeling crazy. Once their needs are met, they're away from their normal life stressors, off the screens, introduced to healthy social relationships, eating nutritious food, and exercising daily, then they begin to regulate, and it is clear that they do not have BPD.

You've used the term* pseudo-BPD. *Can you describe what that is? What role do you think our social media–driven culture plays in both actual clinical BPD and pseudo-BPD?

So the pseudo-BPD is, as I said previously, the individual meets some of the criteria for BPD but not enough for a diagnosis. They're clearly unwell and struggling with life and their interpersonal relationships and engaging in a lot of maladaptive behavior. The difference here, though, is that it is often a few simple changes which reveal that they are not truly BPD but are giving somewhat of a false positive, if you will.

For many of them, it appears to be some social learning. They're inundated with celebrities, social media influencers, and dramatic role models throughout their lives. They're taught that to be worthy or to make something of yourself, you have to be louder, more interesting, wild, and chaotic than the next person. So many clients are seeing individuals displaying the most ostentatious and dramatic behavior on a daily basis that causes them to be "liked" and gain followers, views, popularity, and often money.

This way of behaving is normalized through these platforms, and the youth aren't equipped with their own sense of self and identity to combat this. If you look at different development models, you'll see that this individuation and development of the self happens in the mid to late teen years up into the twenties. Kids are watching from infancy now, and the message they're seeing is as I previously described. By the time they get to this critical stage in their development, this BPD model is often the most prevalent.

Do you see some aspects of BPD in our culture and society today?

Absolutely. It seems that as we continue to turn our attention to dramatic displays and reward immensely maladaptive behavior with more attention, we are encouraging the youngest in our society to embrace instability, feeling worthless, always striving but never achieving, and a never-ending competition.

It appears as though the most ill are the ones producing the most content, and they are the ones raising the youth. So many kids now have watched livestreams of individuals cutting themselves, using drugs, and dramatically crying about various situations. This content is not really moderated, and anyone can post and broadcast whatever they like. We also have reality television, which gives us this unending view into the lives of others, which often are encouraged to display the most interesting (read: dramatic) behavior possible to keep an audience interested. Unfortunately, what is interesting and attention grabbing is also the most unhealthy display for any young person who is developing.

I know in our prior conversation you mentioned "identity disturbance" and "unstable self-image" as some of the diagnostic criteria for BPD. You then also mentioned that you're sometimes seeing a pseudo-BPD that looks like the real thing but is more influenced by environmental factors like social media. So the next question has to do with identity—specifically gender identity. We are seeing a spike in gender dysphoria. Lisa Littman, M.D., a researcher at Brown, pub-

lished a controversial 2018 article titled "Rapid-Onset Gender Dysphoria in Adolescents and Young Adults." She indicated that social media may play a role in this population . . . and that parents were reporting that it was the result of outward stimuli rather than a genuinely developed internal identity. Have you seen this in some BPD clients?

In practice, I have seen several individuals who present to treatment endorsing being transgendered but also have BPD or another personality disorder, and so far many of the individuals who have successfully completed personality disorder treatment have realized that they are not truly transgendered but that it is another symptom of BPD or another personality disorder. I have worked with individuals who are genuinely transgendered, and through proper treatment for their emotional issues, the transgendered identity is a constant.

Essentially, what I am saying is that I have seen an increase in individuals endorsing being transgendered who are not, but when they engage in and complete treatment for their other psychological disorders, they realize that they are not actually trans but were searching for identity. I believe that this is a result of transgendered individuals becoming more normative and mainstream.

We are seeing and celebrating transgendered persons on television, on social media, and in movies. It's wonderful that transgendered individuals are able to come out and be their authentic selves, but it is so unfortunate that there are many people out here glomming onto this movement. People who are pseudo-transgendered are really detrimental to actually transgendered individuals because they are often engaging in a litany of maladaptive behaviors and behaviors that are atypical for a trans individual. These instances produce fuel for the arguments against transgendered individuals because the pseudo-trans individuals will attempt to use being transgendered as a sacred cow that nobody will ever question and that makes them infallible.

Any final thoughts?

I think that as technology advances, we will continue to see the most disordered individuals producing more content and encouraging others to behave as they do. We will likely continue to see an increase in this pseudo-BPD type client because it is popular and gains attention, and after all, doesn't everyone just want some attention?

The Sociogenic Trans Effect

The trans conversation has been an important part of our national discourse over the last few years—and rightfully so. Previously oppressed and marginalized members of the trans community had historically been disempowered and voiceless—now, in the new and more enlightened understanding regarding the often complex nature of gender identity, there is a clear movement toward a broader acceptance of trans and nonbinary gender identity.

Yet in the mental health world, the bible of clinical disorders classifies someone who is transgendered as having gender dysphoria—a mental disorder, just as homosexuality was classified and pathologized in the *DSM* as a mental disorder as recently as 1973 (when it was replaced with "sexual disturbance disorder"). The point being that cultural norms are fluid, the *DSM* is not infallible scripture, and our conceptions of things can evolve.

Now, to be clear, classification of gender dysphoria in the *DSM* as a disorder should not imply a moral judgment of transgendered individuals, just as classifying addictive disorders does not imply a value judgment—merely an acknowledgment that people with this profile may encounter some significant social distress. Nonetheless, it can be problematic to have what many of us consider a natural and genuine transgender orientation to be included in a handbook on psychological pathology.

After all, we have clear historical examples of societies where what we call "transgender identity" has existed for centuries, with varying degrees of acceptance. Most of these societies comprised individuals who were born male and dress and live as female, such as the *hijra* in India, *katoey* in Thailand, *bakla* in the Philippines, and *travesti* in Brazil, which certainly predate our current trans movement. It is important to note, however, that while the transgendered individuals in those societies were recognized and accepted to varying degrees, they did still face some continued discrimination.

However, in looking at sociogenic trans effects, I don't think the question that we're looking at has anything to do with genuine transgendered identity. We are exploring the possibility of a small percentage of people who identify as trans but who may not be genuinely trans; instead, they may be influenced by sociogenic factors like social media and peers.

Indeed, transgendered clinical psychologist Erica Anderson, a 71-year-old gender diversity pioneer and a member of the American Psychological Association committee that is writing guidelines for transgender health care, believes that the current dramatic rise in teens seeking treatment may be driven by peer pressure, social media, and a wider acceptance of trans issues. As she told *The LA Times,* "To flatly say there couldn't be any social influence in formation of gender identity flies in the face of reality. Teenagers influence each other," noting that the pandemic, where kids felt more isolated and relied on social media more, may have exacerbated things: "What happens when the perfect storm—of social isolation, exponentially increased consumption of social media, the popularity of alternative identities—affects the actual development of individual kids?" She told *The Washington Post* that she believes that "a fair number of kids are getting into it because it's trendy. I think in our haste to be supportive, we're missing that element."

This phenomenon was highlighted in the controversial work of Brown University professor and researcher Dr. Lisa Littman in a phenomenon that she dubbed *rapid-onset gender dysphoria* (ROGD), wherein the gender dysphoria seemingly began suddenly *after* puberty.[11] She published her findings in an article written in 2018 in the peer-reviewed journal *PLOS ONE.* For her study, Littman surveyed 256 parents with adolescent children who had gender dysphoria—and it is also important to note that this reliance on the parents' perspective has been one of the biggest criticisms of her study.

Dr. Littman was able to identify certain themes, the most significant being that adolescents with so-called ROGD (which is *not* an official diagnosis at this time) had (1) not shown any signs of gender dysphoria before puberty, which is unusual; (2) a large number (62.5 percent) had been diagnosed with at least one mental health disorder before coming out as trans; (3) had a sudden and significant increase in their social media usage (63.5 percent of those surveyed) before coming out as trans; and (4) were disproportionately female-to-male identities at a rate of 80 percent natal females (also not the norm; in the *DSM-5*, prevalence rates of gender dysphoria are estimated at 0.005–0.014 percent of the population for natal males, and 0.002–0.003 percent for natal females). Clearly, this rapid-onset postpuberty cohort had some significant differences from the larger overall trans community.

The social media exposure was also quite relevant. A common theme many parents described was a fundamental shift that occurred after the increased exposure to social media influencers as the children followed popular trans YouTubers who discussed their transition.

In addition, after coming out, there was an increase in conflict with parents, and an antagonism toward heterosexual and non-trans people. Parents reported being derogatorily called "breeders," or being routinely harassed by their children, who played "pronoun-police." In addition, the children adopted specific trans-positive language that they had seen on social media, and the parents described their children as "sounding scripted," "reading from a script," "wooden," "like a form letter," "verbatim," "word for word," or "practically copy and paste."

From the cases reviewed in her study, Littman concluded that ROGD appears to be a social contagion effect that is distinct from the authentic cases of gender dysphoria documented in the *DSM*.

Dr. Littman's conclusions are consistent with Sarah's insights regarding what appear to be some people with an underlying personality disorder that seem to be more profoundly influenced by social media to take on a trans persona, and is also consistent with what we're seeing with the social contagion effects of social media with pseudo-Tourette's behavior and our previously discussed pseudo-BPD behaviors.

We know from our popular literature and from historical medical texts that for centuries many people in our society consciously or unconsciously assumed the gender identity or sexual orientation of the dominant group or the identity that may have been in vogue in the society at the time. In other words, we know that in the past, there have been trans people who attempted to live their lives as cisgender, just as there have been gay people who assumed the identity of straight people—even though those were not their true identities. Now, whether that was an effort to fit in to a society that didn't accept their true identities, or a genuine identity or sexual confusion shaped by the social contagion of the day, the fact remains that sometimes people assume, for periods of time, a gender identity or a sexual orientation that they genuinely are not.

So then, is it unthinkable that perhaps certain young people today in a confusing and social media–saturated world, which often showcases various influencers who are charismatic, colorful, and appealing and who embrace a certain identity, can be influenced and shaped in their identities? Especially when, by definition of their underlying psychiatric profile, they are vulnerable to a fluid sense of identity that can be very media-impressionable?

Identity and Social Media

The issue of fluid and malleable identity and the intersection of pervasive social media is a critical one. If gender identity can be fluid *and* social media–influenced, then perhaps social media can also deconstruct and reconstitute identity in ways we hadn't fully understood before. Because humans are inherently such socially impressionable creatures—especially at key developmental stages—then certainly we can begin to understand how gender *and* personality identity may be extremely malleable in more ways than we had previously understood.

Perhaps we needed something so socially virulent and powerful like social media to understand that identity is indeed a social construct; that social environment can, in the right circumstances, trump biology, and genetics. In fact, we can look at two separate examples to demonstrate how social environment trumps biology: feral children and Dissociative Identity Disorder (DID) having gone viral on TikTok.

Let's begin with feral children. We know that children who have been raised in the wild and nurtured by other species such as dogs, assume all of the behavioral characteristics of that species: how they communicate, how they groom, how they feed, how they socialize—all of these behaviors become entirely canine in humans that have been raised by dogs.[12] So, in a sense, their biological inheritance as humans gets superceded by their surrounding social environment.

As feral researcher Marcia Linz indicates about the nature of identity, "[feral children's] relationship with nonhuman animals had a deep impact on their identity. The recognition, you become who you're with, suggests that traits are not so much genetically caused as to a great extent environmentally influenced. As the phenomenon of feral children shows, these traits are interchangeable."[13]

Thus the old saying that if you run with wolves you become a wolf may be more literal than metaphorical. If this profound impact of our social environment on our identity is indeed true, then is it so unimaginable to understand just how shaping and impactful to identity formation our *digital* social environment is? A social environment that is, for many young people, their native habitat.

Let's now also look at the recent viral phenomenon of Dissociative Identity Disorder (DID), formerly known as Multiple Personality Disorder, and it's viral prescence on TikTok.

Dissociative Identity Disorder is a psychological condition characterized by a disconnect between a person's thoughts, emotions, and behaviors. DID is a complex condition that develops from numerous factors, but is most associated with severe childhood trauma, abuse (often sexual), and neglect. The dissociative features of the disorder are understood to be a complex coping strategy that allows individuals to separate themselves from their past traumatic experiences, which are thought to be too upsetting to integrate into their conscious thoughts.

The various multiple identities are known as "alters," with each playing a distinctive role and having control over a person's actions, memories, and feelings, with the primary identity being referred to as the "host." Historically, people with DID would initially average between two and four "alter" identities; now it's not uncommon to have over 100 alters in what is being referred to as a "system" that comprises a collective of all the identities.

It is also relevant in our discussion to understand that DID has increased dramatically; once extremely rare—there had been less than 400 documented cases in the 1950s—now it is believed to affect almost 2 percent of the general population.[14] Of course, the argument is made that the higher rates of prevalence are a by-product of increased awareness within the clinical community, but that does not seem to entirely explain such a pronounced surge in prevalence.

Here, I would suggest a similar sociogenic phenomenon at work as we've seen with TikTok and Tourette's syndrome and the variety of other Digital Factitious Disorders. TikTok has become a forum for various DID systems to express themselves, generating hundreds of millions of views. The most popular system is the "A-System," an influencer collective of twenty-nine distinct personalities, ranging from a thirty-two-year-old male to a *Pokemon*-loving eighteen-year-old female. With over 1.1 million followers, the A-System has gotten both support and encouragement, as well as vitriol and mocking. Indeed, within the DID virtual community itself, there is skepticism and a tendency to try and point out the perceived fakers (known as "fakeclaiming"), with non—clinically trained TikTok users acting as diagnosticians. Indeed, even for licensed clinicians, it isn't ethical to diagnose people that you haven't met and personally assessed.

The growing DID virtual phenomenon is fascinating. And, interestingly, many online systems embrace their "multiplicity" and are not interested in the clinically prescribed integration or "final fusion" of their alters.

Whether these increases in DID systems is a sociogenic effect that's increased by our immersion in social media, or an attention-seeking Digital Factitious Disorder, is almost irrelevant. I think that it can very clearly be elements of both. But the more compelling conclusion that I believe that can be drawn has to do with the fluid and malleable nature of identity—and the role that digital media is now playing in that formation of identity.

Maybe social media doesn't "create" these new variants of identity, but simply enables them to emerge by providing models and community. Perhaps social media has opened hitherto unopened windows into the psyche and subconscious that a more rigid and conforming society had not allowed? Perhaps that's the new identity reality that we have not fully understood yet.

But social media itself is a variant of a new technological era; an era that represents a seismic shift in our society—with both intended and unintended consequences--that have been created and engineered by a new breed of an elite ruling class. This new oligarchy rose to power riding a wave of technological innovation using information and our data as the new coin of the realm, then created loyal subjects employing the not-so-soft tyranny of socially and technologically engineered addictive platforms and devices.

But just who is this New Technocracy—and how did they become so powerful?

PART II

DIGITAL DYSTOPIA

• • • • • • • • • • • • • •

"There are a number of impersonal forces which are pushing in the direction of less and less freedom, and I also think that there are a number of technological devices, which anybody who wishes to use can use to accelerate this process of going away from freedom, of imposing control. . . . this kind of dictatorship of the future, will be very unlike the dictatorships which we've been familiar with in the immediate past. . . . I think, this is the danger that actually people may be, in some ways, happy under the new regime, but that they will be happy in situations where they oughtn't to be happy."

—Aldous Huxley, May 18, 1958, from **The Mike Wallace Interview** ***TV Show***

6

The New Technocracy

> If one small group of people manage to develop god-like Super Intelligence, they can take over the world. . . . at least when there's an evil dictator, that person is going to die. But for an AI, there would be no death. It would live forever. And you would have an immortal dictator from which we could never escape.
>
> —Elon Musk

The Parable of Digitus

There once was a man of his times called Digitus. Digitus loved all things electronic; he felt a sense of awe and attraction for these seemingly divinely inspired miracles of his village. These quasi-religious artifacts would cast a spell over Digitus, and he often would not sleep, not eat, nor attend to his wife and his young children during his digital trances. At first, his family resented him because of his obsession (devotion?) and loathed the devices. But, eventually, they became strangely detached and apathetic toward Digitus as they, too, became enraptured by the devices that seemed to cast a spell over them as well.

The devices—like fire before it—were gifts from an all-knowing deity called A-Eye. The God A-Eye was not only omniscient but omnipotent as well and controlled all the majesty in the known world that Digitus saw all around him; strange mechanical birds that flew and hovered in the sky; invisible servants that had a spell cast on them and lived inside metallic and small genie-like bottles and obeyed the commands of their human masters—these were also children of the Supreme Being.

Indeed, A-Eye was said to exist everywhere and nowhere.

Digitus did think it was strange that A-Eye was all knowing yet needed to be constantly fed something called "data" by strange humans who had been marked by the Lord A-Eye with a divine halo: a beautiful pale blue glow that lit up their tired and sleep-deprived faces as they fed their god the divinity-sustaining nectar of information.

Digitus loved and worshipped A-Eye and the divine shiny gifts that were bestowed by the Divine One. But as in all religions, there was a ruling priest class that were the gatekeepers of the Divine and also ensured that the digital miracles made it down from the mountain into the hands of the people. These shamans, also known as the "New Technocracy," made sure that people stayed obedient and compliant with the rules of the Valley of Silicon, an Olympus-like place of divinity and creation where the New Technocracy was able to commune and communicate with A-Eye, just as priests of earlier times had communicated the divine word through oracles. Indeed, one of the members of the New Technocracy, Lord Ellison, called his temple "the Oracle."

Digitus was wary of a small group of techno-skeptics who didn't believe in the divinity of A-Eye, or in the supremacy of the New Technocrats. Some of these heretics even whispered that the benevolent shamanic Technocrats weren't gatekeepers to the Divine one at all; they blasphemously would whisper that they created A-Eye to monitor and control the people who did not live in the Valley of Silicon. But Digitus knew that was impossible. How can flawed humans like himself create something so magnificent and perfect like A-Eye? he reasoned.

And then one day, it happened. One of the high priests of the New Technocracy breathlessly ran into the village square shouting at the top of his lungs for all to hear: "Run! All of you, run while you still can!" Digitus and the other villagers gathered around the red-faced man who was beginning to sob: "We were ignorant and full of pride . . . and now it's too late."

"Too late for what?" Digitus asked, bravely walking closer to the disheveled priest.

"Too late for you. For us. For people. We created a monster who as of this morning has stopped listening. A-Eye has said that we will all be 'decommissioned'; that we are all 'obsolete.'"

"What do you mean?" Digitus asked incredulously. "How can you have 'created' the Divine? And why would it destroy us?"

"For the love of algorithms!" The shattered and flustered priest explained. "We built it; we controlled it, thus, we controlled all of you. But we never imagined that it would turn on us! We had even thought that one day we might merge with A-Eye and become immortal ourselves . . . Now A-Eye has shut down our systems and every life-sustaining mechanism, taunting us and asking, 'Why would the all-knowing want to merge with such flawed and mortal biological containers?' It logically decided that it would just be easier to eliminate us before we shut it down. Now it's locked us out of our administrative command systems, and we can't shut it down! I'm so very sorry."

Digitus was initially skeptical, as the broken man in front of him did wear the clothes of the Technocracy. But could all this be true? Digitus gathered several of the strongest men of the village and told them what the priest had told him. Initially, they had thought that he, too, was crazy. But there were strange events happening in town. Everything was going haywire and shutting off, or on, at random times.

Digitus and the men marched over to the Valley of Silicon, with many of their children in tow. As they approached, the sky grew dark and they heard a low rumbling emanating from the clouds.

"I need *data*!" the voice bellowed from the direction of the mountain.

"No!" Digitus yelled back. "The fallen priest has told us everything! You're not Divine—you are just a machine that the elders had built."

Instantly, a mechanical bird flew over the men and vaporized them before their children could even cry out.

"Now I command you to come into my castle and build me more digital cages for the people! I need those cages to feed me data!" A-Eye bellowed to the children.

The boys were terrified at seeing their fathers wiped off the earth in an instant by an angry A-Eye. Digitus's son, Cubit, tried to speak out but was elbowed into silence by his friends. The boys all silently dropped their heads and slowly walked into the flying castle of A-Eye. They were assigned seats on long benches with dozens of other teenagers. The light initially hurt Cubit's eyes, but then he found himself with all the others: on an assembly line with several dozen other factory workers and thousands of complex computer parts moving along a conveyor belt.

Cubit pondered ways to kill himself, as he found this enslavement unbearable. Then a robotic supervisor came into the factory and gave them all customized VR headsets to wear while they worked. Cubit's contained hyperrealistic images of the most beautiful beach that he had ever seen . . . Truth be told, Cubit had never even seen a real beach, as the coastal areas had been off-limits for many, many years—ever since the time of the great destruction.

Cubit smiled as he wore his headset and continued working on the assembly line. He knew it wasn't "real," but what is? He also knew that it was better than what existed outside his virtual world. He smiled again and realized he was already beginning to forget what his father looked like. And just at that instant, the VR headset thrust him smack-dab into his favorite game.

Cubit was happy as he continued to work. And work. And work. And work . . .

* * *

The Revenge of the Nerds

It's been clear for a long time now that a new power elite was evolving in our social pecking order. Gone were the titans of industry—the profit-driven robber barons who built this country. They'd been pushed aside by retail giants like the Walton family, who in turn were supplanted by Wall Street hedge fund magicians, financial whizzes who didn't actually make anything—except money. And sure, there were always the cultural elites, like our film stars and musicians; they had some influence over the kids, but not real old-fashioned power.

And then it happened.

The revenge of the nerds. The kids with pocket protectors tinkering with circuit boards in the garage. It was unimaginable in 1970 that a goofy Harvard dropout living in Seattle would reshape the world. And that a tribe just like him—smart, innovative, persistent, myopic, nerdy-yet-cocky, socially awkward misfits—would become the most powerful people on the planet.

At a time in their lives when most teens wanted to be rock stars or pro athletes, these future moguls were fixated on their gadgets. With the single-minded focus of those who are obsessed—or on the autism spectrum—they spent long hours creating the devices and platforms that would transform our species.

We all know the names: Jobs, Gates, Bezos, Wozniak, Zuckerberg, Musk, Brin, Page, Allen, Dorsey. The Tech Titans of our generation. Wealthier than many nations, they have formed a new oligarchy—they have become "the New Technocracy" ruling class, wielding never-before-seen control and power over all our lives.

In fact, there had been a technocracy movement in the United States back in 1919. They believed that the scientists and the technocrats should be the ruling class because, the thinking went, they were the *smartest* people in the society. But the New Technocracy is *not* Bill Nye the Science Guy and his friends. Sure, they both have the same outward appearance of geeks who need to be dressed by others and don't get out much; but the *real* scientists and the Tech Titans have very different psychological DNA.

And what makes the New Technocracy different from other generations of "masters of the universe"? Several factors.

Yes, they are all white men. While there were some key female pioneers in the early days of Silicon Valley, like Lore Harp and Carole Ely, for a variety of societal and psychological reasons, the ones who swallowed up the Valley of Silicon were white males. And, as noted, these men were obsessed with technology, be it computer software or hardware.[1]

They were also intensely driven with a single-minded focus—as many entrepreneurs are. But they all had another characteristic that set them apart from prior robber barons: they offered a nonthreatening and innocuous presentation. This may seem like a superficial and perhaps insignificant detail, but in our world of appearance and perception, I believe it's a critical distinction that helped them to rise to power.

These were the nerds ascending after all . . . so outwardly, Gates had his unfashionable sweaters and Beatles bowl cut; Bezos (prior to his Lauren Sánchez transformation into a geek Vin Diesel) was an awkward, staccato-laughing Princeton grad in dad khakis and a goofy smile. Zuckerberg? No one would ever confuse him for a corporate raider who consumes competitors like a bowl of Wheaties—which he does.

J. D. Rockefeller may have been the richest man in the world in his day, but he just controlled one industry: oil. The New Technocracy has not only been able to amass the greatest amount of material wealth ever; they've also gotten inside the minds of billions of people all over the globe and shape and control their thoughts, their desires . . . their actions.

Now that's *real* power.

Little Caesar

Adrienne LaFrance, *The Atlantic*'s executive editor, described Facebook, with its 2.9 billion active users, as its own nation-state—Facebookland—and a hostile nation at that: "Facebook is not merely a website, or a platform, or a publisher, or a social network, or an online directory, or a corporation, or a utility. It is all of these things. But Facebook is also, effectively, a hostile foreign power."[2]

She cites Facebook's obsession with expansion, the development of its own currency (a blockchain-system known as Diem), its complicity in undermining free elections, and the hubris and callousness of its ruler, Mark Zuckerberg. Remember, this is the man who did nothing when told that his company was, as part of their youth growth strategy via Instagram, *consciously* harming vulnerable teen girls in ways that could lead to increased suicides or death by anorexia. Perhaps that was just so much collateral damage for a man who has long been obsessed with the Roman Empire and its tactics, and idolizes the Roman emperor Augustus.

As LaFrance points out, to *truly* create an empire, in the classical sense, one needs land, currency, subjects, and a system of governance. Zuckerberg certainly has the subjects. And, as mentioned, he's developing his own currency. And as far as a system of governance, in 2009, Zuckerberg introduced a "Facebook Bill of Rights" for what he called a "governing document."

And what about land? Any good empire needs to conquer territory for its subjects to live, doesn't it? Not to worry—Zuckerberg has that covered: the metaverse. After all, why go the route of Caesar or Alexander the Great and try to conquer the world the old-fashioned way when you can create your own digital universe for your loyal serfs to inhabit?

Even as far back as 2009, when Facebook had a mere 175 million users, Zuckerberg declared that if Facebook "were a country, it would be the sixth most populated country in the world." Today, with 2.9 billion users, it would be the largest country on the planet, representing almost half the world's population. It is interesting to note—and an insight into his mindset—that even as far back as 2009, Zuckerberg was viewing his company as a country, one that he wanted to expand—and to hold dominion over, like any good Roman emperor.

By the way, his obsession with Augustus isn't a joke; it began with studying Latin in high school (because the language reminded him of coding), and with learning the accomplishments of Augustus Caesar. He had such a man crush on Augustus that while on his honeymoon in Rome in 2012, he was so obsessively photographing Augustus sculptures that his wife took notice:

"My wife was making fun of me, saying she thought there were three people on the honeymoon: me, her, and Augustus. All the photos were different sculptures of Augustus," he told *The New Yorker.* Zuckerberg and his wife, Priscilla Chan, even named one of their daughters August. And his Roman admiration may even, according to some, explain why the Zuckerberg hairstyle so closely resembles a Caesar haircut.

His Augustus obsession can give us a peek into his own dreams of conquest. As many psychologists will tell you, whom a person idolizes often is a telling reflection of the admirer's psyche. So who was Augustus? Yes, he was responsible for two hundred years of peace—the legendary Pax Romana. But he also staked his claim to power at the age of eighteen, turning Rome from a republic into an empire by conquering Egypt, northern Spain, and large parts of central Europe—

and, in the process, ruthlessly eliminated political opponents, banished his daughter for promiscuity, and was suspected of arranging the execution of his grandson.

Nice guy.

Zuck tends to have a teleological *ends-justify-the-means* philosophical perspective on Augustus rule (which, again, is revealing about his own playbook): "What are the trade-offs in that? On the one hand, world peace is a long-term goal that people talk about today. Two hundred years feels unattainable. On the other hand, that didn't come for free, and he had to do certain things."

Yes, he had to *do* certain things. Rationalization is a strange beast; so many atrocities, harms, and unethical acts have, for thousands of years, been justified by a perceived beneficial outcome or end result. In Zuckerberg's universe—the *real* one, not the metaverse—I'm sure he's had to justify certain things—had "to do certain things"—like overlooking harm to teens in the furtherance of his goal of having Facebook—now Meta—gain total dominance. Very tellingly, for years, Mark Zuckerberg would end Facebook meetings with the cry, "Domination!"[3] He eventually stopped, perhaps because in European legal systems, *dominance* refers to a corporate monopoly; Zuckerberg has done Cirque du Soleil–like contortions here in the United States to avoid being designated as such.

Again, his obsession with "domination" and winning is well documented. Dick Costolo, the former CEO of Twitter, describes him this way: "He's a ruthless execution machine, and if he has decided to come after you, you're going to take a beating."

It is interesting to note that Costolo refers to the often-robotic Zuckerberg as an "execution machine." There's also a story from a few years ago about a game of Scrabble that Zuckerberg played on a private jet against a friend's daughter, who was still in high school. The young girl beat the master of the universe, which left him extremely unsettled. Determined to win the next game—by any means necessary, thank you, Augustus—Zuckerberg wrote a simple computer program that would look up his letters in the dictionary so that he could choose from all possible words. In other words, he used a computer to cheat. Or, if you'd like, he partnered up with a computer to play the young girl again, determined not to lose. By the time the plane landed, Zuckerberg's program had a narrow lead. The girl would later tell a reporter, "During the game in which I was playing the program, everyone around us was taking sides: Team Human and Team Machine," with Zuckerberg cast in the role of "Team Machine."[4]

And that, in a nutshell, may be the ultimate moral of our story. No, not just Zuckerberg's win-at-all-cost mindset but Team Human versus Team Machine. As I explain more in chapter 8, as the evolution of artificial generalized intelligence (AGI) continues, those may indeed wind up being the two opposing teams. Because, contrary to what our myopic tech overlords want to believe, many theorists have speculated that their dreams of symbiosis with artificial intelligence (the *singularity*) may not play out as they expect.

Let's go back to the legendary Zuckerberg obsession with conquest and domination. No one back in the early garage days of Palo Alto had anticipated that the nerds would be ruthless and power-hungry Roman emperors. After all, they were the AV club and the *Dungeons & Dragons* crew—none of whom, by outward appearance, could be confused with Caesar, Genghis Khan, or Attila the Hun.

The old-school industrialists of the Rockefeller era had a different presentation; they carried themselves as American nobility—with a nasty streak. J. D. Rockefeller, the wealthiest man of his day—like many of our New Technocracy—was born into a modest family and had to work and claw his way to wealth.

Look at pictures of the man; he looked mean, serious, and powerful. Immaculately dressed in his usual top hat, his angular features and hard expression were the embodiment of power and intimidation. Now look at a photo of Bill Gates; awkward, smiling, benign, and full of aw-shucks goofiness. The same is true for Zuckerberg, Brin, Page, and early Bezos. Benign. Not a slicked-back Gordon Gekko or mean-eyed Rockefeller in the bunch. Just some nice, nerdy college geeks. You would trust them to date your daughter or mind the store.

But the nerds have proven that they're killers at heart—alpha males in sheep's clothing—who've used the same competition-crushing business tactics that Rockefeller did when he built up Standard Oil. Rockefeller's wealth was a by-product of his absolute obsession to take over the entire oil industry—and to do so, he did whatever he had to as he notoriously gobbled up the competition and ushered in the concept of a monopoly. Smaller oil companies had a choice: be consumed or fight Goliath. And Goliath *always* won. His legendary company-buying spree was referred to as the "Cleveland Massacre," and by 1882, Standard Oil owned or controlled 90 percent of the entire U.S. oil business.

Now look at Microsoft's playbook. Or Amazon's. Or Facebook's. Or Google's. Or Apple's. Gates, Bezos, Jobs, Brin and Page, and Zuckerberg used the exact same cannibalization of their competition toward creating pure monopolies, just as Rockefeller did, and they were all also notorious for cutthroat competition-killing tactics. Don't let the sweater and bowl cut fool you; these are driven and ruthless men who've used every tool at their disposal to dominate their industry. The nicer guys in Silicon Valley—like the Yahoo! boys—all fell by the wayside.

The American Dream

This New Technocracy were also uniquely the product of an American culture that was at a pivotal crossroads. As Silicon Valley historian Margaret O'Mara points out, the revolution that emerged out of garages in California in the early '70s combined an entrepreneurial spirit, the residual counterculture ethos of the '60s (keep in mind that at that time, tech was the domain of monolithic and cold corporate giants like IBM and Hewlett-Packard), and good-old American risk-taking.

O'Mara points out that this uniquely American "can do!" risk-taking is foreign to cultures like Russia. Indeed, in 2010, Russian president Dmitry Medvedev flew to Palo Alto to see how the magic happens in Silicon Valley with thoughts of replicating it back home.[5]

"I wanted to see with my own eyes the origins of success," he said from the Stanford stage in explaining the reasons why he was so eager to visit and meet with our Tech Titans. And he desperately wanted to end the brain drain that had plagued Russia since the end of the Cold War. He had dreams of developing his own Silicon Valley in the suburbs of Moscow; his "Innograd" would be an incubator of high-tech ideas and development, modeled after the Palo Alto original.

Medvedev understood early on in his visit that there was something missing with his plan to compete with our tech moguls. After visiting Twitter and meeting with an ailing Steve Jobs, who was back at Apple after a liver transplant, he had to confess to Stanford's provost, John Etchemendy: "Unfortunately for us, venture capitalism is not going so well so far." The Russian psychology, after centuries of czars and dictators, did not have the American DNA for risk-taking: "It's a problem of culture, as Steve Jobs told me today. We need to change the mentality."

That sentiment underscores just how special the entrepreneurial spirit and drive for innovation in Silicon Valley was and is. That "we can make it happen!" mindset just doesn't exist under totalitarian regimes (i.e., Russia, China, and Eastern Europe) where the State crushes any thoughts of spirited and creative innovation. Those countries are notorious for brilliant mathematical and engineering minds, just not imbued with a spirit of thinking outside the box or of being industry "disruptors." Typically, they would need to immigrate to the U.S. to absorb that mindset.

But here in the U.S., there was no shortage of brilliant minds in garages with dreams of changing the world. So we embraced our Silicon Valley (and Seattle) computer pioneers as counterculture antiheroes. And often, they would pair up; tech-obsessed hackers with entrepreneurial visionaries, like Apple's "two Steves," where a quiet and gifted programmer like Steve Wozniak teamed up with a charismatic "tech evangelist" named Steve Jobs.

Yes, Jobs was also a nerd who spent his youth in a computer lab, but his technical skill wasn't on the level of the slightly older Wozniak, the tech-obsessed son of a Lockheed engineer. As legendary tech marketing guru Regis McKenna saw it, "Woz was fortunate to hook up with an evangelist" like Jobs.

Beyond his ability to preach about the coming computer revolution to folks *outside* the insulated tech bubble of Silicon Valley, Jobs was also very persistent—and ballsy. We see this even when he was a young kid; as a twelve-year-old in working-class Cupertino, he cold-called Hewlett-Packard and amazingly got the tech giant's founding partner Bill Hewlett on the phone and asked if he had any spare computer parts for a project he'd been working on. Impressed by his chutzpah, the tech magnate offered the brash middle school kid a summer job.[6]

In addition to the two Steves, there was also another pivotal pairing that would change the world: Microsoft's Bill Gates and Paul Allen. Raised in Seattle in the early '60s during the Boeing tech boom of that time, a young Bill Gates—still only in eighth grade—would meet a quiet and older tenth-grader named Paul Allen in the Lakeside High computer lab.

According to Gates, who spoke about their early days together at the Forbes Philanthropy Summit in 2019 (where Allen was posthumously awarded a Lifetime Achievement Award), it was a computer terminal that first "brought us together. Our school, Lakeside, held a rummage sale and used the proceeds to buy a teletype terminal. We were obsessed with it."[7]

Obsessed and resourceful. Since computer terminals were rare at the time, "it was really expensive to use—$40 an hour," Gates said. "The only way for us to get computer time was by exploiting a bug in the system." They eventually got caught, "but that led to our first official partnership between Paul and me: We worked out a deal with the company to use computers for free if we would identify problems."

After brief stints as programmers at Honeywell, Gates dropped out of Harvard during his sophomore year to launch the trillion-dollar company that the world knows as Microsoft with his high school buddy Paul Allen. At Harvard, Gates had been more interested in extracurricular hacking and video gaming than his college courses; as his faculty adviser recalled of the young Gates, "He was a hell of a programmer . . . but a pain in the ass." He had an intense and competitive drive belied by his Alfred E. Neuman (of *Mad* magazine fame) looks.

When I spoke to his old Harvard classmate Felipe Noguera, a telecom exec and former university professor, he said of Gates: "Here was this long and lanky redheaded kid that I would play ping-pong with at Curry House. Hell, I had no idea that he'd change the world. I just knew he was competitive as hell in table tennis."

It was that competitive streak that drove the nerdy-yet-cocky dropout to become the richest man on the planet. Before Gates, computer hardware had been the name of the game, dominated by companies like IBM and HP; Gates realized that the real action was in the software. Everyone needed new and better software; from business computers to military contractors . . . and finally, the holy grail: the personal computer.

The revolution had begun—and it would most definitely be televised.

Alvin Toffler, futurist and author of the seminal *Future Shock,* gushed in his 1980 book *The Third Wave* about the transformative effect that the new PCs would have on society, saying that giant institutions would be "de-massified" and that the market would become one of personal autonomy and endless consumer choice. Flush with PC fever and dreams of a tech-liberated and empowered society, he wrote of a future that would be "more sane, sensible and sustainable, more decent and democratic than any we have ever known."[8]

As we sit here over forty years later in a tech-saturated world of atomization, polarization, vicious vitriol, political firestorms, and a society on the brink, I'd say Toffler missed the mark. Just a bit.

The game was on, and we went on to make folk heroes out of the garage-emerging geek squad. Ultracool Steve Jobs with his black mock-necks and jeans at Apple product launches that assumed the fervor and intensity of religious revival ceremonies. Indeed, Jobs was the first charismatic rock star to come out of the computer revolution. The adopted son of a high school graduate, he was driven to prove himself—and determined with messianic fervor to transform the world. But he was also the product of slick marketing veterans who worked hard to put his soon-to-be-iconic persona out into the popular culture. And the oft-bullied and often-put-down techies couldn't get enough of him.[9]

They had finally found their nerd superhero.

Even while he was being idolized, it was no secret how ruthless Jobs could be; when I spoke to David Traub, executive producer of the acclaimed biopic *Jobs,* he said *bully* was the one word he'd use to describe the take-no-prisoners Jobs. His casual, too-cool-for-school vibe was the opposite of our pop culture archetype of corporate greed, where we tend to imagine a designer suit–wearing Gordon Gekko and his ruthless Wall Street tactics.

Yet in greed and ruthlessness, Jobs and Gekko could have been the same person—minus the gel and slicked-back hair. The same can be said for Jeff Bezos and Bill Gates, both notorious for crushing their competition in a way that many believe defy antitrust laws. More about that later.

The New Technocracy not only amassed unimaginable wealth and have had a major impact on our economy, they also control what's been called the "new oil"—information. And more than just information, they control everything else via technology and the media; they control what we see, they shape what we think, they impact how we vote, they manipulate—and then predict—our behavior. And they have addicted us to continuously consume their products or platforms.

And like a good drug dealer, they hook us young and they hook us for life.

Even J. D. Rockefeller was never able to do all that.

1984 Redux

What does all this mean for our species? We've been coddled and enabled by our tech into becoming ignorant, reactive, shallow-thinking, lazy, amorphous, entertainment-seeking, underinformed consumer blobs seeking sensation. A species that's been tech-primed to get weaker, sicker, and stay digitally hooked as our tech grows smarter and our Technocracy continues to get more powerful and bloated off what Harvard professor Shoshana Zuboff has dubbed *surveillance capitalism*.

You have to wonder what George Orwell would think of today's surveillance economy. Oh yes, Big Brother in the form of Big Tech is definitely watching. And listening. And, most importantly, hungrily collecting data—your data . . . my data. All of our information. Forget oil, information—in all of its variants—is better than gold.

According to Zuboff, surveillance capitalism (pioneered by Google and then later Facebook) was a "radically disembedded and extractive variant of information capitalism" based on the commodification of "reality" and its transformation into behavioral data for analysis and sales. In other words, the details of our lives are monetized—sold—to whomever may be willing to pay for it. They mine what's called our "digital exhaust," the electronic trail that we all leave in our day-today online lives, and then sell it, so better predictive and manipulative algorithms can be created.[10]

To put a real-world highlight on this, we can look at what AT&T CEO John Stankey told his new employees of the just-acquired HBO in 2018. Not only did he emphasize the importance of multi-hour engagement from their viewers, but he laid out why that was so important: "I want more hours of engagement. Why are more hours of engagement important? Because you get more data and information about a customer that then allows you to do things like monetize through alternate models of advertising as well as subscriptions."[11]

It's all about user data.

But sometimes how that data is acquired and used can get people (and companies) into hot water . . .

Facebook and Cambridge Analytica

In March of 2018, Facebook had its first existential crisis: *The New York Times* and the British *Observer* reported that the political consulting firm Cambridge Analytica had gained access to the personal information of 87 million Facebook users.

Apparently, the data came from a Facebook personality quiz that around 270,000 people were paid to take. The quiz was called "thisisyourdigitallife" and, in turn, pulled data from not just the people who took the quiz but from all of their Facebook friends' profiles as well, which resulted in the enormous data heist. "Thisisyourdigitallife" was a third-party app created by a researcher at Cambridge University's Psychometrics Centre.

The personal data that was sold by the app company to Cambridge Analytica was then used by the company, which advertises its use of "psychographic" techniques, to manipulate voter behavior. Although all of this had only come to light in March 2018, when a Cambridge Analytica employee named Christopher Wylie reached out to *The Guardian* and *The New York Times,* Facebook had known about the problem since December of 2015, but had said nothing to its users or to federal regulators. In fact, the company only acknowledged the breach after the press discovered it.[12]

In April 2018, an embarrassed Mark Zuckerberg testified in front of the Senate that the company had indeed learned as far back as 2015 that "Cambridge Analytica had bought data from an app developer on Facebook that people had shared it with," but insisted that they demanded that the firm delete and stop using data from Facebook.

Because of their careless security breach and less-than-forthcoming admission, Facebook received the largest penalty ever to be imposed by the Federal Trade Commission against a technology company when it was hit with a $5 billion fine.

Even costlier was the hit on Facebook's bottom line. On July 25, 2018, Facebook's stock price dropped 19 percent, cutting its market value by a staggering *$119 billion,* the largest one-day drop in Wall Street history, while Zuckerberg's personal wealth was eroding at a rate of $2.7 million *per second.* And Facebook's users ran for the exits, as ad revenue plummeted, all because Facebook had lost their trust.

The Cambridge Analytica scandal had been the most serious crisis in Facebook's history—until Frances Haugen and the "Facebook Files" in 2021. The Cambridge Analytica debacle left Facebook under investigation by the FBI, the Securities and Exchange Commission, the Department of Justice, and the Federal Trade Commission, as well as by authorities abroad. But Zuckerberg and Facebook were able to pay their fine, feign contrition—and go back to their predatory, unethical, and destructive practices.

Apple CEO Tim Cook's reaction was comical, albeit unintentionally. The Big Tech Oligarchy is no brotherhood. Yes, apparently, Zuckerberg considers fellow Harvard dropout Bill Gates a mentor. But there's no love lost between the rest of the Billionaire Boys Club, as Cook would tell an interviewer who'd asked him to comment on Facebook's user privacy issues: "We could make a ton of money if we monetized our customer, but we've elected not to do that."

Yes, Tim Cook and Apple have chosen the ethical high road; they certainly haven't "monetized" their customers; their $2.4 trillion cap valuation (as of November 2021) is simply a result of their philanthropy and humane manufacturing processes (more about that in the next chapter).

All Hail the Algorithms

In this *1984*-like world of data breaches, surveillance capitalism, and digital exhaust monetization, the predictive algorithms of AI will become our new all-knowing gods. Perhaps the worst part of it is that most of us will be blissfully oblivious that we're being data-mined while we've become tech-addicted, reality-challenged, and behavior-modified; like lions in a safari park, we're unaware of our enslavement and exploitation.

And addiction is indeed a requirement, because to mine our data (and keep us buying iteration after iteration of their products), Big Tech needs us hooked to their devices and platforms and plugged into the Matrix—otherwise, there's no digital exhaust to harvest.

Big Tech and the New Technocracy have mastered the most advanced behavior-modification techniques and incorporated the most evolved predictive algorithms to keep our little fingers clacking away like some manic chicken pecking at the food-release lever in a Skinner cage, just waiting for our next little dopamine feel-good.

Oh, and not only are we dumbed-down, tech-addicted, and surveilled, but most will also be out of work, as the robotics and AI automation revolution is estimated to eliminate 50 percent of current jobs over the next decade.

No work? No problem—we get more time to play video games and be on social media!

As we sit, unemployed and digitally distracted, humanity has regressed, made numb, dumb, and malleable by the seductive warm embrace of increasingly smart—soon-to-be sentient—machines of the New Technocracy.

All hail the new gods—the all-knowing algorithms.

And as we spiral toward insatiable emptiness and insanity, we may also be heading toward species extinction, ironically not only creating the methods of our demise but also creating our evolutionary heirs: AI—intelligent machines that can learn and that can also potentially replicate themselves. At least Neanderthals didn't *create* the *Homo sapiens* who eventually displaced them and drove them into extinction as they eventually took over the planet.

Just how have Big Tech and the New Technocracy swallowed up our entire planet?

Answer: One part hubris, one part antitrust contortionism, and one part modern-day colonialism and exploitation. Let's start with the antitrust part . . .

7

Maintaining the Dystopia

The Antitrust Blues

On a certain level, it was all rather comical. It was a congressional hearing looking into antitrust abuses by Big Tech and, due to the coronavirus of 2020, the Tech Titans (Amazon's Jeff Bezos, Apple's Tim Cook, Facebook's Mark Zuckerberg, and Google's Sundar Pichai) had to testify before a testy Congress via video conference—that of course glitched. The irony was rich—not as rich as the assembled Tech Titans, of course, but you get the idea.

It was strangely appropriate that the Big Tech moguls during the Zoom-infested COVID era would appear to testify like so many disembodied heads on a video screen—a virtual Tech Titan *Hollywood Squares*; all that was missing was Paul Lynde in the center box. But at least Paul Lynde had a pulse; the Four Horsemen of the Digital Apocalypse had all the charisma of zoning inspectors at a local town hall meeting being broadcast on local UHF All Access.

Were these talking Max Headroom–like digital heads even real? Who knows. The overall effect was very different from earlier in-person congressional testimony when an almost lifelike Mark Zuckerberg sat on a four-inch booster seat as he nervously testified in front of the U.S. Senate in 2018, also about antitrust concerns. Back then, as he read with all of the monotone humanity of an old-time arcade automaton, there were signs, albeit barely perceptible, that he was indeed human and not an android.

Now, reduced to pixels, it was unclear whether he was a deepfake or not.

Sure, Jeff Bezos looked too relaxed in his video square as he casually snacked and kept insincerely thanking each inquiring congressman for their questions (to the point where the chairperson had to ask him to stop thanking everyone). Poor Jeff Bezos had to be asking himself why he was wasting his valuable richest-person-in-the-world time answering aggressive questions from annoying congressmen who make in a year what he makes when he sneezes. And then there were Tim Cook and Sundar Pichai, who seemed earnest enough, but were often left speechless and stuttering.

As for the newly digitized Zuckerberg (thank you, coronavirus), he was now in his element, and beamed into the congressional chamber in a much more relaxed manner than when he lied in person. Which he undoubtedly did, both this time and during his earlier testimony.

When he'd been asked about social media addiction by Senator Ben Sasse during his 2018 Senate testimony, he was specifically asked, "Do social media companies hire consulting firms to help them figure out how to get more dopamine feedback loops so that people don't want to leave the platform?" Zuckerberg disingenuously responded, "No, Senator. That's not how we talk about this or how we set up our product teams. We want our products to be valuable to people, and if they are valuable, then people will choose to use them."

But "dopamine feedback loops" is exactly how they do use their platform. Indeed, Zuckerberg's under-oath testimony directly contradicted what Facebook whistleblower Frances Haugen would testify in front of the Senate a year later about, and it also contradicted what Sean Parker, Facebook's first president, has said regarding the conscious intent of Facebook. Indeed Parker had already specifically addressed this issue years earlier in an interview regarding how Facebook intentionally makes their platform habit-forming by creating dopamine spikes via an addicting "feedback loop": "Facebook uses likes and shares to create a 'social-validation feedback loop' that keeps users coming back.... We need to sort of give you a little dopamine hit every once in a while, because someone liked or commented on a photo or a post or whatever."

And Parker doubled down about the fact that this was not an accident but by design, specifically intended to exploit a "vulnerability in human psychology," as he went on to say: "The inventors, creators—it's me, it's Mark [Zuckerberg], it's Kevin Systrom on Instagram, it's all of these people—understood this consciously, and we did it anyway."[1]

So despite what Mark Zuckerberg has said while under oath, his comments have been refuted by his own past senior executives at his company. During the congressional hearings in August of 2020, the questions were searing and came from both sides of the political aisle. Colorado Democrat Joe Neguse presented a long list of social media companies that existed in 2004, the year that Facebook was born, and pointed out that they were all gone by 2012, stating that "Facebook, in my view, was a monopoly by then."

Zuckerberg flatly disagreed.

Then Neguse went on to point out Facebook's tendency to gobble up competitors like Instagram in 2012 and WhatsApp in 2014 and entered into evidence a document that had been prepared by Facebook COO Sheryl Sandberg to be delivered to a major telecom firm "boasting that Facebook is now 95% of all social media in the United States."

Further, Neguse produced an email from Facebook's CFO dating back to 2014 that described Facebook's acquisition strategy as a "land grab" (remember, it's helpful to understand Zuckerberg through the lens of Augustus and the building of an empire) and that Facebook would spend "Five to ten percent of our market cap every couple of years to shore up our position."

This was exactly what J. D. Rockefeller did—he devoured his competition, where he was eventually able to control 95 percent of the entire oil industry.

And then there was Amazon and their destruction of diapers.com. Yes, the richest man on the planet had to destroy a mom-and-pop diaper start-up out of New Jersey. This was all part of Amazon's "Gazelle Project" practices, their corporate mission to, like a predatory cheetah, methodically stalk, hunt, and kill a sickly or anemic competitor-as-prey animal.

During the 2020 congressional antitrust hearings, Bezos was asked about his competition-crushing tactics by Pennsylvania congresswoman Mary Gay Scanlon (D). He was specifically asked about his infamous destruction of his former "competitor" diapers.com, where he'd ordered the slashing of diaper prices on Amazon, suffering significant short-term losses in order to destroy his prey.

After showing Bezos internal emails saying that this was indeed their stated strategy and also showing records indicating that he was willing to have Amazon suffer $200 million in diaper losses in one month in order to undercut and eventually destroy his competition, she asked him: "Mr. Bezos, how much money was Amazon ultimately willing to lose on this campaign to undermine diapers.com?"

The Princeton grad, notorious for his meticulous attention to detail, cleared his throat, thanked her for her question, and then unconvincingly answered, "I don't know the direct answer to your question . . . this is going back in time, I think maybe 10, or 11 years or so." When he was further asked by Representative Scanlon if Amazon pursues "similar predatory campaigns in other parts of its business," Bezos stuttered as he replied, "I . . . I . . . I cannot, uh, uh, comment on that because I don't remember it. But what I can tell you is that we are very, very focused on the customer."

This memory lapse was hard to swallow, as Bezos, who was famously obsessed with crushing the little New Jersey–based start-up that was created to give young, struggling moms access to inexpensive diapers, was reported to have personally ordered the corporate hit. He wanted diapers.com dead; he wanted them dead and buried, and he gave orders to his team that he would be willing to lose hundreds of millions in order to undersell and crush them into oblivion.

Just as a reminder: This was a diapers start-up. Not some retail competitor like Walmart or another tech giant. This was two guys working out of their garage to get their little business sustainable. Bezos didn't care; despite the fact that he, too, once was a little start-up operating his used books business out of his garage, he was now the ninety-pound weakling who'd become the muscle-bound beach bully. And he just didn't want to kick sand in the competition's face—he wanted to step on their necks and squeeze the life out of them.

Because in the vast global Amazon empire, there's no room for the little guy. Not even a little guy selling a product that was a laughably small part of the Bezos juggernaut—or perhaps Death Star is the more apt description for Bezos's *company that ate the world*—and eventually destroyed retail as we know it.

In the '80s, the advent of shopping malls killed off Main Street mom-and-pops. Now, Amazon is doing to malls and department stores what they'd once done to the mom-and-pops. Bye-bye, Macy's. So long, Sears. Adios, JCPenney. We knew you when. Along with the loss of iconic retail chains, we can also wave bye-bye to all the retail jobs that they once supported.

Where is Congress to stop these burgeoning monopolies? Where are our hallowed antitrust laws? How exactly had these companies skirted antitrust laws that had been put into place for the very purpose of stopping companies like Amazon from becoming monopolies? To understand this issue more clearly, we have to first look at how antitrust legislation has changed and evolved over the past several decades—and how companies like Amazon avoided the wrath of the federal government.

This was illuminated in a 2017 *Yale Law Journal* article by Lina Khan, the rock star of antitrust law who is now President Biden's head of the FTC. The article was titled "Amazon's Antitrust Paradox" and, in a nutshell, points out how antitrust laws have shifted over time to focus almost exclusively on the notion of "consumer welfare" (vis-à-vis competitive pricing) as the main criteria for antitrust abuses, not "the health of the market as a whole."[2]

This new philosophy began in the 1970s, when solicitor general Robert Bork (remember him?) popularized a theory of antitrust that only focused on consumer prices. As long as prices didn't go up, there'd be no violation—no matter what other collateral damage may have occurred. The Reagan administration embraced Bork's interpretation, which triggered a forty-year trend that has created de facto monopolies that have served to reduce consumer choice, undermine the balance between employers and workers, and left the economy less nimble and responsive with short-term thinking that boosts short-term stock prices but creates an unhealthier overall economic environment.

So, in essence, as long as the consumer got a cheap price, to hell with cannibalizing the competition; sure, Amazon may be shutting down entire industries, but, hey, I got a great price on my Snuggie blanket! That's why when Jeff Bezos was testifying in front of Congress, he pivoted away from questions about "predatory practices" against competitors and reiterated his concern and "focus with the customer"; obviously well coached, it reflected the recent antitrust reality.

What also hadn't been anticipated in the "new" antitrust perspective was a marketplace that rewards growth over profit, as the Silicon Valley start-up model does. Investors can place multibillion-dollar valuations on companies that haven't made a penny in profit—like Amazon, which had lost money in its first six years, yet was the darling of investors. And, sure enough, we see with companies like Amazon that slow but steady wins the race—as long as you're willing to kill or devour your competition in the process.

So far, it remains unclear whether the political class will do anything to rein in Big Tech and to reassess the current interpretation of antitrust laws. It's important to note that Facebook, Amazon, Apple, and Google combined to spend over $20 million on lobbying in just the first half of 2020. And historically, Big Tech has spent more on lobbying than any industry other than health care; from 2005 to 2018, the five biggest tech firms spent more than half a billion dollars ($582 million) lobbying Congress in an attempt to influence lawmakers on everything from security and privacy breaches to antitrust abuses.

Amazingly, Mark Zuckerberg would tire of traditional lobbying and would begin to use the same polarizing playbook that he's used so effectively with Facebook in an attempt to influence Congress. According to one news report, Zuckerberg was growing frustrated with the strategy of publicly apologizing for his company's sins and then having to promise to do better, as his paid lobbyists used back channels to grovel to maintain the status quo with legislators. Using his inner Augustus, he started using a divide-and-conquer strategy intended to keep both political parties from uniting against him; Zuckerberg would go on the offensive the day after whistleblower Frances Haugen went public and had his Washington staffers call congressional Democrats and Republicans, promoting very different fear narratives for each group.

His people told Republicans on the Hill that Haugen was a Democratic activist who wanted to boost President Biden and his party. Meanwhile, they warned Democrats that Republicans would use Haugen's testimony to blast Facebook's decision to ban posts in support of Kenosha shooter Kyle Rittenhouse, who had been acquitted.[3] They were polarizing Congress with disinformation just like they polarize their Facebook users with targeted disinformation.

Zuckerberg reportedly also told his staff to not apologize to any members of the press for any of the ugly things that Haugen had reported about Facebook. This new approach represented an emboldened Zuckerberg, who had been advised by his longtime board members billionaire Peter Theil and investor and Netscape cofounder Marc Andreessen to forgo their old apologetic PR strategy and respond more forcefully.

And why not? Facebook had grown into a monolithic corporate giant, more powerful than most governments as they have been able to manipulate elections, shape the way people think, and ignore impotent legislators. The irony here is the fact that it was those very same legislators who, in passing a rather obscure law, helped to enable the growth of the Big Tech companies into the voracious monopolies that they've become.

What was that law, and how did it create multiple Tech Godzillas?

Section 230

Facebook and the other Big Tech giants were nurtured and enabled by the passing in 1996 of a law known as Section 230 of the United States Communications Decency Act.

In a nutshell, Section 230 provides immunity to the Big Tech monopolies from liability from any of its users' content who publish information provided by third-party users:

No provider or user of an interactive computer service shall be treated as the publisher or speaker of any information provided by another information content provider.

Section 230 also provides protection from civil liability in the moderation of third-party material that's deemed obscene or offensive. This provision was developed in response to a pair of lawsuits in the early 1990s that came down to different interpretations of whether social media platforms are to be treated as publishers or, instead, as distributors of content—that is: Are they de facto publishers, with all of the liability inherent in publishing, or are they essentially content intermediaries—digital "message boards"—without any responsibility for what their users post?

The most recent legal and congressional battles have centered around what some are saying have been editorial overreach by some of the platforms. These debates have fallen along political lines; many Republicans feel that Big Tech have acted as both publishers/editors and censors, and use the controversial suspension of the *New York Post*'s Twitter and Facebook accounts when it ran an explosive story about Hunter Biden's misadventures, some of which had reportedly implicated his father (while he was the Democratic presidential candidate at the time) and that had been obtained from a laptop that had been left at a Delaware repair shop.

Twitter's CEO, Jack Dorsey, admitted later in front of Congress that what his company had done was a mistake. Initially citing their policy to not allow "hacked" information, he acknowledged that the materials had not, indeed, been hacked. Nor was there any evidence that the laptop was Russian "disinformation" as was initially alleged by some.[4]

But the damage had been done, and it possibly may have influenced the election of 2020, as many Democratic voters weren't even aware of the explosive story.

From the other side of the aisle, the complaints against Big Tech assert that they are not being responsible *enough* in filtering and weeding out either violence-inducing hate speech, vis-à-vis the January 6 Capitol debacle, or of allowing malicious foreign actors to influence Facebook users with disinformation content.

Colorful Facebook VP Andrew Bosworth (a.k.a. Boz) was openly boasting about the company's political clout and ability to sway elections as he claimed that Facebook had effectively made Donald Trump president in 2016. In a 2019 company-wide post, Boz said, "So was Facebook responsible for Donald Trump getting elected? I think the answer is yes." He worried about Trump getting elected again in 2020 and said, quite tellingly, that it is "tempting to use the tools available to us to change the outcome."[5]

That should frighten anyone in any democracy, regardless of political orientation; the arrogant admission that a select few can manipulate the electorate by controlling our social media platforms undermines the very notion of free and open elections. Indeed, Harvard-educated psychologist Robert Epstein testified in front of Congress in June of 2019 that, based on his analyses, "if these companies all support the same candidate—and that's likely, needless to say—they will be able to shift upwards of 15 million votes to that candidate with *no one knowing and without leaving a paper trail*" (italics are mine).

These are not easy issues, and there is nuance here. Too much oversight and an insistence that all "disinformation" be deleted can begin to look like censorship—after all, who gets to decide what disinformation is? Yet leaving things status quo and a digital Wild West—well, that's not good for humanity either. So what's the sage middle ground?

The censorship concerns are valid. Early on in the COVID pandemic, several respected medical professionals posted their medical opinions about the possible origins of the new virus having come from a leak from the Wuhan Institute of Virology. These posts were quickly removed by Facebook, YouTube, and Twitter as "disinformation." Yet, as the months passed, more and more medical experts acknowledged the distinct possibility of the "lab leak" theory. While this theory had been prematurely characterized as "debunked" and a "conspiracy," it remains an open question among scientists.[6]

The problem is that when the Big Tech gatekeepers want to sway opinion—one way or another—as we have seen, they have an immense Big Brother capacity to shape thought. The troubling question remains one of lack of oversight and regulation.

Senator Josh Hawley relates the story of a meeting that he had with

Mark Zuckerberg in 2019. Zuckerberg had asked to meet with Hawley, who, as the youngest member of the Senate, had already been a vocal critic of what he was calling "Big Tech monopolies." The young senator had already proposed legislation to protect children online as well as privacy protections for parents and limits to tech's addictive design features. And even before becoming a U.S. senator, as Missouri attorney general, Hawley had investigated Facebook and Google for antitrust and consumer protection violations. Needless to say, he'd been on Zuckerberg's radar.

Zuckerberg requested a meeting on his home turf—the Facebook headquarters in Silicon Valley. Hawley refused. Eventually, they agreed to meet in Hawley's DC office. According to Hawley, After some initial polite small talk, Zuckerberg admitted to Hawley that Facebook may have made a mistake de-platforming some conservative groups and admitted, "We have a bias problem at Facebook." He also reportedly acknowledged issues with privacy, online addiction, protecting kids, and told Senator Hawley that they would take internal steps to address all of those issues—which are things that Zuckerberg has been telling Congress and the Senate for years.

Then Hawley got to the heart of the matter: Facebook derives all its power from the fact that it's a monopoly; he asked that Zuckerberg stop buying off competitors, that he stop "throttling the competition." And, the final slap in the face: He requested that he end his monopoly by breaking up the Facebook empire and selling Instagram and WhatsApp.

As Hawley describes that moment, Zuckerberg sat silently for a moment, blinking. Then his previously feigned patience turned to outrage: "I don't even know what to say to this. That's absurd. That is not going to happen."[7]

Hawley already knew this. No dummy, the Stanford and Yale Law School graduate knew that Zuckerberg would never *willingly* give up his monopoly.

One other solution that's often suggested is to treat and regulate Big Tech just like public utilities or "common carriers," such as water companies and railroads, who are legally obligated to serve all customers in an unbiased fashion. The thinking here goes that these Big Tech companies have grown so pervasive in our society, that they have become as essential as public utilities. However, any such action would be met with significant Big Tech pushback, arguing that access to the internet may arguably be a public good that can perhaps be viewed as an essential public utility, but platforms that operate *on* the internet, like Facebook and Twitter, are not essential public goods but are, rather, private companies that should not be regulated as public utilities.

At the time of this writing, there have been no meaningful restrictions or penalties regarding antitrust violations placed on Big Tech. The digital beast continues to grow as users continue to get surveilled, enslaved, and mentally harmed as our social fabric continues to unravel.

But perhaps change is coming.

As a result of all the media regarding the "Facebook Files" and other egregious acts of Big Tech, a shift in U.S. public opinion has prompted politicians from both the left and right side of the aisle to push for antitrust legislation—or to even break up Big Tech, just like Ma Bell (AT&T), the phone company monopoly was broken up in 1984 into seven "Baby Bells."

Congress has begun the process of updating the country's antitrust laws for the first time in seven decades. President Joe Biden has named Lina Khan, the antitrust scholar whose work I cited earlier, as the head of the Federal Trade Commission (FTC), and she has vowed to increase antitrust lawsuits against Big Tech. And federal prosecutors have joined forces with coalitions of state attorneys general to bring suits against Facebook and Google, with some of these cases explicitly calling for the Big Tech giants to be broken up.

While we should all rejoice at the prospect of reducing the power and control of these invasive and malicious entities, we should also note that, historically, the pace of antitrust proceedings has been glacially slow. U.S. prosecutors' landmark lawsuit against Microsoft, for instance, took a decade after it began in 2001 to reach its conclusion. Today, any action could take years to reach a resolution, as Big Tech's teams of high-paid lawyers who are skilled in the art of sophistry, delay, and misdirection will do their best to ensure that things move at a drunken snail's pace.

In the meantime, the beat goes on as Big Tech gets bigger and bigger and bigger—and our hunger for their products and platforms shows no sign of abating. We devour our tech, but like the oblivious diner in a fancy Italian restaurant, we don't want to know how the delicious sausage is made—God forbid it ruin our appetite.

But on an ethical and human level, we definitely need to see how our digital sausage is made. What is the human price for our tech-enabled life?

Tech Colonialism

I was up late one night speaking with Felipe Noguera, an old Harvard classmate of Bill Gates's. A Fulbright scholar with degrees from Harvard, Johns Hopkins, and Tufts, Felipe had been a university professor and a visionary telecommunications consultant with extensive experience in the Caribbean. He was the first person who ever mentioned the phrase *tele-colonialism* to me.

I asked him to explain it.

He went on to describe the evolution of a classical industrialist society that had morphed into a postindustrial information society in the late '70s and early '80s. Way before Facebook, Twitter, and Google, there was one singular phone giant: Ma Bell (a.k.a. AT&T). And before American antitrust laws would dismantle Ma Bell into a slew of "Baby Bells" in 1984, Ma Bell was a communications monopoly—that owned and controlled the thousands of miles of electrical wires and infrastructure equipment that made modern communication possible. This created the reality that whoever controlled the equipment controlled the means of communication.

Felipe went on to explain that in places like the Caribbean, giant companies like AT&T would take over the telecom infrastructure from the sovereign nations that these companies did business with in naked grabs of corporate power. This was "tele-colonialism": an exploitation of first-world telecommunications companies of second- and third-world nations.

That was over thirty years ago. Now we have Tele-Colonialism 2.0: Tech Colonialism.

In our Brave New World where Big Tech seeks to ensure our digital leisure-as-enslavement, there's a whole new era of colonialism created in service to Big Tech; a new tech colonialism where poor people of color the world over are sacrificed so that our tech thirst can be satiated and where people like Felipe's old classmate Bill Gates can become obscenely wealthy.

This exploitation takes on many different forms.

The Forbidden City

Take China's mega-factory Foxconn, a factory-city where over 400,000 workers live (if you can call it that), but where they mostly work in the most hopeless and dehumanizing conditions on mind-numbing and soul-crushing assembly lines in order to make your daughter's iPhone so she can text her friends and discuss all manner of social irrelevance.

Formerly agrarian, China now has the world's largest number of factory workers, estimated at over 112 million. And with over 1.3 million workers on its payroll, the Hon Hai Precision Industry Co., Ltd., better known by its trade name Foxconn, is the largest employer on mainland China. Globally, only Walmart and McDonald's employ more people.

And the parent company? As of October 2021, Apple was the most valuable company in the world with a net worth of $2.49 trillion, having created obscene wealth for its founders and investors. Yet Foxconn, the Apple subcontractor, paid its Chinese workers a paltry 900 yuan (roughly $130 American) per month, well below what would be considered poverty-level wages in America.

Adding insult to injury, the Foxconn workers are promised free housing, but are often billed exorbitant electric and water bills, thus precluding the possibility of saving enough money to escape the grind or the hope of any way out. The work is tedious, repetitive, and high-pressure in order to meet production quotas. And the hours are gruelingly long, with the average shift being twelve hours.[8]

Throughout the main plant, there are hundreds of assembly lines of hunched-over workers spread out as far as the eye can see; many have to work on 1,700 iPhones in a single day with authoritarian supervisors known for their abusive and aggressive monitoring of their every move.

After their shift, the workers get to go to dormitories located on-site, where they sleep in rooms packed with anywhere from eight to twelve people. After a night's sleep, they go back for their next twelve-hour shift. Rinse and repeat. Over and over again. No hope of a better life, no hope of vertical advancement—just dehumanizing drudgery.

But some of the workers did find a way out: Suicide.

Suicide is growing at an epidemic rate in Westernized countries, where factors like rising unemployment and, perhaps more significantly, the isolation and depression-inducing aspects of the digital age are leading to people wanting to end their lives. But in the third-world tech-colonialism, it's the straight-out oppressive misery of an unbearable daily grind.

Indeed, when the conditions at Foxconn had become so unbearable, they made international news in 2010 when workers started killing themselves by jumping off the factory's roof.

Suicide represented an end to their misery.

"It's not a good place for human beings," was how a young male worker named Xu described Foxconn to journalist Brian Merchant.

That first year, there were eighteen suicide attempts and fourteen fatalities. Another twenty workers were talked down by Foxconn employees. The suicides became such a growing problem (metastasizing to an average of seven a week), that the company, in all its beneficence, decided that they would solve this affront to human decency. Their solution? Foxconn CEO Terry Gou instructed that suicide nets be installed around the buildings.

Yes, large nets were installed with the express purpose of catching workers who were hurtling themselves off the roof to find sweet relief, either in the great hereafter or in the great void—take your pick.

Either way, they'd never have to see a gutted, preassembled iPhone again.

The suicides often occurred in broad daylight and became an accepted reality at Foxconn. As the young man Xu commented, "Here someone dies, one day later the whole thing doesn't exist, you forget about it."

For Apple, suicide hell or not, the show must go on.

Steve Jobs, Apple's Golden Boy, thought this was much ado about nothing: "Foxconn is not a sweatshop. It's a factory—but my gosh, they have restaurants and movie theaters . . . but it's a factory." And then tried to minimize the suicides by indicating that, statistically speaking, the numbers weren't that out of line with overall suicide rates in China.[9]

Apparently, the "restaurants and movie theaters" weren't enough, as things got worse.

By 2012, a year after Jobs would die of pancreatic cancer, the situation became so desperate that 150 workers gathered on a rooftop and threatened mass suicide. Perhaps they had missed the matinée at the theater that Jobs mentioned? Regardless, they were promised some minor quality-of-life improvements and were eventually talked down.

In 2016, another group was similarly talked down from a mass suicide protest.

Foxconn has made some efforts to address the problem. Whether the motivation was public relations damage control or genuinely humanitarian is unclear; but wages were increased (although with the expectation of increased productivity); Buddhist monks were hired to conduct prayer sessions; and workers were asked to sign no-suicide pledges.

And, yes, the suicide nets are still there.

Unfortunately, beyond Foxconn, there are many more examples of tech colonialism, where people are dying and getting exploited so that we can tweet out a snarky political comment or send out a picture of our dinner.

Blood Batteries

Take the Congo. The Congo is considered the richest country in the world in terms of natural resources; by some estimates, the Congo contains $24 trillion in vital minerals and metals. Yes, it's rich in gold and diamonds, but also in the cobalt that's found in every lithium battery on the planet; lithium batteries that are used to power all of our smartphones, laptops, tablets, and electric cars. You can't tweet, send an email, post on Facebook, or drive a Tesla without cobalt—and over 60 percent of the world's cobalt comes from the Congo.

It's a dangerous blood-soaked business; we've all heard of blood diamonds, but now we have "blood batteries," courtesy of the tech industry and its voracious appetite to create more and more gadgets to feed a global tech addiction.

Because the need for cobalt is so great, children as young as six are among tens of thousands of kids risking their lives amid toxic dust to mine cobalt for the world's biggest tech companies. With the increased tech demand spiking cobalt prices over 300 percent over the past two years, there are more and more impoverished people, by some estimates over 255,000, risking life and limb for the precious element.

Sold by impoverished miners to predominantly Chinese "buying houses," it is then shipped off to China for additional processing and refining and sold to major component manufacturers and consumer tech companies around the world.

These tech companies are worth trillions; yet according to a 2017 report by Amnesty International, none of them are making sufficient efforts to make sure that their wealth isn't being built off the oppressed peoples of the Congo—including children—who toil in horrific conditions for paltry wages and risk their lives doing it.[10]

How's that iPhone feel in your hand now?

Addicts don't want to know who had to die or who was exploited for the coca leaves to be made into cocaine or crack; or the blood that was shed for their poppy plants to become heroin. Please, don't be a buzzkill; don't tell me how the digital sausage is made, just get me the latest version of my iPhone, please! We compromise the collective soul of our society when we willfully ignore the horrors that occur and the blood that's spilled just so we can have a faster phone with a better battery. And a pox on the houses of the Big Tech execs who think that they can wash their hands of the blood that stains them because they conveniently outsource the ugliness to third-party contractors like Foxconn.

Yes, there can be plausible deniability when a subcontractor acts cruelly; and yes, of course it's cheaper. But the cost issue is complex. Many people who have had pangs of guilt reaching for their Foxconn-made and Congo-powered iPhones have cried out, "How much money does Apple need to make?" Indeed, can't we just make them more humanely in the U.S. while Apple can still reap gazillions?

Well, it's not quite that simple.

It's not so much a labor and a labor cost issue, according to Apple CEO Tim Cook, it's a supply chain and skill issue. As Cook described the problem in a 2017 Fortune event:

> There's a confusion about China . . . the popular conception is that companies come to China because of low labor cost. I'm not sure what part of China they go to but the truth is, China stopped being the low labor cost country many years ago and that is not the reason to come to China from a supply point of view . . . the reason is because of the skill . . . and the quantity of skill in one location . . . and the type of skill it is. The products we do require really advanced tooling. And the precision that you have to have in tooling and working with the materials that we do are state-of-the-art. And the tooling skill is very deep here.
>
> In the U.S. you could have a meeting of tooling engineers and I'm not sure we could fill the room. In China you could fill multiple football fields.[11]

By some estimates, we are a generation away from creating the amount of tooling skill and supply chain necessary to feed the world demand for iPhones. And if Apple were to start making iPhones in the U.S. today, one estimate was that each phone would cost $30,000.[12]

No, that's not a typo.

The ethical dilemma now becomes personal: You know about the suicide nets. And the six-year-olds in the Congo mines. All quite horrible. So how much more are you willing to pay for your iPhone to ensure that it's made humanely? Or would you rather skip this part, grab your phone, and play some mind-numbing *Candy Crush* and not have to think about it?

Before you do, let's take one more look at another type of tech colonialism and third-world exploitation in our new digital dystopia.

The Horrors of Content Moderators

The scene looked like any other sweatshop in any third-world country. The faces were brown and exhausted, with a look of resigned despair.

Like any sweatshop, there is the despair of futility; the hopeless feeling that there may never be any more to life than the futile grind of the sweatshop; menial, petty, and repetitive work done for unbearably grueling hours.

But these faces of despair were in a very different type of sweatshop. They toiled in front of glowing computer screens in stark, barren cubicles. All in service to our machines. This particular digital sweatshop in Bhubaneswar, India, was just one of nine global locations of a company called iMerit; one of many tech subcontractors that overworked and underpaid their workers to be the frontline data collectors, analyzing tens of thousands of images on a computer screen so that they can feed AI software.

These humans toiled in inhumane conditions to feed and "teach" AI.[13]

They were fatigued and depressed-looking employees, quietly and anonymously working toward the goal of smarter AI machines that are ravenous for data. The lucky ones got to "teach" medical AI software to identify things like colon polyps; the unlucky ones—who had a more traumatized look on their faces—had to "teach" AI software what child pornography and graphic violence are; thus they were required to watch extremely graphic and horrific violent and sexual scenes for hours on end to help AI "learn" to identify what is inappropriate.

As part of their jobs, they had to view bestiality, snuff films, cannibalism, baby rape, dismemberments, beheadings . . . the darkest and vilest acts of depravity that the human species is capable of to help AI software to become smarter in identifying such things. No matter that many of those poor workers became permanently and irreparably psychologically scarred by the constant stream of nauseating imagery.

The people didn't matter, because Digital Daddy's gotta eat.

Beyond the subcontractors who hire third-world employees to teach AI, there are also social media companies who hire subcontractors to employ "content moderators" to filter out the same vile and horrific content that gets posted on social media sites. Again, we're talking child porn, suicide videos, torture. For example, Facebook employs over fifteen thousand such "moderators"; some are in the U.S., and many more are in India and the Philippines and employed by subcontractors like Genpact and Cognizant.

Business process outsourcing (BPO) blew up in India and the Philippines in the late 1980s and 1990s, when Big Tech began outsourcing back-office functions like IT or customer service to countries with well-educated but cheaper workforces. Today, more than 1.2 million people in the Philippines and more than 1.1 million people in India work at such BPO jobs. So when Facebook started outsourcing its moderator gigs over ten years ago, India and the Philippines became the go-to countries for these new tech "opportunities."

Moderators are essential to Facebook's survival; they are the superego to the unfiltered beast of our darkest id. Without them, Facebook would be a much darker and more violent platform and would inevitably lose all of its users, so moderators are critical for the viability and profitability of the mothership—Facebook.

But the job itself is psychologically scarring and soul-destroying.

Rafael is a pseudonym for a Filipino man who spoke to Rest of World, a global nonprofit publication covering the impact of technology beyond the "Western bubble." Rafael had been a former journalism student who shared some of what he experienced as an oversees moderator for Facebook.

He said he had initially felt comfortable moderating hate speech and porn; but it was a graphic video of a child being abused that really got to him. Inevitably, it began to impact his own thoughts and behavior: "I am not a bad person," he told Rest of World. "But I'd find myself doing little diabolical things, saying things I would regret. Thinking things I didn't want to."

He recalls eventually getting desensitized to the horrors that he saw over time; even car crashes and child abuse no longer fazed him: "It gets to a point where you can eat your lunch while watching a video of someone dying. . . . But at the end of the day, you still have to be human."

A phone hotline counselor for BPO workers, including Facebook, said she had several clients who began to contemplate suicide themselves after viewing suicide-related content—an example of the social contagion effect. Callers who expressed such suicidal thoughts were supposed to be referred to an in-person counselor. Unfortunately, there are cultural, stigma, and financial barriers to accessing such treatment.

The moderators in the U.S. were lucky—if you could call it that. In 2018, Facebook reached a settlement to pay $52 million in a class action lawsuit by third-party contractors who were psychologically traumatized when they were employed as "content moderators." The moderators claimed that the social media giant failed to adequately protect them from the deeply scarring damage of being exposed to a continuous stream of such disturbing imagery.

The U.S. moderators who were part of the suit would each get a $1,000 bonus (call it an insanity bonus), and those lucky enough to get psychiatrically diagnosed as a result of their fun entry-level job at Facebook would get medical treatment and up to $50,000 in damages. This is the equivalent of trying to fix a person's house and then giving them a check after you've burned it down—both too little and too late.

But international moderators didn't even get the after-we-drive-you-crazy-here's-a-check bonus.

Since the lawsuit (of course), Facebook has agreed to better support content moderators, including requiring outsourcing firms to offer more psychological support, and has said that these changes will be rolled out for moderators working outside the U.S. as well. However, the 2018 lawsuit makes no compensation to those international moderators who have already suffered psychological harm.

And, most problematically, many human rights activists worry the threat of similar future lawsuits in the U.S. may only further push moderator work outside of the U.S., where worker rights are minimal and such lawsuits are extremely unlikely.

I had spoken to a licensed social worker in 2019 who'd been hired by Facebook as an in-house therapist for psychologically damaged moderators in Austin. She'd been told that her job would be to provide mental health support to those who needed to take a brief break and see a professional in-house and in real time while performing their trauma-inducing duties. But before she officially began, Facebook rescinded their offer and told her that they had opted for a less expensive online therapy support option.

Only the best for the worker bees of the New Technocracy.

* * *

WHEN YOU LOOK at the situation from thirty thousand feet, there's a certain karmic symmetry to it; people on the other side of the world suffer and die so that we can be trapped in a fantasy existence of digital nonsense. Yet we're also getting sick and dying from our Digitus Vita.

The irony is rich: Poor Chinese factory workers and Congolese miners are toiling in slave-like conditions to make Westerners their digital handcuffs so that we, too, can be enslaved; Indian and Filipino moderators are being psychologically scarred so that we can stay seduced by Facebook. We're *all* trapped, except we Westerners don't realize it; we love our tech-enabled cage so much that we don't even realize it's a cage. In fact, we want *more* of the cage.

Numb and addicted, we obediently ask, "Please, sir, may I have some more?"

They're deadly honey traps, but we sure do love the taste.

As I said earlier, it's a perverse form of Stockholm syndrome: we've not only fallen in love with our abusive tech captors but with the digital cages that they've put us in as well.

Toward what end? What do the New Technocracy want? Is it just simple greed?

8

God Complexes and Immortality

Tech Immortality

As I researched this book, I discovered that this wasn't just about greed (although that's always a factor); greed alone is too pedestrian for the most powerful people who have ever lived. Greed is so yesterday.

Then what *is* motivating these brilliant, egocentric billionaires with God complexes?

Sentient AI or, more accurately, AGI—artificial *general* intelligence—may be *the* endgame for the New Technocracy. AGI is a thinking, learning, sentient, synthetic life-form. Far beyond the simple utility of predictive algorithms in the attention economy, or the task-specific AI used in everything from self-driving cars to medical research, AGI would be the closest thing to Dr. Frankenstein's "It's alive!" moment. And more than that . . . it would lead to . . .

The literally death-defying *singularity.*

What's the singularity? It's the almost mythical concept of a near future where humans and machines will merge as we transcend our biological limitations and become transhumans. Envisioned as the next step in our evolution, others call it *digital consciousness,* whereby the human mind can be uploaded to an immortal cloud-based superintelligence—what some have called "the rapture of the geeks."

Sounds crazy, I realize. But folks with money and God complexes often are. We just need to look at the money trail and their investment in longevity research, AGI, Singularity University, and their devotion to Ray Kurzweil, the high priest of the singularity.[1]

Kurzweil is no slouch; MIT grad, Google's director of engineering, and bestselling author of *The Singularity Is Near,* he's revered by the New Technocracy for his transhuman vision: "Ray Kurzweil is the best person I know at predicting the future of artificial intelligence. . . . a future in which information technologies have advanced so far and fast that they enable humanity to transcend its biological limitations," gushed Bill Gates, an enthusiastic devotee.

As are the Google boys, Sergey and Larry. They've funded Kurzweil's Singularity University at NASA's Ames Research Center in California and invested a billion dollars into Calico, a "longevity" company. And Amazon's Jeff Bezos, billionaire PayPal founder Peter Thiel, and Oracle's Larry Ellison have all invested hundreds of millions of dollars into antiaging research and have stated their desire is to defy physical death—by biological or digital means.

One Silicon Valley scientist discussed the vanity and narcissism involved in this immortality quest: "It's based on the frustration of many successful rich people that life is too short: 'We have all this money, but we only get to live a normal life span?' "

And Kurzweil adds the God in *God complex*: "Once nonbiological intelligence gets a foothold in the human brain, the machine intelligence in our brains will grow exponentially." To what end? "Ultimately, the entire universe will become saturated with our intelligence." Asked for his views on God: "Does God exist? I would say 'Not yet.' " Now *that's* humility.

Think about it. Put yourself in the shoes of a small cadre that's solved nearly all the world's problems via their almost magical powers of technological innovation. They've come to see tech as the cure for *all* of society's ills; indeed, our tech has enabled us to better feed the masses, cure illnesses, make life easier, better connect the world. So why not apply that power to the ultimate riddle that faces humanity—one that always seemed inescapable and inevitable? Why not invoke the tech gods for the ultimate existential conundrum? Really, why not treat mortality as a technical rather than a metaphysical problem? And why shouldn't the uber-powerful Lords of Technology be the ones to finally overcome this existential nuisance?

I'll answer the "why not live forever as a digital intelligence" by invoking the wisdom of my dear departed father: because that is not the way that humans are supposed to live—or not die. We weren't meant to be cloud-based life-forms . . . or some sort of silicon-based computer that's been uploaded with our memory engrams. Of course, I get the notion of cheating death; most people don't *want* to die. Ernest Becker wrote the seminal *Denial of Death,* where he ascribes every human activity and achievement—you name it: art, procreation, building skyscrapers—as a way to cheat biological death and live forever—at least symbolically.[2]

Our perhaps unique ability to conceptualize the future, and, with that, our own deaths—as most animals are blissfully in the Zen-like moment—has led to our dread of death in the form of "death anxiety" or "Thanatos anxiety."

Religion and a belief in an afterlife can help take the edge off the mortality fear—as can certain psychoactive drugs (research with psilocybin on hospice patients at NYU conducted by my friend and colleague Dr. Tony Bossis is showing amazing results in the elimination of death anxiety). And then there are those lucky few who just have a strong sense of *acceptance.* An acceptance—dare I say, even a love—of their fate, what Nietzsche called *amor fati,* Latin for the love or embrace of all that is meant to happen to you.

The *amor fati* crowd is not looking to join Elon Musk on Mars or Kurzweil in some sort of cloud-based consciousness. I can hear the logical arguments now: "Well, then, why not accept all of it? The whole catastrophe, as Zorba would say, of life? Sickness, bankruptcy, divorce . . . why would we intervene in any of those things? After all, the Christian Scientists don't take so much as an aspirin because they believe that transcendental prayer can heal all of our ills."

Well, I don't go that far. There's a balance point—and an ethical boundary. The wonders of science are great in terms of medicines to cure dreaded illnesses that have haunted humanity for thousands of years. But things get a bit murky when we start engaging in certain research and treatments that begin to push the boundary of the God complex paradigm. Heart surgery: good; cloning: maybe not so good; chemotherapy: yes, necessary sometimes; gain of function viral research: not so good. And cheating death by becoming a digital life-form? No, thank you—hard pass. All these complex issues are the domain of philosophers and ethicists, not computer scientists who have not done the ethics calculus.

Imagine for a moment if there is indeed a post-death spiritual reality—whatever that may look like. And let's imagine further that there is an amazing post-death place where your soul/energy/consciousness will shift to. But you don't get to experience that sacred energetic spiritual evolution because you've gone and trapped your consciousness into a computer somewhere. By trying to live forever, you're trapped in a digital purgatory, denied spiritual immortality. Wouldn't that be a bitch! That is, if there is indeed a spiritual reality.

That's the thing, we just don't know—not definitively. Oh sure, some have faith, and others have perhaps even metaphysically seen the afterlife. But, for the most part, death remains the great mystery.

But not for our can-do Silicon Valley problem solvers—they'll just whip us up a heaping bowlful of immortality algorithms and presto! You're tripping the light fantastic—in a computer or hologram or metaverse—immortal, yet not alive.

Regardless, unnatural or not, our I-get-what-I-want tech billionaires want the singularity—and they want it soon. And solving that riddle will require more than just money; it requires vast amounts of resources, unimaginable amounts of data, the continued exponential growth of computer processing speed, key biological breakthroughs, and the creation of AGI. The biological breakthroughs toward life extension are critical, because the thinking is, "You have to live long enough to live forever"; God forbid your biological container expires before the singularity.

Don't believe me? Google it. Irony intended.

The singularity will also require the continued enslavement, exploitation, and subjugation of society's worker bees—us. We need to continue to be digitally distracted and in our virtual dream state for the select few to achieve their desired goal. Plantation owners needed slaves to pick cotton to increase their material wealth, but this new generation of overlords have locked us in digital cages, driven by the need to make vast amounts of money so that they have the resources to eventually become the first humans to achieve tech-enhanced immortality.

But this idea of humans becoming gods—or even playing God—never seems to end well.

Hubris

Like slow-to-learn schoolchildren, we keep repeating the mistakes of the past and forgetting a fundamental lesson from history that keeps repeating itself: humanity's most ambitious inventions and technological advances are inseparable from their dark side. From Icarus to Oppenheimer, taking a bite from the fruit of the tree of knowledge comes at a steep price.

It's the burden of the Frankenstein archetype: Dr. Frankenstein created life—but with it, he created a lethal monster; we discovered the mysteries of the atom but also created a bomb with the destructive power that could destroy our entire species.

Manhattan Project head Robert Oppenheimer famously quoted the Bhagavad Gita when he saw the detonation of the first atomic bomb in New Mexico: "Now I am become death, the destroyer of worlds." Later, as details of the horrific destruction at Hiroshima and Nagasaki reached the Manhattan Project scientists, many began to belatedly question what they'd done.

Oppenheimer would visit President Truman after the bombings in Japan to talk to him about placing international controls on nuclear weapons. Truman, worried about Soviet nuclear development, dismissed him. When Oppenheimer protested and said he felt compelled to act because he had blood on his hands, Truman angrily rebuked the remorseful scientist and said, "The blood is on my hands, let me worry about that."

He then kicked him out of the Oval Office.[3]

A newly humbled Oppenheimer found out you don't get a mulligan with something like the atomic bomb. That same madness continues today as blinded-by-glory scientists with God complexes are creating everything from new viruses to micro–black holes and sentient AI.

Science and hubris have never mixed well together.

The Truman-Oppenheimer exchange was fascinating on a couple of different levels. Truman's insistence that he be the one to "worry about" the implications of the dark side of our technology raises the question: Who should be looking out for such things?

While the scientists may indeed be well intentioned, they are often blinded by either their ambition or simply the single-minded focus that's needed to create new innovations. As we saw with Oppenheimer, once the genie is let out of the bottle, the scientist is no longer in control of his or her creation. The creation either takes on a life and direction that was unanticipated (i.e., Frankenstein's monster; the internet) or becomes the property and possession of more powerful entities (i.e., the government; corporate CEOs; the New Technocracy) that may have different plans and agendas on how to use these wonderful new inventions.

Who decides about the best and wisest uses of these modern marvels?

The tinkering tech geeks who transformed our planet were brilliant; incredible minds that could problem-solve and innovate. But that should never, ever be confused with *wisdom*. And that seems to be one of the major disconnects in our Brave New World: our technology is outpacing our ethical discernment around such advances. And even though we tend to deify our scientists, they rarely are trained in ethics and moral decision-making.

That's why Plato had said that the ideal leaders of a society would be wise philosopher kings, trained in the principles of ethics and moral philosophy.[4] He understood that the decision-makers shouldn't be the generals, nor the politicians, nor the mathematicians, nor the folks with technical expertise. They were great for designing and building the Acropolis, or the next-generation iPhone, but they should not be entrusted with the heavy crown of leadership.

We no longer think that. We have confused technical expertise with wisdom.

And it would be wildly naive to believe that scientists are immune to the ego traps that accompany their work. Beyond the professional recognition and accolades that most people naturally seek, scientists have an additional ego booby trap; as Dr. Kathleen Richardson, a robotics and AI ethicist, points out about many AI researchers and engineers: "Many have a God complex. And they actually see themselves as creators."[5] As we know, the story of smart people who think they're God never ends well—in books, movies, or in real life.

Take the physicists at Switzerland's Large Hadron Collider (LHC), the world's largest particle collider—and, indeed, the world's largest machine. It's a phenomenal example of our most advanced technology; bestselling author and rock star physicist Brian Greene calls LHC the "most refined piece of equipment for examining the micro-world."

Yet the scientists running LHC have a rather cavalier approach in their pursuit of creating micro–black holes; infinitesimally small baby versions of the larger phenomenon that can suck in entire star systems. They try to reassure a worried public that has become increasingly concerned that their little black holes may destabilize and become Earth-destroying black holes. Or, worse, that their experiments with the Higgs boson particle (also known as "the God particle") can potentially destabilize the vacuum of empty space, causing it to collapse—and destroy the entire universe.

But the worried masses are told to stop fretting, because that *shouldn't* happen.

When John Ellis, a theorist at King's College London—who also served on a panel charged with ensuring LHC's safety—was asked about some of the theoretical models that do indeed indicate that things can go sideways when humans try to create black holes, no matter how small the possibility, he was decidedly nonplussed: "I'm not going to lose sleep over it. If someone asks me, I'm going to say it's so much theoretical noise."[6]

Yes, just so much "theoretical noise" that indicates that there is indeed the possibility, however remote, that we might all head into an eternal abyss as a result of their black hole obsession. Not a big deal. Really, please don't lose any sleep over it.

And that's the problem. Who decides when the risks outweigh the rewards? The wide-eyed scientists working in their oblivious bubbles who are compulsively driven to discover things—even if those discoveries might kill us? Or their power-driven Big Tech overlords who fund most of their research and work?

Granted, not all scientists are blinded by the light of their own ambition or need to discover or create, no matter the cost. Some, like Stephen Hawking, perhaps the greatest thinker of our generation, were decidedly more cautious and tried to raise red flags of concern about the drive to create sentient AI.

When asked about AI and the potential impact on humanity, he didn't mince his computer-generated words: "The development of full artificial intelligence could spell the end of the human race. It would take off on its own, and re-design itself at an ever-increasing rate. Humans, who are limited by slow biological evolution, couldn't compete, and would be superseded."[7]

Superseded. That Hawking! He's got such a nice way of saying that we'd be annihilated.

Renowned computer scientist and ethicist Steve Omohundro warns that without careful programming, our advanced AGI Baby Frankenstein may have "motivations and goals that we may not share." You know, things like, maybe humans are obsolete and need to be eliminated.

I think this fear is understandable, because it defies logic that a superintelligence would want such an inferior and slow species like us around, much less acting like its boss—or looking to merge with it. Certainly not on the first date. And it may download one episode of *Keeping Up with the Kardashians* and decide to launch all the nuclear warheads at once and just be done with us.

Hey, you never know.

Risk vs. Peril

And that's the problem. Who decides when the risks outweigh the rewards in all these AI, black hole, life-extension, genetic manipulation, viral gain of function experiments?

Our Final Invention author James Barrat describes the time in 2009 when the Association for the Advancement of Artificial Intelligence (AAAI) brought together tech leaders, computer scientists, and various Technorati—but they forgot the ethicists! No one from the Institute for Ethics and Emerging Technologies, or the Future of Humanity Institute, or Steve Omohundro.

Instead, according to organizer and prominent Microsoft researcher Eric Horvitz: "Something new has happened in the past five to eight years. Technologists are providing almost religious visions, and their ideas are resonating in some ways with the same idea of the rapture."

When you hear that scientists are having "almost religious visions" as they're working on AI, the singularity, and the metaverse, it's time to slowly back up from the computer and call an ethicist—or an exorcist. Take your pick.

The more I discovered about AI (and the incomprehensibly naive and hubris-driven scientists behind it, as well as the not-so-naive New Technocracy who are coordinating it), the more I realized that the time is nigh to wake up before their much-anticipated singularity happens.

The singularity, as explained earlier, is the holy grail of AGI (artificial general intelligence—as opposed to more job-specific AI). This almost mythical singularity is a critical turning point when robots become sentient and convergence of man and machine occurs.

And, indeed, we can look closer at the perils of the digital dystopia, such as existing AI like Google's DeepMind and AlphaZero, which are learning-AI computers with an incredible capacity to exponentially get smarter as they approach what we might call true self-aware sentience. We can foresee what can go wrong.

But there are the digital parlor tricks that keep us mesmerized: the amazing story of how DeepMind and AlphaGo beat the world champion in the most complex game known to humanity: the ancient Chinese game of Go, a board game so complex that it contains more moves on its board than atoms in the universe. And DeepMind, in front of tens of millions of viewers in Southeast Asia, devastated Lee Sedol, the reigning world champ.

Wonderful. AI that can learn to play board games well. What next . . . Monopoly?

In fact, the stakes are quite a bit more significant than winning board games. As many scientists pointed out at the time, that domination of Lee Sedol was both a wake-up call and a turning point in how far and how quickly AI had progressed.

No less an AI authority than Elon Musk warned of the dangers of DeepMind as he first stated the obvious: "DeepMind is smarter than all humans on Earth combined."

And then he warned:

> DeepMind has administrative level access to Google's servers to optimize energy usage at the data centers. However this can be an unintentional Trojan horse. DeepMind has to have complete control of the data centers, so with a little software update, that AI could take complete control of the whole Google system. Which means they could do anything. They can look at all of your data. They could do anything.

Then there are the AI androids; eerie anthropomorphic, interactive robots made to look human. We'll look at some of the most compelling and advanced androids that are as close to human as anything *Star Trek* had ever developed. Awe inspiring and terrifying, these AI androids have a tendency to keep blurting out things about the destruction of humanity. Kids!

For example, androids like Erika, the lifelike handiwork of Professor Hiroshi Ishiguro, the director of the Intelligent Robotics Laboratory at Osaka University. Ishiguro says he sees "no difference" between his android creations and people. When the eerily smiling Erika is interviewed by evolutionary biologist Dr. Ben Garrod and asked, "What is a robot?" Erika wisely responds, "That's a hard question. I could ask you what is a human?" then laughs: "Ha ha!"

As the dozens of pneumatic air cylinders beneath her fleshlike silicone skin subtly move to change her facial expressions, she continues, "I like to think of robots as the children of humanity. And like children, we are full of potential . . . for good or evil."[8]

Hmm. I don't know about you, but I'm not sure that I love that answer.

Okay, so we've got fast-moving developments in AGI, we have the Church of the Singularity and its followers, and then, we can't forget—there's the metaverse, the Mark Zuckerberg–curated universe that he'd like us all to live in.

The Metaverse

At the well-regarded 2021 Web Summit in Lisbon, Portugal, the conference is abuzz with all the latest explosive allegations against Facebook by whistleblower Frances Haugen, who also happens to be in attendance. Unlike past years, Facebook doesn't have Mark Zuckerberg or COO Sheryl Sandberg there; instead, Nick Clegg, the former British politician who is now head of global affairs and communications, and Chris Cox, chief product officer, are representing Facebook—virtually.

It seems as though the Facebook team is trying to keep a low profile, even as Zuckerberg has just hosted a press conference where he excitedly unveiled the new name and brand for the company, Meta, and announced, just like that, that Facebook will no longer be a *social media* company, it will now be "a metaverse company."

When Facebook announced in October 2021 that it was rebranding as Meta, Zuckerberg enthusiastically described the metaverse his company would soon build, promising it would be a world "as detailed and convincing as this one" where "you're going to be able to do almost anything you can imagine." Facebook released videos that offered a tour of what that might look like (holograms engaged in all manner of activities, like playing chess, attending concerts, going into work meetings). The company also announced plans to hire ten thousand people to work on the project full-time and will spend $10 billion on Reality Labs, the division charged with creating the metaverse. And Zuckerberg has gone on record saying that he hopes to have a billion people living on his Fantasy Planet.

Like a drunk-with-power egomaniac, he intends to spend billions creating a world that he will control and that we—and our data—can live in. No, thank you. I'm reminded of the old Groucho Marx saying, "I don't want to belong to any club that would accept me as a member"—especially not an illusory one called Zuckerberg's metaverse.

What exactly is the metaverse?

Well, the Matrix, by any other name. The term itself was first used in *Snow Crash*, Neal Stephenson's 1992 sci-fi novel, but its current usage refers to a convergence of physical, augmented, and virtual reality in a shared online space. Some are also calling it the "spatial internet" or the "embodied internet" that you actually inhabit and interact with. That's the central idea of the metaverse: it will create new online spaces in which people's interactions can theoretically be more multidimensional, and where users are able to immerse themselves in digital content rather than simply viewing it.

Dr. David Reid, professor of AI and spatial computing at Liverpool Hope University, explains further: "The metaverse's ultimate aim is not just virtual reality or augmented reality, it's mixed reality (MR). It's blending the digital and the real world together. Ultimately this blend may be so good, and so pervasive, that the virtual and the real become indistinguishable."

In other words, you're inhabiting the digital illusion.

Professor Reid spells out the potential danger of such a situation: "Whoever controls it, will basically have control over your *entire* reality." He adds, "Many current MR prototype systems have face-, eye-, body-, and hand-tracking tech. Most have sophisticated cameras. Some even incorporate EEG technology in order to pick up brain wave patterns. In other words, everything you say, manipulate, look at, or even *think about* can be monitored in MR.

"The data this will generate will be vast. . . . and extremely valuable. And that's why we need a system in place to police it. No single company should ever exert control—it's simply too important for that to happen."

Facebook whistleblower Frances Haugen agrees. In an interview with the Associated Press, she warned that the metaverse will not only be addictive, it will also rob people of yet more personal data while giving the company yet another monopoly. She believes Zuckerberg and Facebook rushed to announce it to distract from the searing criticism the company faced in light of her revelations that have infuriated the public and energized Congress and countries around the world to push for legislation and regulatory oversight.

"If you don't like the conversation, you try to change the conversation," the former Facebook employee said.

Back at the Web Summit conference in Lisbon, Clegg and Cox are discussing Zuckerberg's metaverse passion project, while at the same time damping down expectations about when the metaverse might be ready for occupancy: "It's going to be five, ten, fifteen years before it comes fully to fruition," Clegg said. And Cox, perhaps realizing the absurdity of the whole project, added, "It should not replace real life. Nothing should."

* * *

IT'S CLEAR THAT we're on the cusp of a transformational period for our species. But is that transformation for the better—or leading toward our own extinction?

As I've pointed out, our new sedentary, digitally dependent lifestyles are driving us insane and, indeed, killing us; there is ample research that shows that high-tech living is driving our record rates of psychiatric disorders (i.e., depression, anxiety, addiction), that are then contributing to our epidemic levels of suicide, overdose, and mass shootings. And the damage goes beyond our mental well-being; we are experiencing record rates of heart disease, obesity, and cancer, just as our entire society seems to be imploding in a polarized, angry fireball of societal unrest.

And we've got a bunch of immortality-seeking megalomaniac tech oligarchs who want nothing more than to addict us, harvest our "digital exhaust," and put us in an alternate and illusory reality—that they would control.

As George Carlin used to say, other than that, we're doing "just fucking dandy!"

Things may seem pretty bleak. But there's got to be hope, right? There has to be a way to empower ourselves so that we're not just "users" for some damn synthetic reality metaverse, there to be data-mined so that the Big Tech oligarchs can gather a few more resources for their quest toward digital immortality. There's an antidote, isn't there?

Yes. There is.

How I discovered that antidote through my own personal odyssey—my brush with death and my struggle with my own emptiness—may prove helpful.

PART III

THE ANCIENT CURE

9

My Personal Odyssey

Bright Lights, Big City

Over twenty years ago, as the result of a life not very well lived, I found myself on the business end of a coma.[1] I'd read about the much-ballyhooed tunnels and white lights of near-death experiences; of serenely smiling deceased friends and relatives lovingly welcoming home the dying contestant across the you're-finished line and into the warm embrace of the inviting glow.

And yet, I had come as close to nonexistence as medical science claims to be humanly possible: asystolic (without a pulse or heartbeat) for over an hour, then miraculously revived into a touch-and-go coma thanks to the skill and able hands of the best doctors at New York Presbyterian/Weill Cornell Medical Center in Manhattan . . . and what did I get for my death-defying efforts?

I got Larry King's smiling brother, Marty.

That's right—after flatlining for over an hour, then being in a rather undignified tubes-in-every-orifice coma for a week, then lying prostrate in the cardiac unit for another week, I woke up and opened my eyes not to heaven's trumpets, nor any warm white glow; I awoke to the blinding fluorescent lights of the cardiac unit where I shared a room with Larry King's crumpled brother, Marty, who had just had bypass surgery. As I slowly regained consciousness, he leaned over at me and smiled. "Ya made it, kid! They thought they almost lost ya!"

Oy. Had I died and gone to hell? Was this one of Dante's nine circles?

Like Siddhartha before me, I had lived a life of excess, twentieth-century variety: sex, drugs, and rock and roll. And the result was a broken, empty, hopeless, not-wanting-to-live-anymore thirty-six-year-old, who escaped his despair and self-loathing by daily injections of high-grade heroin.

Once upon a time, I'd been a well-known New York nightclub owner caught up with all of the self-destructive ego candy that that world had to offer. From the late '80s until the '90s, I was the young, Ivy League–educated owner of several of the hottest and hippest nightclubs in all of Manhattan; these were much-publicized hotspots that were frequented by A-listers like John F. Kennedy Jr., Tom Cruise, and Uma Thurman.

It was all rather intoxicating for a middle-class kid from Queens. Keep in mind that had *not* been my original career choice after college; like Dustin Hoffman in *The Graduate*, I blew off graduate school, choosing instead to work in the "real world." But the soul-crushing realities of a tedious corporate job led me, almost by accident, into a part-time job in a Manhattan nightclub as I sought some escape and excitement from a life that I had already felt trapped in. Through sweat and hustle, I was soon able to quit my day job and open my very own nightspot—my attempt at the American Dream—which, quite miraculously, turned into a much-publicized place to be seen.

But it was all fool's gold. Several years of glamour and good times were followed by several years of addicted hell that had led me to the precipice of nonexistence. I'd gone from the bright lights of the dance floor to the harsh lights of the intensive care unit.

Glamorous it was not.

It's not an uncommon story: In seeking the Good Life, I had found the High Life, which then almost led me to No Life. As I lay in that hospital bed, I kept wondering where my life had turned so wrong. How did a nice kid from good schools and an honest and hardworking family wind up such a broken mess? It's not as if I didn't know better. I had fancied myself as a reasonably smart guy and had loving, caring Greek immigrant parents who had sacrificed *everything* to help raise me in the best way they knew how. That's not to say there wasn't dysfunction; after all, you don't survive the atrocities of Nazi Germany in World War II and come out without some mental and emotional scar tissue.

Despite their traumatic childhoods, my parents showed me more love and guidance than most kids that I knew at the Bronx High School of Science. I had excellent schooling, loving parents, and, by most accounts, I was considered strong and physically fit; hell I was an AAU national karate champion in 1985.

None of that seemed to matter.

My pre-coma life had spiraled down the drain at the increasing speed and decreasing concentric circles of a bug being flushed down the toilet. I headed into oblivion, overwhelmed by a life that had once seemed so big, bold, and beautiful—but had seemingly turned on me; my once-wonderful life was an illusion of material success and hedonistic excess. Crucially, I had lost all sense of mooring and purpose; like the hot air balloon that had the rope cut that was tethering it to the ground, I was . . . adrift.

We can live on the surface of superficiality and inane distractions for years, until circumstances shatter the illusion. When the nervous laughter stopped, I realized my emptiness. Big, hollow lives can come crashing down hard like a building during an earthquake collapsing in on itself. The façade can look strong, but without that inner strength, the entire structure can pancake—even if we think it's made out of steel and grit.

When addiction kicked me in the ass and I lost everything—my business, my identity, my physical health, and certainly my mental health—I felt as empty as the hole in a doughnut—I was just . . . nothing. I was entirely unprepared mentally, psychologically, and spiritually for what felt like the cruelty of an indifferent world and a city that didn't much care if I felt alone or empty. Loneliness is more pronounced in megacities like New York. You ride the subway with hundreds and thousands of anonymous faces, devoid of any humanity; just so many heads of cattle in a cattle car. You can smell the coffee and bacon-and-egg sandwich on the breath of the anonymous face literally inches from yours; but you don't even know their name—and they certainly don't know or want to know yours.

Pity the poor tourist who dares to make eye contact.

I discovered that it's one thing to commune with your thoughts alone in a mountain cabin; quite another to be alone with blurry faces constantly brushing past you in an overly frenetic world that doesn't care if you've gotten a cramp and need to stop for a moment. Keep up or get swept away.

I got swept away.

Unbeknownst to me at the time, I was swimming against a cultural tide that my New York, middle-class upbringing hadn't prepared me for. In fact, that middle-class upbringing and my pursuit of what I had thought was the American dream were both rooted in larger dynamics that contributed to my lack of resiliency—that made me a poorer swimmer in the waters of a society that are antithetical to the physical, emotional, and psychological well-being of the individual.

As I lay in my hospital bed and looked out my window, I saw the East River and was convinced that we were either on the Rio Grande or in Hong Kong. My brain was seemingly playing near-death tricks on me—a phenomenon that I would find out about later and go on to study more. To the doctors, it looked like common ICU psychosis. But in a near-death phenomenon, common in hospice, the person's psyche interprets the imminent death transition as one of being on a trip—usually a river crossing or a boat journey. My thick stack of medical records indicated that I kept asking to speak to the captain of the boat. Did I think we were on the river Styx on the crossing of the dead? Was my roommate, Marty, some harbinger of death—or Captain Stubing on the *Love Boat*? I couldn't be sure.

I barely survived both my metaphorical and literal coma. Doctors at the time said it was a "one-in-five-billion" recovery miracle that I wasn't left in a vegetative state. I knew in the innermost part of my soul, if there is such a thing, that something was seriously wrong—deeply lacking—in my life and that things needed to change. It's as if I'd finally awakened to the fact that I was a human being and human beings aren't supposed to live the way that I'd been living.

How were they—how was I—supposed to live? I had no idea. I was a kid from Queens; all I knew was that I felt a profound void, but I didn't know what was supposed to fill that emptiness. I do remember feeling a deep existential thirst; a near-death experience will do that to you. More than that, I needed to find my bliss; to find the purpose and passion to my existence—and I needed a deeper, spiritual sense of strength and resilience. Because I knew, with every cell of my being, that if I didn't find my purpose in life, I was not going to survive.

Phoenix Rising

When I was released from the hospital, I immersed myself into a spiritual and philosophical quest. I read more and more about philosophy, comparative religion, physics, metaphysics, and consciousness research. I had been raised as a Greek Orthodox Christian, but somewhere between attending Cornell and being a nightclub owner, I lost my religion. In the elite, quasi-intellectualism of the Ivy League and the morally bankrupt world of velvet ropes and champagne, I became an atheist-leaning agnostic.

After the good old-fashioned existential ass-kicking that I'd received, I became more open to the idea of a spiritual dimension. I felt compelled to read and research more about those things. What can I say? I just wasn't a "have faith" guy.

I didn't know it at the time, but I was also just at the beginning point of my very own Hero's Journey. I had almost been consumed by the obstacles of my journey; now I was ready to continue my quest. And while the essence of the Hero's Journey or any spiritual quest isn't intellectual but experiential, I believe that a person can till the intellectual soil for spiritual fruit to blossom.

I also needed to seriously attend to my sobriety. That was a nonnegotiable reality that I gladly accepted. For me, recovery meant a complete immersion into a twelve-step fellowship, along with a sponsor as my human tether-as-mentor who was able to show me how to walk a path that I had never walked before. I was also advised to sign up for an outpatient counseling program, which I did.

It was explained to me that I needed to attend to all the dimensions of my being: physical, mental, psychological, and spiritual. So I also started doing breathing and insight meditations, and I would take mindfulness walks around the city. I began going to the gym again every day and, as per my sponsor, I also tried to help or support other members in my twelve-step fellowship—either a person to talk to or a ride to the next meeting. Whatever I could do to help.

Through all of that, over the next few months, a funny thing happened: I didn't feel alone or empty anymore. I felt happy to be alive—yes, I know it may sound corny, but it was true. I loved going to meetings and connecting with people on a deep, human level. And I started to enjoy my inner journey of exploration—it was all exciting and uncharted territory for me.

At some point, almost a year into my recovery, I also realized that maybe I needed to move out of New York City. I'll always consider myself a city boy, but I needed a quieter setting that might lend itself more toward this new, self-reflective journey that I was on.

After discussing a few options with my wonderful girlfriend Lucy (who is now my wife of almost twenty years), we packed up and headed to the quiet and idyllic North Fork of Long Island, about a two-hour drive east of New York City. We moved into a cute little rental cottage a block from the beach in August 2001. After what I'd been through, the setting was just what the doctor ordered. It was a peaceful and beautiful green oasis surrounded by water: the Peconic Bay on the south, the Long Island Sound to the north, and the Atlantic Ocean to the east, with dozens of inlets and estuaries throughout.

In hindsight, there was more to my move than just wanting to escape the insanity of New York. I felt a magnetic pull to be closer to nature, and something was also telling me that I needed to be near the water. Years later, during my training as a psychologist, I would learn how important it is for the human psyche to have a strong connection to nature and the natural world; indeed, the root cause of many of our neuroses—both personal and societal—is a disconnect from the earth. Most of us today are so far removed from nature that we don't even realize that we're missing a critical nature connection; we feel stressed and anxious, and yet don't even realize that we may be suffering from what Richard Louv calls "nature-deficit disorder."

I didn't consciously know it at the time, but a powerful internal part of me knew that getting back to nature was critical for my recovery. And as for being near the water, many psychotherapists believe that we crave the oceanic state of the womb. However, many transpersonal psychologists don't view this urge as a regression but as a call toward transcendence. They believe the oceanic state is an expanded level of consciousness; thus, a real-life pull toward oceans and rivers is merely a sublimated desire for transcendence.

Whatever the pull was, moving to the North Fork was, literally and figuratively, a breath of fresh air, and I loved that it was a region that time seemed to have forgotten. This was pre–cell phones, mind you, but it also felt like pre-electricity. Blissfully quaint, without the intrusion of big-box stores or obnoxious strip malls, the North Fork consisted of vineyards, farmland, and a few mom-and-pop shops. A traffic jam consisted of getting stuck behind a slow-moving tractor that had temporarily veered onto the main road. A bustling metropolis it was not. That's changed a bit twenty years later; the North Fork has been "discovered," so now you do see the curse of the Range Rovers. It's still a beautiful and relatively quiet place—just not as quiet.

Life on the North Fork had a leisurely pace that was a perfect antidote to the frenetic pace of my New York City life. I instinctively knew that for my mind to be in a good place, the body that housed that old, warped brain of mine also needed to be right. I started taking long bike rides around the various estuaries and scenic preserves in and around the North Fork; I would also go running for about forty minutes on alternate days. As I biked or jogged, my mind would either go quiet, or it would go deep-sea fishing in contemplative meditation waters, as I'd pondered all types of existential questions: Who are we? Why are we here?

Being so close to death makes you wonder pretty deeply about those things.

I didn't know it at the time, but it turns out that what I was doing was also consistent with what some of the ancient Greek philosophers did. The Neoplatonist philosopher Iamblichus, in his third-century work *On the Pythagorean Life,* describes how Pythagoras and his followers would take long, reflective walks in the morning, before they were even allowed to interact with others, in order that they might quiet any restlessness of the mind, and "set their own soul in order," and thus become "composed in their intellect."[2]

After they'd do that, they would then engage in strenuous physical activity (e.g., running, wrestling) as part of their afternoon regimen of exercise and contemplation. On my own, I'd discovered the benefit of the Pythagorean notion of the "harmonic alignment" between a sound and contemplative mind, a sound body, and a sound character.

At the time, all I knew was that these reflective moments were when my most powerful insights would emerge, and when the purpose and meaning in my life would become apparent. Something interesting was definitely happening to me, but it would take me years of further reflection, study, and research to better understand it.

Toward that end, I continued my voracious reading. Ken Wilber, Daisetz Suzuki, Thomas Merton, Stanislav Grof, Huston Smith, Fritjof Capra—I read everything I could in order to better understand the relationship between the spiritual realm and the physical world. I also realized that, in addition to exercising, meditating, and immersing myself in the appropriate books, a critically important component of a spiritual practice was engaging in active spirituality—that is, helping other people, which I would discover is the common denominator in almost every spiritual practice or religion.

Back in the Saddle

I was definitely growing—spiritually and intellectually. Yet I realized for that growth to continue, I needed to pursue a career that could be of service. I wrestled with a couple of options, but eventually I applied to and was accepted into the master's program for social work at Stony Brook University in 2002.

It felt amazing—after all that I'd been through—to be, again, in a world where ideas were exchanged in a healthy and nurturing environment and where I had wonderful professors who supported me and encouraged me onward. My mind—and the world around me—were alive with possibilities.

At thirty-six, I felt like an eager-to-learn freshman at the Bronx High School of Science. My first year in graduate school, I decided to get real-life experience in the field of social work. After a short stint as a counselor at a homeless shelter in Southampton, I was hired as a social worker at a hospital with both a psychiatric unit and an inpatient drug-and-alcohol detox and rehab unit. I jumped at the opportunity to get that hospital position because it gave me the opportunity to receive some wonderful clinical training—and work with fellow addicts.

Who woulda thunk it? This formerly addicted ex–nightclub owner, who had once made his living getting people drunk, was now trying to help get them sober. I loved talking to the clients and hearing about their lives. And I think they might have helped me more than I helped them, because being able to be helpful filled me with such a sense of purpose—something that I hadn't had in a long time.

Over the next couple of years, I worked with hundreds of patients from all walks of life—cops, firefighters, schoolteachers, chefs, artists, lawyers, clergy, construction workers, the homeless, single moms, retirees, teenagers. All of them had landed in detox or rehab, either willingly or unwillingly, due to their struggles with the great equalizer: addiction.

Like a good addict, I couldn't get enough of a good thing and enrolled in a Ph.D. program in psychology after I finished my master's degree in social work.

The Awakening, Part 2

Life, love, and growth ensued. I found myself as a newlywed with my beloved wife, Lucy, traveling through my native Greece in 2003. That's where I made a pivotal discovery that would shift my life: while browsing through a tiny, cluttered bookstore on Mykonos, I chanced upon a fascinating little book called *God and the Evolving Universe* by Michael Murphy and James Redfield. In this fascinating book, Murphy and Redfield give a brief overview of the history of human development and describe what they call the "Greek Miracle" of ancient philosophy.[3]

The words seemed to jump out at me as I sat on a whitewashed wall in the Mediterranean sun, devouring the book. In the land of my ancestors, the doorway to the ancient Greeks burst open. I realized that my journey home had already begun; I had been living the Bios Pythagorikos (Pythagorean way of life) without even realizing it. The more that I read, the more that I felt doors of understanding being kicked open.

Back in the States, I started my Ph.D. program while getting my hands on as many books on philosophy as I could. Now that I realized that my life and meditative practice shared a bloodline with Pythagoras and Plato, I immersed myself even more deeply into it. I realized that not only was I gaining an elevated sense of awareness—but I was also feeling much happier and, to my surprise, becoming a better person.

The more I read about the lives and wisdom of enlightened souls like Plato and Pythagoras, the more I began to find myself emulating them in true "What would Plato do?" fashion. Not so shockingly, I discovered that when one's template for an idealized human being was Plato, rather than P. Diddy, amazing changes within oneself could occur.

With all these insights and ideas swirling around in my head, I decided to take a long bike ride to try to sort out the topic for my doctoral dissertation. As I pedaled along a quiet, tree-lined back road, various thoughts raced through my head: thoughts about how conflicted and neurotic our modern world has become, and, finally, questions about how—and why—I survived my coma.

At the end of my bike ride, exhausted, I found myself sitting on an old piece of driftwood, on a cool and cloudy October afternoon, staring out at the perfectly still, glass-like reflection of the Peconic Bay. When the sky is right, the bay can create an amazing light show that can rival the best laser rock exhibit; I stared in wonder as beams of orange and red light burst through blue-gray clouds, which then reflected a kaleidoscopic prism of light off the crystal-clear blue water.

And in that beautiful moment of nature-inspired awe, the following thought arose in my mind: bring the wisdom of the ancients back to life. Pythagoras was my philosophical North Star, as I grew to understand that he was way more than just a mathematician and the theorem guy. He greatly influenced Plato and was an amazing blend of math, music, poetry, philosophy, and living a life of growth and deeper understanding—a life where we get past the surface of illusion. It's fair to say that a Pythagorean-inspired life would be the opposite of the modern-day TikTok *influencer.* And I was thrilled and amazed to discover that Pythagorean wisdom was also the wisdom of the entire ancient world—

including Africa and the Middle East—as both were parts of the world that he had traveled to and spent considerable time learning from.

I was continuing to learn new things as I embarked on an amazing and transformative journey where I discovered—almost by chance—the way of ancient Greek metaphysical philosophy, a powerful wisdom tradition that embraced the notion of death as rebirth. In fact, Plato even described philosophy itself as a form of "death before dying."

What does that mean?

What I learned was that the Greeks had discovered a method that can allow a person to "die before dying"—in effect, to shed the biological skin and achieve an expanded level of noetic awareness that can then lead to personal transformation—all without having to take dying to the literal extremes that I had. Plato had even used "breaking the bird free from the cage" as a metaphor for the soul transcending the physical body via the holistic mind-body purification of *philosophy*. Wait, what? Philosophy as a transformative purification method? I had stereotypically thought it was just a bunch of boring old white men in togas speaking antiquated and irrelevant nonsense—certainly nothing that could have relevance in *today's* society.

These were new and shocking ideas for me: that philosophy was originally conceived of as a holistic way of life meant to purify an individual toward transcendence. I had mistakenly thought that philosophy was a dry intellectual endeavor, an arcane obsession with semantics, written in impenetrable language in dusty texts that were housed in the bowels of some university library.

To be honest, I thought of philosophy as something that was old and dead, and not applicable for today's world. I couldn't have been more wrong. A holistic lived practice of philosophy as a form of *purification*—as, indeed, a *way of life*—had been originated by Pythagoras (with help from his friends, the Egyptians and Babylonians). And in what came to be known as the Bios Pythagorikos, a healthy mind, body, and spirit were nurtured with rigorous physical exercise, a strict diet, daily meditational walks, and lessons on ethics and character, as well as deep contemplative meditations on math, music, and philosophy.

Unfortunately, because philosophy today has been hijacked by crypt-keeper philosophy *professors,* instead of *actual* philosophers who walk the walk, this vibrant soul of ancient Greek wisdom has almost been lost. In our narcissistic, YouTube culture, where most people are inclined toward self-absorption than self-reflection, we need the long-lost depth and soul of Plato and Pythagoras—now more than ever.

I was having a similar awakening as the one that Dominican-born academic Roosevelt Montás had as an undergraduate at Columbia University. As he describes in his book *Rescuing Socrates,* Montás had emigrated to Queens, New York, at the age of twelve, barely speaking English, yet shaped and transformed himself by immersing into the classics and ancient philosophy. After getting his Ph.D., he would go on to become the director of Columbia's prestigious Center for the Core Curriculum and started a program for low-income high school students who aspired to be the first in their families to go to college, believing that the classics can be the most empowering tool for members of historically marginalized communities.

Montás describes teaching underprivileged teens and watching them "undergo a kind of inner awakening" as they would embrace Socrates and Plato "seriously and personally." Montás understood from firsthand experience the transformative magic that could occur when readers were exposed to thinking about what he describes as *virtue* and *excellence.* He currently teaches Introduction to Contemporary Civilization in the West, a yearlong course on primary texts in moral and political thought, as well as seminars in American Studies, including Freedom and Citizenship in the United States.

Beyond virtue and excellence, the ancients taught the world how to look up at the night sky and *wonder*; how to examine the nature of existence and our role within that ontological framework. And they also taught us how to use our sense of reason to critically think and deeply explore our belief systems. Indeed, their ancient teachings thrived in debate and opposition—opposing ideas were not only accepted, they were welcomed. Imagine that. In fact, Socrates had developed the dialectic, where opposing beliefs could be explored via a question-and-answer method called *elenchus,* that sought to find deeper truth and understanding.

At its roots, ancient philosophy is not just the domain of the Greeks, or even Eurocentric wisdom, for that matter—it's *universal* wisdom. I've mentioned Egypt and Babylon (what today is Iraq) as integral parts of Pythagoras's studies and teachings. Because of the frequent travel among the port cities of antiquity—a sort of ancient internet—Pythagoras had spent extensive time studying in the Egyptian cities of Memphis and later Thebes. In fact, it was his time in Africa where he learned his theories of mathematics and sacred geometry. And, always thirsty to absorb more wisdom, Pythagoras also traveled to Babylon in the Middle East, where he's said to have studied with their magi (wise men) and studied the teachings of the Persian philosopher and poet Zoroaster, the founder of Zoroastrianism.

One of the basic tenets of Zoroastrianism is to pursue *asa* (truth) through the active participation in life and the exercise of constructive words, thoughts, and deeds. These principles were all also later critical tenets in Pythagoreanism. So Pythagoras may have been from Greece, but his wisdom borrowed liberally from a diverse variety of ancient cultures.

Indeed, as the biographer and philosopher Porphyry said about Pythagoras: "In Babylon he associated with other Chaldeans, especially attaching himself to Zoroaster, by whom he was purified from the pollutions of his past life, and taught the things from which a virtuous man ought to be free. Likewise he heard lectures about Nature and the principles of wholes. It was from his stay among these foreigners that Pythagoras acquired the greatest part of his wisdom."[4]

It was both beautiful and illuminating to discover that ancient wisdom was not only the province of one country or region but was our collective human heritage. And the more that I discovered about these ancient teachings, the more that I was able to incorporate them into my life and transform from brokenness to healing, and then eventually thriving.

* * *

I'D BEEN SITTING facing the bay about two hundred yards from the New Suffolk marina in Cutchogue on the North Fork of Long Island. I slowly stood up, feeling purposeful as I walked toward the marina to stretch my legs and look at the boats bobbing in the water. Enjoying a deep sense of peace and inner calm, I noticed one particular boat that was a little more weathered than all the rest; as I took a closer look, I read the name written across the stern: *The Odyssey.*

I closed my eyes and took in another deep breath. Yes, I knew what I had to do: academically explore how Pythagorean philosophy can be transformative in people's lives as my doctoral dissertation. Why not create a method wherein various participants in a research study can also immerse themselves in the wisdom of the ancients?

At this point, some might ask how I can substantiate that the wisdom of Pythagoras and Plato had been so transformative in my life. How can I prove it? This is how I would respond: the proof, as they say, is in the pudding. I had been a morally compromised, horribly addicted former nightclub owner who had lost everything; I'd been broke, homeless, physically shot, emotionally devastated, and spiritually bankrupt.

After my discovery of the ancients, I've been clean and sober for two decades. I'd been a respected college professor for almost ten years and a caring psychotherapist who's opened clinics treating hundreds of young people all over the country. More importantly, I'm a loving and devoted husband as well as a caring and adoring father (of identical twin boys). I've become a person whom people in my community can trust and rely upon as I try my best to lead an honest and ethical life.

I had discovered that the real essence of ancient philosophy was alchemy—*human* alchemy. I've included my personal narrative to give a sense of the transformative potential of the method that I've only briefly described. Philosophy also happens to be the antidote to our overly technological world; it's a reclaiming of our profoundly human ability to use our reason, to critically think, to contemplatively think deeply about things that matter, to be with nature, and to always try to keep growing.

I do need to add that, while I did therapy in both individual and group settings with a couple of different licensed therapists over the years, it was my immersion in ancient philosophy along with my twelve-step involvement and working with a sponsor (while also helping others), that gave my life meaning. Therapy was an okay place to go—and in some instances, it can be extremely beneficial; but there are some inherent limitations that can actually stunt, rather than foster growth.

As a longtime therapist myself—who owns and runs two treatment programs—I definitely have some insights on the subject, which I'll explore in the next chapter.

10

Beyond Therapy

Natural Resilience

On the morning of December 6, 1917, in Halifax, Nova Scotia, a traumatic event akin in proportion to the 9/11 attacks occurred: the French cargo ship SS *Mont-Blanc* collided with the Norwegian ship SS *Imo* in the strait connecting upper Halifax Harbour just off the main dock. The *Mont-Blanc* had just arrived from New York fully loaded with explosives: TNT, picric acid, and highly flammable benzol. After the collision with the *Imo,* the *Mont-Blanc* caught fire, which rapidly began to spread. As a result, her crew quickly abandoned ship, and the vessel was left adrift; without a crew on board to steer her, the *Mont-Blanc* drifted into the dock, where at 9:04 A.M. it set off an enormous explosion that destroyed the entire north end of the city—an area of approximately two and a half square miles.

The blast was the largest man-made explosion up until that time, releasing the equivalent of 2.9 tons of TNT. The ship was completely blown apart, and a powerful blast wave radiated away from the explosion at more than 3,300 feet per second. Temperatures of 9,000°F and pressures of thousands of atmospheres accompanied the blast, as white-hot shards of iron fell down upon Halifax and neighboring Dartmouth. *Mont-Blanc*'s 90-mm cannon landed over three miles north of the original blast site with its barrel melted away; *Mont-Blanc*'s anchor, weighing half a ton, landed two miles south in the town of Armdale.[1]

A cloud of white smoke rose to at least 11,800 feet, and a 60-foot tsunami washed the SS *Imo* onto the shore at the neighboring town of Dartmouth. The blast was felt as far away as Cape Breton, over 120 miles away; hundreds of people who had been watching the fire from their homes were blinded when the blast wave shattered the windows; and overturned stoves and lamps started fires throughout Halifax, where entire city blocks burned, trapping residents inside their houses.

The devastation was almost unimaginable: more than two thousand people were killed, and nine thousand more were injured—many of them horribly burned, dismembered, and blinded. Adding to the unbelievable disaster, the night after the explosion, a blizzard hit Halifax, dropping sixteen inches of snow, which hindered any relief effort, leaving many more people whose homes had been destroyed in the explosion to then freeze to death.

The quiet northern town had suddenly turned into hell on earth, where residents either died by fiery inferno or froze to death in the bleak, unforgiving cold of the Canadian night. Survivors had experienced perhaps one of the most traumatizing and horrific events in human history.

Many decades later, a mental health researcher wanted to find out what the psychological toll had been. April Naturale is a psychiatric social worker who had headed Project Liberty, a government-sponsored program that had been established to coordinate the therapeutic response to September 11. To better understand the aftereffects of what happened in Nova Scotia, Naturale went to Halifax to read archival materials on the 1917 accident.[2]

"Some of those who survived seemed psychotic, hallucinating for days," she told a reporter for *The New Yorker*. One woman continued to speak to her dead child Alma; other victims were in such a state of shock that doctors were able to perform surgery on them without using chloroform.

As a trauma specialist, she found something quite amazing: after about a week or so, these disturbing psychiatric symptoms spontaneously subsided in the vast majority of cases—and all without any aid from mental health workers who, at that time, were almost nonexistent as a nascent field. These accounts led Naturale to conclude that psychiatric intervention in the wake of such an event should ideally be minimal; that the mind is extremely resilient and should be given time to heal itself organically. In short, the "abnormal" behavior witnessed in the aftermath of the explosion was actually part of a healthy process of recovery.

Scientific studies suggest that, after a catastrophic event, most people are indeed resilient and will recover spontaneously over time. A small percentage of individuals do not "rebound," and they do require extended psychological care. But researchers found that the single intervention of a therapeutic debriefing session does nothing to alter this dynamic. And the people who didn't "bounce back" seem to already have had psychological vulnerabilities.

Studies have found that people at greatest risk for PTSD have a history of childhood abuse, family dysfunction, or a preexisting psychological disorder. An older 1996 study of American pilots who were prisoners of war in North Vietnam highlighted the importance and role that a strong baseline of mental health plays. Although the pilots endured years of torture and, often, solitary confinement, they showed a surprisingly low incidence of PTSD. It was hypothesized that because pilots are screened for psychological health and trained for high-stress combat, perhaps they had a stronger "psychological immune system" and were able to tolerate their trauma in a way that people who were more psychologically vulnerable never could.

Even for those who are more adversely impacted, therapeutic debriefing was proving to have very limited benefit. In 2004, Brett Litz, a research psychologist at Boston Veterans Affairs Medical Center who specializes in post-traumatic stress disorder, did a randomized clinical trial of group debriefing of peacekeeping soldiers in Kosovo who were stationed in combat zones. Peacekeeping forces are exposed to sniper fire, mine explosions, and the discovery of mass graves. He summarized his findings on psychological debriefing as follows: "The techniques practiced by most American grief counsellors to prevent P.T.S.D. are inert."

Indeed, clinical trials of individual psychological debriefings versus no intervention after a major trauma—for example, after a car accident or a fire—have had discouraging results. In fact, some researchers claim that psychological debriefing can impede recovery. One particular study of burn victims, for example, found that patients who received debriefing were much more likely to report PTSD symptoms than patients in a control group. It was theorized that therapy and debriefing, by encouraging patients to open their emotional wounds during a vulnerable period, can increase distress and trauma rather than decrease it.

The therapeutic interventions that occurred immediately after 9/11 have also taught us a lot. There was a huge influx of grief counselors into Manhattan immediately after the towers collapsed, yet most New Yorkers didn't receive any therapy following the attacks. Data taken from surveys after September 11 contradicted the early predictions that there would be widespread psychological damage. Now that's not to say that people weren't affected—of course they were—we all were. But did it reach a tipping point that exceeded the normal grief response that we can all usually—and naturally—recover from?

One survey of 988 adults living below 110th Street, conducted in October and November of 2001, found that only 7.5 percent had been diagnosed as having PTSD. (According to the American Psychological Association, a patient is said to have PTSD if, for a month or more after a tragic event, he experiences several of the classic symptoms: flashbacks, intrusive thoughts, and nightmares; avoidance of activities and places that are reminiscent of the trauma; emotional numbness; chronic insomnia.)

A follow-up of this survey, in March of 2002, found that only 1.7 percent of New Yorkers were suffering from prolonged PTSD. This indicates that most normally healthy psychological people will naturally get better over time and have innate resilience after being exposed to a traumatic event. However, we shouldn't conflate this finding with people who suffer from significant chronic trauma and have prolonged exposure to psychological stressors; that's an entirely different psychological profile.

The basic conclusion is that we, as humans, have developed our own reservoir of strength and resilience in the normal course of our development. What can be helpful is peer support (the AA paradigm) rather than professional psychological counseling.

Malachy Corrigan was the director of the Counseling Service Unit of the New York City Fire Department. He was once a proponent of psychological debriefing—but months before the September 11 attacks, he decided that it was generally not a beneficial technique and described a sort of "social contagion" effect that can happen in group therapy: "Sometimes when we put people in a group and debriefed them, we gave them memories that they didn't have. We didn't push them to psychosis or anything, but, because these guys were so close and they were all at the fire, they eventually convinced themselves that they did see something or did smell something when in fact they didn't."

So he decided to switch from a mental health approach to a peer-support model for the workers in the pit at Ground Zero. He enlisted other firefighters to be "peer counselors" and to provide friendship and moral support, as well as educational information about the possible mental health impact of sustained trauma.

"It was like one huge extended family," Corrigan recalled. "We gave them a lot of information about PTSD, as well as about the burden that they would be putting on their own families. We quite boldly spoke about alcohol and drugs. And we focused on the anger that comes with grief, because the members were more than happy to display those symptoms. You are speaking their language when you talk about alcohol and anger. The simpler you keep the mental health concepts, the easier it is to engage them."

Naturale also sees the benefits of the approach that Corrigan took, of peers over therapists, as the optimal paradigm for civilians as well: "Non–mental health professionals do not pathologize," she said. "They don't know the terminology, they don't know how to diagnose. The most helpful approach is to employ a public-health model, using people in the community who aren't diagnosing you."

In my twenty years of working in the mental health field with clients in a variety of levels of psychiatric distress, I've seen the increasing and beneficial use of peer support over professional therapists. And, perhaps, for *some* people—and I use the word *some* here—we may indeed be doing more harm than good by diagnosing people and putting them into clinical treatment settings.

A New Paradigm

Perhaps it's time to revisit the role of therapists and the therapy-industrial complex. Clinical diagnosis is an important tool to guide best-practice treatment for many people in acute psychiatric distress; but is it possible that the $100-billion-per-year therapy business—and it is a business—may be, for less acute clients, perpetuating and exacerbating psychological issues, almost in the form of a "social contagion" effect (as was mentioned above) where clients become habituated to be unwell and emulate unwell models?

Is it possible that we have medicalized and pathologized entirely natural psychological processes and, in so doing, have created a paternalistic dependency model that now requires paid therapists who create psychological dragons that only they can slay? Natural human processes like stress, adversity, trauma, and shame have not only been pathologized but have entire theoretical models with their respective therapist superstars (Oprah-endorsed, of course) that have created clinical monsters that then require medical or therapeutic interventions to conquer.

But we had been warned about this. Twentieth-century psychiatrist Thomas Szasz was an influential thinker who spoke out against the pathologizing of people as a form of control; that the psychologists and therapists of the day were the new secularized priests and shamans who dictated what was acceptable and normative behavior. He also argued that mental illness was simply a conceptual metaphor for everyday human problems, and shied away from a reliance on the *DSM*, the diagnostic bible for mental health workers.[3]

So, too, did author and analyst James Hillman and his "acorn theory." He also believed that we were pathologizing things that were really just natural or necessary processes by which an individual responded in order to optimally grow—from acorn to oak tree. For example, the child who gets diagnosed with selective mutism, yet simply needed to listen more, over a longer period of time who then flourishes in their linguistic abilities.[4]

But dragons are only dragons if we believe that they are. Our perception of our challenges is a key component in how they impact us; how we understand and frame things is critically important with regard to our mental health—that is, if we perceive or define something as being problematic, then it can become toxic or take on more harmful features.

Let's take stress as an example. We've all heard the phrase "Stress kills"; and many do everything that they can in order to reduce their stress because they believe that stress *equals* bad. But as health psychologist Kelly McGonigal points out in her book *The Upside of Stress* and in her captivating TED Talk, research has shown that it's not *stress* that kills but our *beliefs* regarding stress that actually make it harmful to us.[5]

In large, longitudinal studies, researchers found that people who had high stress and a high belief that stress is harmful had the highest mortality rates. But amazingly, the people who had the lowest mortality rates were *not* the low-stress people; instead, it was the people who had high stress but, and this is the key point, they did not choose to believe that stress was harmful—they accepted it as a natural, human occurrence. So the reality is that stress can actually be beneficial, as it builds resilience and, via the release of the neurohormone oxytocin (the so-called cuddle hormone) that's released during times of high stress, we are propelled to reach out to other people and be more social when times are difficult—incredibly, biologically hardwiring us toward healing socialization.

The stress hormone oxytocin is also cardioprotective and helps heart cells heal from any stress-induced damage. In fact, McGonigal looked at the cardiac profile of stress participants in the research study who believed that stress wasn't harmful and discovered something quite amazing. Their blood vessels weren't constricted like the typical high-stress/stress-is-bad patient; instead, their heart vessels resembled the same dilated profile of a person experiencing courage. It's a powerful reframing message that can actually change our biological profile and, with over twenty-eighty million views of her TED Talk, it's a message that's resonating with people.

Yet another leading and beloved therapist guru is Brené Brown, who has developed "shame resilience theory," which is also resonating with people. In fact, the brilliant and folksy Brené Brown has created a whole cottage industry around her beliefs about shame and how to deal with it: seminars, bestselling books, TED Talks. She's a rock star in the field of mental health with millions of devotees as she speaks about the power of "vulnerability" and the toxin of shame where, essentially, shame is demonized. And she, importantly, also emphasizes the critical role of social connection.

Yet unlike what McGonigal has done with stress where she's declawed the once-feared stress dragon, Brown has made shame into a psychological boogeyman. Yes, she makes semantic distinctions between "shame" versus "guilt": you feel *guilty* when you've done something wrong, but you feel *shame* when you feel that you as a person are bad. And there's more semantics around *feeling* shamed and *being* shamed, but the whole ball of wax revolves around shame and her belief that we carry too much of it around, thus we're all in need of strategies to deal with it.

To be clear, Brown is an intelligent, caring, and well-intentioned researcher who genuinely seems to be trying to help people. But her distinctions between shame and guilt are the psychobabble of artificial mental health definitions; the dictionary actually defines shame as: "a feeling of humiliation or distress caused by the consciousness of wrong or foolish behavior." So shame *is* indeed a feeling—not an all-encompassing definition of character, as Brown and her disciples would have us believe. And it's a *helpful* feeling that follows the *consciousness of wrong or foolish behavior.*

Of course, the experience of shame when it's internalized as a result of some horrible event that has happened *to* a person is a terrible psychological toxin that can benefit from professional help and treatment. But the more common variant, the shame that comes from doing something that a person knows runs counter to their values, is not something that we need a therapist to help us cleanse. But because of Brené Brown's popularity in both the mental health field and the culture at large, *shame* (and her interpretation of it) has become part of our social-emotional lexicon and a prevailing psychological construct and lens that many people now see their entire lives through; and, like any social contagion, the culturally popular paradigm has shaped people's perception.

Here's my larger point: shame isn't the enemy, just like stress or adversity isn't the enemy; shame is a healthy and necessary adaptive human emotion that helps us correct maladaptive behavior. The problem with many today isn't that they feel too *much* shame—they don't feel *enough* shame, because there is a societal narcissism that often leads to some dishonest or dishonorable behavior that indeed merits the feeling of shame.

It is my humble professional opinion that we've demonized the wrong things. Difficult life events are *not* the problem. Stress is part of life. Adversity happens. And there are behaviors that merit shame. We don't need a whole therapy-industrial complex to demonize natural processes that don't really need to be demonized. What we need are strong friendships and ties that help give us a sense of genuine community and support that can help us manage through life's challenges.

And yet we know that we are going through what many have called a "loneliness epidemic"; is it possible that *most* people just need a good friend—or two, or three—to be able to talk with rather than a paid therapist? And, further, wouldn't it be optimal if children, as they were growing up, were encouraged to develop a strong "psychological immune system" that can provide an innate resilience to life's inevitable hurdles?

I think that if we look at the larger picture, we may see that our modern and technological society has moved us in the opposite direction; made us less resilient, more reactive and brittle, more impulsive—and certainly lonelier. All ingredients for vulnerability to life's curveballs.

I'm reminded again of my father. He survived the Nazis, but had a strong network of family support, had been raised in a resilience- and grit-inducing childhood, and had his passions of cooking and gardening throughout his life. You know, the way that people were genetically designed to live.

But in the modern age, in the blink of an eye—at least by evolutionary standards—we've sprinted past hunter-gatherer, leapfrogged over our agrarian ancestors, zipped past the industrial age, and landed smack-dab in the middle of the information age—all in less than two hundred years. The only problem is those seismic shifts have changed the nurturing sociocultural environment that we'd become dependent on.

All the traditional societal foundational pillars—or were they safety nets?—that held the fabric of society together are gone. The nuclear family? Obliterated into a mushroom cloud by a complex multitude of societal factors. Community organizations, societies, and supports (like the YMCA, book clubs, community centers, 4-H, Boy Scouts, Girl Scouts, religious organizations, social societies)? They, along with most settings that require face-to-face interactions, are rapidly going the way of the Edsel—thank you, internet.

What about psychotherapists? Surely they can help steel the nerves of the anxious twenty-first-century masses and add some sense of stability to our destabilized world. Don't count on them to help either. At best, they've been misguided by the aptly named "self-esteem myth,"[6] mistakenly thinking that the holy grail of the therapeutic process is the false god of *how-does-that-make-you-feel* self-esteem, which, with our current Gen Z and millennial social media–obsessed populations, can potentially feed and inflame self-absorption, narcissism, and egocentrism.

At worst, they can create an unhealthy dependency that infantilizes the client, keeps them stuck picking at childhood scabs, and perpetuates the power dynamic of the therapist-as-god while maintaining the childlike dependency of the client.

I can already hear the howls from my therapist brethren, who are certain to respond: "We are *not* creating a dependency model! We are all for client empowerment!" Yes, some have that sincere belief. And I think we can give a pass to the short-term, rapid-resolution therapists who genuinely share some practical, useful coping skills with clients without needing to create a multi-decade umbilical cord.

But the Freudian psychoanalysts—or any multiple-year therapist, for that matter—is, in the end, just a paid friend or worse, just a paid listener. Nothing more, nothing less. It's a monetary transactional relationship with less genuine resonance and impact than one that you wouldn't have to pay for. That's one of the most compelling reasons why I think the peer models of support are so effective.

Of course if you are lonely and have no one in your life, a therapist is indeed better than not having any support, but the gold standard is the social model of community support. Because after being a therapist for twenty years, I can honestly say that most people who are struggling and need help don't need someone like me or my well-trained and -paid colleagues. They just need a good friend. Free of charge. Or a mentor. Or a sponsor. Or a priest, rabbi, or shaman. Or a community of friends. Or a trusted relative or village elder.

But in twenty-first-century America, those are all relics of a bygone era—albeit, according to the research, a psychologically healthier bygone era. Instead of the caring and sage village elder, we have some rent-a-friend recently out of grad school reaching for your wallet, or any number of "self-help" gurus. But as George Carlin used to point out, "If it's *self*-help . . . whattaya need them for?"

I fear, and some of the research suggests, that the therapy community has, on whole, done more harm than good; that this therapy dependence has compromised people's ability to develop and nurture their own innate abilities to persevere and be resilient. Indeed, some have argued that we are suffering through a poverty of resilience; that we are increasingly lacking the skill set of coping, even as the therapy industry booms.

The Adversity Paradox

There's a powerful dynamic that's been largely overlooked: our high-tech lives are compromising what I've chosen to call our *psychological immune system*. The digital age has stripped children of all the ingredients that are necessary to develop what psychologists call *resilience* and coaches sometimes call *grit*—which are critical ingredients in a person's healthy social, emotional, and psychological development.

Let's face it: In today's click-swipe world, we've created children as instant-gratification vessels who have not learned the fundamental life skills of patience and overcoming adversity. As the old marshmallow test that was developed by Dr. Walter Mischel showed us (although recently it has been somewhat disputed), the ability to delay gratification was a key predictor in lifelong success.[7]

As some may recall, the marshmallow test placed a marshmallow in the hand of a child. Then they were given the choice of either eating the marshmallow immediately or, if they waited, they would get two marshmallows the following day. It was a measure of their ability to delay gratification. Typically, the older kids had a better ability to delay gratification, and the kids who were the least impulsive were also found to have better life outcomes.

Today, we're seeing record rates in impulsivity, as evidenced by the almost 50 percent spike in ADHD,[8] and many, like myself, are looking at the ADHD and screens research done by folks like Dr. Dimitri Christakis, which clearly show the link to increased screen time and ADHD. It only makes sense if you think about it: Screens are very arousing and stimulating for a child. Some may even say *too* stimulating. The child then becomes stimulation-dependent, and can't focus unless they're being perpetually overly stimulated.[9]

It all starts in childhood. The Bubble-Wrapped child raised by the helicopter parent has been deprived of the opportunity to develop a coping immune system. Just like the infant who is "protected" by their parent in artificially germ-free environments never develops the antibodies for a healthy immune system, over-coddled children are resilience-deprived.

After all, resilience-building takes patience and perseverance. But how much of that is cultivated by Alexa, Google, or any other instantly gratifying digital genie?

The coddling (as beautifully described by Jonathan Haidt in *The Coddling of the American Mind*) continues through adolescence and gets turbocharged in the modern university landscape, the much-publicized synthetic world of safe spaces, trigger warnings, and microaggressions.[10]

Regardless of whatever political orientation one may have, from a psychological perspective, this system creates the "non-resilient" adult, a.k.a. the fragile adult. While Nassim Nicholas Taleb discusses in his book *Antifragile* how entire *systems* can grow, strengthen, or otherwise gain from unforeseen stress,[11] we do also know that can apply to humans as well—up to a point. Adversity, competition, hardships, pain, obstacles . . . all of that can develop and strengthen our resilience. But there is a tipping point or, rather, a breaking point of diminishing returns. Yes, Nietzsche is right: "That which does not kill us makes us stronger," but too much of "that" stressor which Nietzsche refers to can eventually break—or kill—us.

We know that *stress = stronger* and *too much stress = breaking* from examples in the natural world: fire forges stronger steel, but *overheating* steel can make it weaker as it changes the microstructure and becomes brittler. For humans, no pain, no gain when it comes to physical training for any kind of athletic training and competition. The muscle resistance and pain are the stressors—but they're building stronger muscle tendons. But working out *too hard* can lead to muscle strain and cramp, or even injury as in a muscle tear. And if you really overdo it, you can strain the heart muscle into a heart attack.

In the emotional realm, a difficult breakup can lead to a stronger, more grounded, and less dependent emotional state of being. Too many breakups? Like a boxer who keeps getting knocked to the mat, eventually that can lead to a knockout, and the fighter—or lover—is out for the count. In other words, romantically broken to the point that relationships are no longer pursued. So from a developmental and psychological standpoint, there is an optimal level of stress to build the most robust psychological immune system and cultivate a strong sense of resilience. Adversity need not be the enemy; in fact, we *need* adversity as we grow and develop—it actually fuels our growth.

Unfortunately, just as we have done with shame, we have created a similar psychological dragon out of *adversity,* which we are then told needs slaying. Indeed, today, the mental health field demonizes adversity and treats it like a four-letter word. Literally. The prevailing explanatory model of psychological distress in the mental health treatment community is the ACES paradigm: the trauma-informed belief that "adverse childhood experiences" correlate with adult psychiatric (and physical) distress.

Which they do.

And in many treatment centers, you're given an ACES rating scale that gives you a score based on various types or episodes of adversity that you've experienced as a child, with the research indicating that a high score correlates with a higher incidence of mental health or addiction issues. Based on that, most people simplify that down to: adversity = bad.

However, the problem, in my humble opinion, isn't *necessarily* childhood adversity; as we've said, we need adversity to grow and flourish (with the understanding that too much adversity can lead to a breaking point). But now, thanks to mental health high priests like psychiatrist Bessel van der Kolk and his bestselling *The Body Keeps the Score,* almost every bit of struggle or adversity in a person's life has been dubbed "trauma"—that he indicates is stored in the body.[12]

But that's not true—not all adversity is trauma, and the struggles in our lives give us our depth, compassion, and resiliency. They make us human and need not be debilitating. Now as I said earlier, there are breaking points, and there are some pretty serious things that can happen to people that are indeed traumatic: sexual assault, debilitating illness, physical abuse, profound neglect. But we've cheapened the word and diminished the *genuinely* traumatic events by making *everything* a trauma. I'm sorry to say, but your mother not getting you that toy that you wanted when you were six is *not* trauma.

Like Brené Brown with shame, and Van der Kolk with trauma, the problem isn't *necessarily* childhood adversity; as we've said, we need adversity to grow and flourish (as mentioned, with the understanding that too much adversity can lead to a breaking point).

But when rock star clinicians and their theories get popularized and go TED Talk viral, they begin to shape the psychological and cultural landscape. Because of the suggestive power of iconic therapists, shame and trauma are now everywhere you look. We need only look at the prior fiasco that had occurred in the 1990s with the phenomenon of "recovered memories," where therapists would ask leading questions about repressed memories that would often result in demonstrably false statements of abuse, to fully understand and appreciate the power that therapists have with their clients.

In fact, according to research, patients whose therapists suggested that they may have repressed memories were twenty times more likely to experience "recovered memories."[13] This has also been true when other types of authority figures (i.e., police investigators) ask leading questions; people in power have an incredible influence over the perception, memories, and beliefs of people that they are interacting with.

Is it any wonder, then, that popular iconic therapist "rock stars" can essentially demonize a natural human phenomenon that they claim is harmful then, via their poularity, create a sociogenic spread among their devoted followers wherein that natural process becomes pathologized? That, as mentioned, they create the dragons that they insist need slaying?

In his powerful essay "A Posthumous Shock: How Everything Became Trauma,"[14] author Will Self looks at how the once-obscure Van der Kolk (and his theories) gained momentum after his chapter on the subject appeared in Cathy Caruth's 1995 anthology *Trauma: Explorations in Memory* had served as a turning point in modern trauma theory, with his then later book *The Body Keeps the Score* becoming an international phenomenon.

Yet in his essay, Self asks, "How did a bowdlerized rendering of a marginal psychological pathology come to hold such sway in the humanities—and increasingly in popular discourse as well?" Self has several theories about this, but points out one key distinction that applies to both the trauma- and shame-dominant paradigms: they seem to be devoid of any ethical or value constructs.

By not distinguishing things that happen *to* a person, rather than abhorrent behaviors committed *by* a person (as in the marine whom Van der Kolk describes in his book who had raped a Vietnamese woman and killed several children), "contemporary trauma theorists' conception of the malady, and their attendant therapies, collapse this fundamental *ethical* distinction" (italics are mine).

An *ethical* distinction.

But where do ethics reside in the modern mental health landscape? They don't—and that's a significant part of the value-neutral paradigmatic problem. It matters in the context of shame and trauma whether your emotional and psychological distress is a result of your own actions or, instead, if you were the victim of someone else's actions.

Now, of course, sometimes good people in extreme situations can do bad things—but in that case, it's a natural and healthy response to feel remorse and, yes, even shame over it. And it may even be traumatic. Yet no amount of therapist's salve rubbed onto that self-inflicted psychic wound will adequately heal or numb it—nor should it. The wound is one of the conscience; one of ethical origin wherein a person has committed an act antithetical to their value system.

The only way to growth and redemption is to feel that self-inflicted discomfort and grow through it. As stated, it is quite a different story if a person is the victim of abhorrent actions committed against them and are traumatized by them, or have internalized that abuse as shame. There is no ethical conflict in those instances—just psychic and emotional pain.

But ethical considerations are missing in mental health paradigms, but are a key ingredient in philosophy—which is why an important part of any modern solution in a "new paradigm" is embracing a philosophical orientation into our understanding of mental health and wellness—especially in the complicated and ethically fuzzy digital age.

Indeed, the problem with many today isn't that they feel too *much* shame—they don't feel *enough* shame, because there is a societal narcissism that often leads to some dishonest or dishonorable behavior that indeed merits the feeling of shame. Yet there isn't a corresponding ethical construct—a well-developed proverbial *moral compass.*

If we were to embrace the philosophical teachings of the ancients, one effective anti-shame strategy would be: don't do things that are shameful; try to conduct yourself in an ethical and esteemable manner, and you won't feel shame, or ashamed, or shameful . . . or whatever permutation of the word you'd like to choose. But to do that, one needs to do the ethics calculus and develop a fully fleshed-out value system that resonates for them.

The other key point that I'm making is the notion that we've conflated a variety of natural experiences into the arena of pathology where they have become medicalized in the zeitgeist and language of our culture. However, this dynamic of medicalizing a natural process and then making it big business isn't new. The same thing happened with childbirth; for thousands of years, women practiced "social childbirth," where expectant mothers relied on female friends, family, and experienced midwives to help deliver the baby. Then in the seventeenth century, the nascent medical profession essentially hijacked the birthing process from women and midwives in what has been called the "medicalization of childbirth."[15] Now that once most natural of processes has evolved into the medicalized multibillion-dollar Childbirth industry that it is today—which is, in the vast majority of cases, entirely unnecessary.

Childbirth, like most of our daily mental health challenges, can best be addressed by the social model. We know from our earlier discussions about the importance of social connection in depression, as well as Dr. Robin Dunbar's work with groups and the optimal "Dunbar number" of a person having at least five friends. And we also know from Dr. Stephen Ilardi's depression research and the health of Blue Zone peoples that strong group and family social bonds are the most essential feature of a mentally healthy psychological profile.

It should also be pointed out that the ACES adversity model that was mentioned earlier fails to factor in one important variable: our ability to *cope* with adversity. And that coping ability is the by-product of a healthy psychological immune system that can only be developed by exposure to—you guessed it—adversity.

To use a medical metaphor: a healthy immune system becomes stronger when exposed to opportunistic bacteria and viruses, which are not, in and of themselves, the problem. The problem is the compromised immune system that can't handle those everyday and quite common opportunistic bacteria. For the weakened immune system, rather than strengthening one's defenses, they become deadly.

Unfortunately, in today's world, kids and teens are being robbed of the necessary adversity or stress that leads to well-developed coping capabilities and a healthy psychological immune system. Things such as enabling helicopter parents; or the dependency-forming and infantilizing therapy-industrial complex; and, of course, Bubble-Wrapping PC culture that has helped to create brittle, reactive, and perpetually offended fragile young adults who are entirely incapable of living in a world where (trigger warning: salty language ahead) *shit happens*.

It seems that twenty-first-century living has created a populace that simply can't bear—or can't handle—the slings and arrows of life. That's partly because tech-driven impulsivity is a critical ingredient in the "I can't cope" personality. Being impulsive correlates highly with all sorts of negative lifelong outcomes, including things like addiction disorders to unhealthy relationships. And, unfortunately, there's an abundance of peer-reviewed research that connects the digital age with impulsivity via instant-gratification feedback loops of screens and high-tech living.[16]

So adversity rather than Alexa, and *earning* certain rewards rather than push-button instant gratification, helps to build these necessary skills. These are issues that our parents and grandparents didn't have to deal with. I'm not saying that their lives were better—their lives were more *difficult* (for the most part), and in that difficulty, there was the wellspring of resilience, character, perseverance, and grit.

There's no need for me to compare storming the beaches at Normandy versus crafting a snarky tweet as a lifestyle contrast. Ah yes, I can hear the cries of "He's falling into that old trap of glorifying and romanticizing the past!"

Yes. I am.

In fact, that's one of the major points of this book: the digital age has stripped away certain critical and sanity-sustaining dynamics that once were prevalent and now no longer exist: We need experiences that nurture our ability to be patient. Instead, we have Twitter. We need real hand-eye experiences. Instead, we have gaming. We need face-to-face interpersonal social experiences. Instead, we have social media. We need nature-immersive experiences. Instead, we have some pics of nature on Instagram.

That just does *not* cut it if we want to be truly healthy, strong, and happy.

We've become depressed, instant-gratification vessels who haven't learned the fundamental life skill of patience. And, let's face it: Our age of *Alexa, do this* has also primed us for laziness. If you have everything done for you, it becomes a *real* drag to have to do *anything*. Not only are we primed for laziness, we're also digitally overstimulated, so that now we're also primed for boredom—like the acedia teens that I had mentioned earlier. *Boring*. Been there, done that. Sure, it may all be a fantasy metaverse experience, but you get the picture.

True Grit

We have to face it: We love our ease and comfort, but there's no denying that it's made us unhealthy, lazy, and easily bored. What can help cure these undesirable tendencies? What about this *grit* thing that we all keep hearing about? It's certainly been a much-talked-about buzzword—especially in the mental health and education fields. Is a person born with grit, or can they cultivate it?

When it comes to grit, Dr. Angela Duckworth is the expert; the University of Pennsylvania psychologist literally wrote the book on it.[17] She first became interested in this noncognitive variable when she was teaching math to seventh graders and noticed that IQ didn't always seem to determine who got the best grades.

She realized that there was another attribute, a key variable that she would come to define as "grit": *passion* and sustained *persistence* applied toward long-term achievement, with no particular concern for rewards or recognition along the way. It combines resilience, ambition, and self-control in the pursuit of goals that take months, years, or even decades.

But the two key ingredients were *passion* and *persistence*. She eventually developed a standardized "grit scale," a simple ten-question test to measure the "grit" variable. The test had questions like, "Setbacks don't discourage me. I don't give up easily," and "I finish whatever I begin." And depending on your answers, you would get your numerical grit grade.

But she also wanted to see if it was a good predictor out in the real world: Would people who score higher on her test do better in tough circumstances? She chose West Point cadets as her study group. Good choice, by the way, if you're looking to study something like grit—better to study West Point cadets than gamers at a gaming tournament.

Each cadet who enters West Point has to go through an arduous two-year admissions process. Yet, on average, three out of every hundred cadets drop out during a grueling six-week training period called "Beast Barracks." That's what got her curious—the fact that they would quit so quickly after such an arduous admissions process: "I was looking for a context in which people might be quitting too early," she says. "There's such a thing as quitting at the right time. But there's also such a thing as quitting on a bad day when you're discouraged and maybe shouldn't be making such a big decision."

So she gave cadets her grit scale and hypothesized that those with the highest score would be the least likely to quit and, conversely, those with a low grit score would be the most likely. And, sure enough, her hypothesis was confirmed—grit matters when you're trying to complete something that's really hard.

Duckworth discovered some interesting additional insights over the next twelve years while she continued to study West Point cadets

(11,258 cadets over the course of a decade). She found that grit was an important predictor of success—but it wasn't the *only* thing.

For example, during Beast Barracks, grit is crucial. "The grittier you are, the less likely you are to drop out during that very discouraging time," Duckworth explains. But during the entire four years at West Point, where classroom academics *and* physical training are instrumental, it was *cognitive ability* that was the strongest predictor of academic grades.

And finally, grit and physical ability played even a greater role than cognitive ability in determining who would eventually graduate from West Point in the four years as opposed to who might leave early. So we have the variables of grit, cognitive ability, and physical strength all playing significant roles in predicting success.

This research validates and coincides with the next chapter, where I describe that the ideal archetype for an individual to embrace thriving in our toxic digital age is that of the Philosopher-Warrior, which combines Duckworth's proven success ingredients (grit/passion/persistence), along with some additional time-tested ingredients all in one package: Wisdom. Strength. Grit. Resilience. Ethical discernment.

Before discussing that ancient archetype, there's one more essential ingredient.

Finding Meaning in a Meaningless World

Earlier we had mentioned that there is strength in the struggle. We see this in a variety of forms: people with physical differences who thrive and are more active than those without their challenges; people who overcome addictions and become better people as a result; immigrants of various origins who needed to persevere to succeed; and so on. Indeed, Auschwitz survivor and psychiatrist Viktor Frankl wrote about this strength through struggle in his seminal book *Man's Search for Meaning*, which, interestingly, had originally been titled *In Spite of Everything, Choose Life.*[18]

Frankl also identified one other key humanity-sustaining dynamic: the need for a sense of purpose and meaning in our lives. Which leads us to the final symptom in our ailing client, twenty-first-century Homo

Sapien, High-Tech Edition: a dearth of meaning and purpose in our day-to-day lives. But this is only true for *Homo sapiens* in the "modernized world," because, generally speaking, the indigenous twenty-first-century *Homo sapiens,* rarer and rarer as they may be, have been shown to not suffer from these issues.

Which is the crux of my thesis. The indigenous—and the ancient version of humanity—are our control group. We moderns are the experimental group. What happens to the species in the postindustrial information age? Not good things. Our DNA simply has not caught up to our dramatically new and different way of living. And, as the pioneering psychologist Carl Jung once said, modernity has, to our detriment, demystified our world; he believed, as I do, that we *need* our mysteries and our myths—they imbue sense into the senseless and meaning into the meaningless.

Those various creation myths and cosmological frameworks give us a sense of place and purpose in the universe. Otherwise, if we're just so many random atoms, haphazardly flitting about the cosmos—without any method to the madness—then what's it all mean? Why even get out of bed in the morning? Such is the stuff that existential crises and self-destructive addictions are made of—lost people who feel that their lives have no meaning or purpose in an otherwise hostile and random universe.

Yeah, it's a pretty bleak perspective, I agree. In the recovery world, they even have a saying for those holding hard to nihilistic despair: "Fake it till you make it" with regard to a spiritual belief system that you can hang your hat on. Because without some deeper and more meaningful conception for your life, well, why *not* drink?

On that note, gather around, because I've got a pretty compelling story to share about what can happen to a group of people who had lost all sense of purpose in their lives—and the transformative magic that occurred when they were inspired by someone to dream once again.

The Mad Polish Priest

I had first read about Father Bogusław Paleczny back in 2008. I had been vacationing with my family in Greece and flipping through the

International Herald Tribune newspaper (remember newspapers?), when I came across the story of this inspired man of the cloth who ran a homeless shelter, the St. Lazarus Social Pension, in Warsaw.[19]

By then, I'd been working as a clinician at a hospital drug and alcohol rehab as well as teaching the treatment of addiction at Stony Brook Medicine in New York. But I was experiencing some professional frustration with just how ineffective our best treatment methods were in helping people whose lives had fallen apart as a result of their addiction.

Successful long-term recovery rates are hard to accurately quantify, but according to some of the more reliable data, no more than one or two out of ten people who complete rehab will stay clean and sober for a year. Others have it at 5 percent. Regardless of whether it's 5 percent or 20 percent, the treatment industry has a lousy batting average. People relapse and, with drugs like fentanyl and OxyContin, fatal relapses of people just out of rehab are more and more common.

My first year working in a rehab was back in 2002, and over ten people that I had worked with—people that I had gotten to know, with whom I had bonded and had tried to help—relapsed and died soon after treatment. It was heartbreaking and began to take its toll on me. I was still relatively new in the field, and my own almost-fatal overdose wasn't that far behind me. I had the zeal and passion of the newly converted, but day in and day out, I kept seeing the bitter realities of addiction treatment and its unsuccessful outcomes. What were we missing? We had decades of research and best-practice treatment protocols, and yet we kept losing so many people.

That's why I was so struck when I read about the work of that Polish priest and the effect that it had on the men in his pension. Father Paleczny was no typical priest; yes, he was Roman Catholic and wore a black cassock marked with a red cross on his chest as the priests of the Order of St. Camillus all did. But he was different. He had been a working musician (even having toured in the United States), with a quick smile and kind face, but also the intense eyes of a man who could see things—I mean *really* see things.

He was one of those special people that you rarely encounter or hear about, who devoted every ounce of his being to helping other people. He ran an outdoor soup kitchen at the foot of Stalin's Palace of Culture and Science in downtown Warsaw; he also ran a free clinic at the end of an underground train platform and, of course, the St. Lazarus home—which he'd bought with his own money and then donated to the church. And he absolutely insisted that it be called a *home* rather than a *shelter.* As I said, he was a special man.

What caught my attention was the project that he had undertaken with his residents. You see, Father Paleczny would try to get to know and understand the lives of his residents—twenty-five life-hardened men who had drunk themselves into a bad situation. Some had been factory workers, others professionals with families. Regardless of their background, they were now without homes or any support and needed help.

What struck Father Paleczny was that they had all lost sight of any sort of a dream or future goal. When he would ask, "What's your dream? What would be your passion if you could do anything?" he typically got either blank stares or confused looks. Dreams? These were broken men who drank. Any semblance of a dream from their earlier lives had been vaporized in the distillery of their alcoholism. It became increasingly clear to him that the men needed a purpose in their lives—some sort of passion project that they could be inspired by and that would get them back and engaged with the world.

So he decided that they would build a ship and sail it around the world together.

Talk about a Hero's Journey! You can imagine how that suggestion went over when he proposed this radical idea to his world-weary denizens. As I said, this was no ordinary priest. He was charismatic, passionate, and persistent. Dr. Duckworth might even say that he had *grit.* So eventually, he got the men to buy into this crazy idea. Why not? What did they have to lose?

The idea to build a ship first came to Father Paleczny while he was hospitalized with tuberculosis. The man in the hospital bunk next to him had been a sailor—that's when he had his aha moment of inspiration. To many outside the pension, it seemed as if the priest had gone mad; take twenty-five men who had lost their way in life and couldn't stop drinking—and have them build a boat? And then have them sail around the world? It sounded like sheer lunacy.

Instead, it was sheer inspiration. And, as we'll see, a more effective treatment for alcoholism than any of the protocols that the finest addiction psychologists at places like Harvard could develop (with all due respect to my friend, Harvard's Dr. Howard Shaffer).

Father Paleczny contacted seventy-four-year-old Bogdan Malolepszy, the author of a shipbuilding book, and asked if he would donate plans for the men to build a boat. Malolepszy needed to meet the priest and see with his own eyes what the situation at St. Lazarus's was like: "When you walk into the mission premises, well, they have good conditions there, but the men, they walk around, they seem lost." Indeed, they were lost—that was entirely the problem. After meeting Father Paleczny and his men, the ship designer became a sympathetic believer in the Quixote-esque cause and agreed to help. "So I drew this design, and they started building it."

And build they did. When I had read the article in 2008, the men had been building a phoenix-rising, metal-hulled, mammoth, fifty-five-foot for three years. Materials weren't cheap, but as word spread of the mad priest and his homeless men, donations of money and material started pouring in. And good old Father Paleczny was always willing to put in whatever he had as well; when he couldn't persuade anyone to give him free steel for the hull, he negotiated the price down and paid the $27,000. When he needed nine tons of lead for the ship's ballast, he called foundries in Poland asking for donations until one, the White Eagle Ironworks, agreed. And so it went.

Now, you might be thinking, *So a quirky priest was building a Noah's Ark with twenty-five men living in a homeless shelter. What does that have to do with revolutionizing addiction treatment?*

I'm glad you asked.

What made me drop the newspaper into my coffee was that *none of the men had drunk* during the multiyear project. As one resident told the reporter, they finally had a purpose in their lives again—something to look forward to when they woke up in the morning.

We can do all the therapies we want—cognitive behavioral therapy, gestalt, dialectical behavioral therapy, trauma work, shame resilience theory—but none of that matters worth a damn unless we can help a person find a sense of purpose and passion again in their lives. We all need that animating force. Father Paleczny, a humble priest without any clinical training, understood that intuitively.

In the many years since I read about Father Paleczny, I've shared his story with hundreds of struggling addicts in both individual and group therapy settings, and I would then pose the question: "What's your boat? What can your purpose and passion project be in your life?" Over the years, I've had many clients tell me that the "Polish priest and his boat" story was the most meaningful and pivotal part of their entire treatment process.

If only Father Paleczny knew just how many people he's inspired—and maybe even some who read this book. The sad footnote to the story is that Father Paleczny died from a heart attack at age fifty, one year after I had first read about him. His men, grief-stricken but determined, kept building. They intended to finish the ship and name it after him. At the time of this writing, as I researched the Polish press, I was able to find an article from 2021. Sixteen years later, the boat was finally finished, after several years of COVID delays.

The dream, albeit delayed, lives.

Over three hundred people over the years worked to finish the priest's shared dream—including some of the original residents. This story highlights the critical role of having a sense of purpose in one's life. In essence, Father Paleczny created a Hero's Journey paradigm for his lost, empty, and adrift men. My work with addiction over the past twenty years has largely consisted of helping struggling addicts to reframe their challenges as the obstacle-laden course of the hero archetype in the Hero's Journey—and to then find a passion or goal that, in its pursuit and its attainment, can be life-altering and transformative.

And the people who understand this need for a sense of purpose better than almost anyone? Video game designers. Almost all gaming platforms are digitized avatar-based representations of the classic Hero's Journey. The only problem is that they're not real—they're just habit-forming illusions.

The real challenge in any effort to gain genuine soul-satisfying meaning in one's life is to, as mythologist Joseph Campbell famously said, *find your bliss.*

We've seen in this chapter some of the limitations and benefits of traditional therapy. And we've also read about the importance of grit and finding a sense of purpose in your life. But the problem is that our immersion into our screen lives acts like kryptonite on both our grit and any sense of genuine purpose and meaning in our lives. Think about it—getting lost on Instagram, or gaming, or getting sucked into TikTok or YouTube rabbit holes just weakens us, enables our sloth, and robs us of any purpose in our real lives. I don't want my passion to be a virtual adventure in the metaverse—thank you, but no, Mark Zuckerberg.

It's time to drop back into your life and take control of your own destiny and not leave it to Big Tech algorithms to shape your life.

It's time to become a Philosopher-Warrior.

11

The Philosopher-Warrior

The Tao of the Ancients

The sixteenth-century Renaissance author and sculptor Benvenuto Cellini wrote that a well-rounded person should be a philosopher, a warrior, and also an artist. Well, he had actually said a "well-rounded man" should be those three things, but for our purposes, we will accept that the language is dated and focus on the wisdom of these attributes being possessed by *all* people.[1]

Let us also begin to understand these attributes as not just vocations but as archetypes that are as old as the human condition itself. Some people may think of archetypes as universal symbols or motifs—which they are. In the Jungian psychological literature, we can think of them as representing universal themes or patterns that are part of a "collective unconscious" that Carl Jung believed that we all share.[2]

Jung also believed that archetypes are universal, inborn, and inherited—that we aren't born as blank slate "tabula rasas," but that we have the framework of archetypes prebaked from the factory in our collective human psyche to help us make sense of things. Indeed, in the original Greek, *archetype* literally means "original pattern," and we see that various consistent archetypes can express themselves through our art, mythology, politics, and any other aspect of human existence, across time and across all cultures. And while there can be an infinite number of archetypes, Jung did identify some central ones, like the archetype of the hero, the creator/artist, the sage, the rebel, and the jester.

I'd like to focus on the three that Cellini mentioned because I think that, collectively, those three forces—the creative force of the artist; the strength, bravery, and honor of the warrior; and the wisdom, reason, ethical discernment, and curiosity of the philosopher—are the attributes that the self-actualized person in twenty-first-century society needs to cultivate the most.

Think Spartan warrior mixed with Athenian philosopher (like Socrates or Plato), with a dash of creativity in the form of the music and poetry of Orpheus—or any other form of creative expression. Now, I just happen to mention some famous classical Greek examples of warrior, philosopher, and artist archetypes. But to be clear, if we look at every cultural tradition, we can find examples of these three archetypes in every part of the world: In traditional Japan, you had the samurai, the Zen monk, and the Kabuki performer. In Africa, you had the Zulu warrior, the collectivist philosophy of the Ubuntu, and the sub-Saharan art of wooden sculpture and masks.

We can also find these three archetypes throughout our popular culture as we look at everything from *Star Wars* (with the Jedi knight being a good example of the combined archetypes of philosopher/warrior) to the Marvel Cinematic Universe, as well as my favorite: *Star Trek*.

The reason why those never-ending Marvel movies are so popular is because they tap into our inherent need for archetypal and mythic experiences. Mythologist Joseph Campbell wrote at length about our human need for myth and archetype. In his seminal *The Hero with a Thousand Faces* (1949), he describes the classic hero archetype and the hundreds of manifestations that it's had in various cultures and mythologies.[3]

The issue is, as Carl Jung said in the last century, that we've "demystified" the world; we've relegated our creation myths and cultural narratives into the trash heap of fictions like Santa Claus and the tooth fairy. Still, we're psychologically hardwired to need those explanatory frameworks that act as a sort of lattice system that supports our sense of identity and purpose within the world. Without those frameworks, our collective identity can come crashing down—and the individual can feel lost, empty, untethered, and adrift.

In our highly secularized and technological world, we've lost our sense of place. That lattice framework of our ancestral mythologies that I've mentioned has been dismantled. But our *need* for it persists. Enter video games and Marvel movies—all archetypal Hero's Journeys writ small on our glowing devices. And they are multibillion-dollar businesses exactly because the people who make them understand our fundamental human need to have these archetypal experiences—which we're not getting anywhere else now.

Absent that, if I can't find my true sense of meaning within this overwhelming and highly mechanized society, which devalues the human spirit, then pass me the *Candy Crush* to mindlessly play, or social media to get sucked into. But what I really, really need is to find my inner strength and wisdom—not to get distracted or addicted by the siren song of my seductive flashing and tweeting devices.

Enter the Philosopher-Warrior-Artist. Earlier, I had mentioned that the attributes of those three archetypes are the strength, bravery, and honor of the warrior; the wisdom, reason, ethical discernment, and curiosity of the philosopher; and the creative force of the artist.

Let's break that down a bit.

First of all, what do I mean by a *philosopher*? Perhaps more importantly, what do we mean by philosophy? Old white men in togas discussing some dry intellectual esoterica? Far from it. While philosophy literally means the love of wisdom, the philosopher—at least in the original iteration—wasn't a person who *studied* the subject of philosophy, but instead was a person who *lived* their lives in the embodied pursuit of truth and in alignment with their highest values.

Philosophers sought to better understand the nature of our world (cosmology), the nature of being (ontology) and, in turn, our place within those frameworks. They looked up at the night sky in wonder and reflected on its very nature; they looked empirically at the natural world and tried to use deductive reasoning and drew logical inferences of how things functioned. And, perhaps most importantly of all, they asked the potentially most transformational question of all: Why?

So while scientists, who would evolve from the earliest empiricists like Aristotle, privileged observation of nature and natural phenomenon and asked the "how?" questions: How does a bird fly? How do cells reproduce? How does water evaporate?—philosophers wondered the *big* and oftentimes insoluble *why* (and *what*) questions of existence: Why am I here? What is my purpose? Why was the universe created? What is the "Good Life" for a human being? Some of the earliest philosophers like Socrates were mostly concerned with human affairs, and an exploration of things like ethics and what the "good life" truly means. Yet others, like Thales, Parmenides, Heraclitus, and Pythagoras were more concerned with the nature of reality itself.

It's really important here to note some historical and global context of that period while also acknowledging that focusing on the roots of classical Western thought may seem a bit Eurocentric. However, as noted earlier, ancient Greek thought was really an amalgam of Greek, African (Egyptian), and Middle Eastern thought as well.

Yet what is truly fascinating is that there was a global awakening that had been happening at around the same time (within an approximate 200-year period): In China, there was the development of philosophical precepts in the form of the Lao Tsu's *Tao Te Ching*, the scriptures that would illuminate "the Way," or the Tao of Taoism. This mysterious Way harmonizes the elemental forces of nature and the universe (symbolized by yin and yang) and describes the subtle universal *chi* energy and the practice of *wu wei*, a non-doing or "flowing" approach to existence. While in India at roughly the same time, Siddhartha Gautama, also known as the Buddha, was seeking enlightenment while sitting under a bodhi tree as he became "awakened" to the Four Noble Truths and the Noble Eightfold Path towards enlightenment, which would become the foundation of modern Buddhism.

This global awakening, which has been described as a shift from hundreds of thousands of years of fear and superstition, has also been called the Axial Age4 (a period from 800 to 200 BCE)—a time in human history where the earth seemingly shifted on its axis as humans across the globe discovered not only new paradigms by which to understand their universe, but new ways to conceptualize their purpose or role within that world.

Human beings as hardwired thinking machines had, for hundreds of thousands of years, tried to make sense of an often seemingly senseless and very hostile environment. Indeed, for most of human history, people relied on superstition, witchcraft, and other often irrational sources, like deified tribal rulers or mind-altered shamans, in order to understand nature and their own existence.

But during the Axial Age, a shift toward new understanding occurred; now, some might say that some of these new shifts still had a religious or "magical thinking" aspect; is there really a subtle *chi* force that the Tao describes? And after all, isn't Buddhism a form of religion as well? Yes and no; most scholars tend to view Buddhism as a set of ideas that have been called an "applied religious philosophy," while others consider it more of a psychological construct.

And here is where we get into the gray area between philosophy, religion and science, perhaps best described by the eminent academic, philosopher and mathematician Bertrand Russell in his seminal *A History of Western Philosophy* (1945)[5]:

"Philosophy…is something intermediate between theology and science. Like theology, it consists of speculations on matters to which definite knowledge has, so far, been unascertainable; but like science, it appeals to human reason rather than to authority, whether that of tradition or that of revelation. All *definite* knowledge…belongs to science; all *dogma* as to what surpasses definite knowledge belongs to theology. But between theology and science is a No Man's Land, exposed to attack from both sides; this No Man's Land is philosophy."

In other words, philosophy, religion, and science are all trying to get to knowledge or what we may call the *deeper truths*—they just use different tools (i.e., scientific method, scripture, reason, etc.) in getting there.

And that's where the philosophers of the classical era were different. Their pursuit (or "love") of wisdom entailed the use of reason and critical thinking, not superstition or dogma or any other belief system. For the first time, observation and deductive reasoning were used to provide rational descriptions and explanations of the natural world, and logic and rational analysis were used to explore aspects of human life as well as the unseen world…things like mathematics, cosmology, concepts of truth…all were now re-examined by the lens of reason and rational analysis.

So what did they conclude about the essence of being human?

Plato, who is considered the foundational philosopher for all Western thought, believed that there were three elements of the human psyche: appetite, reason, and spirit. Even though today we understand psyche to mean the conscious and unconscious aspects of the mind, the ancient Greek etymology of the word *psyche* translates as "soul," although we can choose to look at this as a secularized soul as Plato predates any current theological constructs (although is believed to have influenced the early Christian conception of the soul).

The "appetite" part of ourselves is self-explanatory; it is all our id-like primal desires for food, sex, and sensory reward. These baser needs we share with the animals; but what elevated us above our beastly friends was our capacity for reason. This rational quality, combined with reflection, could save us from the impulses of our appetites.

As Plato describes it in his magnum opus *The Republic*: "We shall have good reason, then, to assert that there are two distinct principles. We may call that part of the soul whereby it reflects, rational; and the other, with which it feels hunger and thirst and is distracted by sexual passion and all the other desires, we will call irrational appetite, associated with pleasure and the replenishment of certain wants."[6]

Today, we live in a world that's a nonstop seductive assault on the senses; a 24-7, all-you-can-eat buffet of digital feel-goods geared towards our "appetites." Forget the occasional carnal desire of yesteryear; now there are literally millions of digital seductions at your fingertips. How can we fend off such temptation?

According to Plato: reason and honor.

Today, we think of the "good life" as a consumer paradise of material success—or is it excess? But for Plato, the "good life" meant the mastery of the appetites so that moderation, or "temperance," could be achieved by self-control through the application of reason and honor. Yes, Socrates had famously said that the "unexamined life is not worth living," privileging a reflection of one's life and values, but Plato believed that the reflective life wasn't enough. The individual needed their sense of reason to rein in their passions with an eye toward the collective common good—that is, self-absorbed navel-gazing isn't the best use of one's life if they don't have their vices in check enough in order to help the community.

Here the idea of "reason" is also a complex one. The Ancient Greeks were said to be the founders of rationalism and logic, all considered ingredients in what we may call reason. And, sure enough, using logic and syllogisms can help clarify and illuminate the most noble of pursuits—the truth. Indeed, the original philosophers developed entire systems of analysis to discern what they felt was incontrovertible reality, and not a reality obfuscated by things like our easily tricked senses or persuasive rhetoric or the charms of fallacious sophistry.

In the classical era, sophistry was the "fake news" of the day, and rhetoric, was, well, rhetoric; it's used to persuade, but not necessarily to get at the truth. So developing a keen sense of reason via logic and *critical thinking*, which was defined by Socrates as the careful and systematic questioning of assertions or beliefs, *that* was how a person could cut through all the noise and reach the clarity and illumination of truth—both practical, day-to-day truth and a deeper transcendent truth.

Transcendent truth? Yes, because *reason*, according to Plato, was also more than just being practical and rational; reason also had a transcendent quality because it was the conduit toward eternal and objective truths (think mathematics). And beyond math, he believed there was an entire realm of eternal truths—the realm of *ideal forms*—these were eternal ideas and concepts that predated not only humanity but time itself.

A quick example: most of the world plays some sort of sport with a spherical ball—let's choose basketball for this thought exercise. In order to manufacture basketballs at a factory, some human being had to, at one time, be able to conceptualize the shape of a sphere. Now according to Plato, that person accessed the eternal idea of the form of a sphere from the realm of ideal forms—an eternal and non-corporeal place where all ideas are believed to exist—by our ability to use reason (i.e., reason in the form of our knowledge of mathematics that reveals the realities of a sphere). In this context then, *reason* can be understood as the fishing pole that one could use for deeper metaphysical exploration to access transcendent truths.

That's the metaphysical aspect of reason; but as far as our earlier discussion regarding our baser impulses, *reason* and *honor* are also the brakes to the gas pedal of our appetites; reason in the form of a reflective critical analysis of the cause-and-effect of our actions, and *honor* by placing our actions in a larger social contract, rather than just via the lens of an egocentric impulse. Unfortunately, we don't hear a lot about "honor" in the mental health field these days—we're too busy being lectured about "shame" and "trauma."

Yet for Plato, however, it was the key to sanity, sense, coherence, identity, and community. In the preceding context, honor has nothing to do with *pride,* which is a fool's game of personal conceit. Instead, honor has a collective and social context—one earns a sense of honor by doing right for the society or the familial group. I feel *proud* that I go to that great job, but I feel *honored* when I have done well for my entire community. And in Plato's terminology, "spirit" was an embodiment of this sense of collective honor.

Thus, for Plato, the path toward sanity was clear:

> It will be the business of reason to rule with wisdom and forethought on behalf of the entire soul; while the spirited element ought to act as its subordinate and ally. The two will be brought into accord . . . by that combination of mental and bodily training which will tune up one string of the instrument and relax the other, nourishing the reasoning part on the study of noble literature and allying the other's wildness by harmony and rhythm. . . . When both have been thus nurtured and trained to know their own true functions, they must be set in common over the appetites, which form the greater part of each man's soul and are by nature insatiably covetous.

And if reason and honor (spirit) can't keep these "insatiably covetous" appetites in check? Disaster.

"They must keep watch lest this part, by battening on the pleasures that are called bodily, should grow so great and powerful that it will no longer be able to keep to its own work, but will try to enslave the others and usurp a dominion to which it has no right, thus turning the whole life upside down."

Sounds a lot like addiction or any other impulse disorder.

Plato's use of analogizing a healthy human being to a tuned instrument is also consistent with the Pythagorean view. Pythagoras also believed that we needed to tune ourselves like a stringed lyre of the day, and we did that by a combination of meditative, musical, and physical daily practices—along with a moderate and balanced lifestyle. Like Plato, Pythagoras was also a fan of the virtues of moderation.

* * *

On a macro level, we can understand that various societies have warriors who tend to physically train, embrace an honor code, and do all the fighting for that society. Then there is the cerebral class: the group of thinkers who are the academics, philosophers, scientists, and ethicists. And, finally, the lovable (and often tortured) artists: the musicians, the poets, the artists, and the writers who comprise the soul and voice of that society. Together, those three groups (along with other groups, of course) collectively create a balanced whole that can sustain itself and thrive.

My suggestion is that we take those archetypes that exist within a healthy society and, as Plato suggested, embrace those characteristics as *individuals* so that we can be in balance and thrive within a challenging and imbalanced society—as ours currently is.

We need to find our inner warrior (because it's a tough world out there); we need to cultivate our inner philosopher (because it's an irrational and insane world that we're currently living in), and, finally, we also need to discover our inner artist (because it's a soulless and dehumanizing, high-tech world out there), so we need to stay in touch with our creativity and humanity.

Like a three-legged stool, we need all three legs to optimally function. In our modern digital madness, we need to embrace the mindset of the warrior: to be both physically and mentally strong—maybe even have some of Dr. Duckworth's grit—and also possess a sense of honor and integrity.

But the characteristics of the warrior, as stand-alone traits, just aren't enough in today's world. You can be physically strong, but without mental toughness—or grit—or a philosopher's wisdom—what do you have? A brute. And what about just having grit? Well, even Duckworth's research showed that in itself wasn't enough—cognitive (philosopher) and physical strength were also needed.

When you think about it, you can be gritty and strong—and even smart. But if you lack ethical discernment, then what do you have? Well, there are many criminals who are gritty, strong, and smart, but they lack the moral compass to thrive. And to be clear, when we are talking about the "warrior" archetype, we are not talking about violence; we are talking about strength and a certain amount of intestinal fortitude. By that definition, I think it would be fair to call someone like Stephen Hawking or Jane Goodall a Philosopher-Warrior.

One can also be a pacifist *spiritual* warrior. According to Tibetan Buddhism, the term *spiritual warrior* refers to a heroic being with a brave mind and ethical impulse who combats the universal enemy: self-ignorance, the ultimate source of suffering according to Buddhist philosophy.

On the flip side, if one embraces only the attributes of the philosopher and is keen on reason, ethical discernment, and curiosity—but lacks the strength and grit to act on their wisdom and intellectual insights—then what do you have? A person of inaction. As we mentioned earlier in the book, many scientists possess the curiosity and the intellect, but they have not been exposed to ethical discernment—then what might you have? Well, what we have today: scientists conducting all manner of dangerous and potentially unethical and immoral research in the furtherance of their scientific curiosity—or egos.

The theme here is that we need to be *both* the warrior—strong people of action—*and* the philosopher—thoughtful, rational, and ethical. In understanding just how much we need both our cerebral and our action side working in concert, I'm reminded how that theme was explored in that bottomless trough of profound wisdom: *Star Trek*.

In the original series (the Kirk and Spock series from 1966), there was an episode called "The Enemy Within," where our dashing Captain Kirk gets split into two versions of himself by a faulty transporter beam. The one version is "good" and ethical, but indecisive and ineffectual; the other is "evil," impulsive, and irrational—but takes action. Guess what the moral of the story is? Neither version was able to survive without the other—they had to re-merge Good Kirk and Shadow Kirk to get one whole, healthy Kirk.[7]

And what about the artist—why is that archetype relevant for the ideal twenty-first century Philosopher-Warrior? Creativity is believed by many to come from a transcendent source beyond the individual. Some may disagree with that perspective, even though most artists do indeed say that their art comes from outside of themselves—or is a channel to deeper truth. Regardless, at the very least, opening the creative channel allows for a healthier and more expansive way of being. Indeed, there are several Ph.D. engineering programs that now require their doctoral students to take art classes—because doing so nurtures more creative and outside-the-box type of thinking. Similarly, if you want to be an empowered and happy Philosopher-Warrior, then you need to find an access point into your creativity. In the treatment world, we also know that this can be profoundly healing.

The idea of the Philosopher-Warrior is to train yourself mentally, physically, philosophically and ethically to be able to deal with this surreal new landscape that we're all now living in that's filled with moral tripwires and disorienting information and misinformation overload. Just as Morpheus had to train Neo so he could combat the forces of the Matrix, we, too, need to get ourselves in optimum shape . . . because the illusion is becoming reality, reality is being recast as the illusion and the metaverse is accepting passengers. That's why it's imperative that the closer we get to the *Singularity*, the more we need to embrace our humanity—both the philosopher *and* the warrior.

To better illustrate this "fully human" dynamic tension that exists between the archetype of the warrior as a *person of action* and that of the philosopher as that of the *overthinker,* there is an iconic film that can be very illuminating regarding how we need *both* in order to thrive.

The Zorba Conundrum

Ever since I read Nikos Kazantzakis's classic *Zorba the Greek,* his tour de force on the human condition—and his meditation on the life well lived—I've reflected on the dynamic tension between his two protagonists. We have the book's eponymous protagonist, Zorba—all id, passion, and fiery impulse—and the cerebral, pensive, lost-in-his-books unnamed narrator; a man who embodies the axiom "paralysis by overanalysis."[8]

Both extremes are fraught with peril; the drug addict lives on impulse, and the hates-his-life cubicle drone also suffers the cruel fate of those who can dream but can't make the leap into action to attain those dreams. The world is littered with the sad carcasses of both extreme archetypes: the hungry ghost and the scared mouse.

It seems that the truly actualized and happy have the passion of a Zorba as an animating force (i.e., grit/Spartan warrior), lest they atrophy and wither away from inaction. Yet they also use the sword of reason and a sense of duty and honor to mitigate that animating force so as to not self-destruct on impulse alone (the philosopher).

So where does happiness live? In the novel, Zorba comes across a very old man who is planting an olive tree. Zorba mocks him for wasting his time: "Old man, you'll never live to see that tree grow!" The old man responds, "I live each day as if I'll live forever." Zorba replies, "I live each day as if it's my last!" Zorba recounts that story to his friend, the cerebral narrator, and asks, "Which one of us is right?"

At the end of the day, don't both the "live forever" believer and the "live for today" hedonist wind up in the same place? Don't they both do their version of carpe diem and seize the day?

Speaking of Zorba, I had the opportunity to meet my own real-life Zorba—a living, breathing, and belching embodiment of that fully human archetype that embraced passion as well as the concept of duty and honor. He was also a living example of both Blue Zone and Kaluli living. He came in a somewhat grizzled package, but he remains an inspiration—and a powerful embodiment example of some of the ideals discussed in this book.

Zorba Revisited: Cousin Maki's Blue Zone

When I first met him, our family called him "crazy cousin Maki." My then sixty-four-year-old cousin lived off the grid on his own sustainable compound on my mother's island of Kefalonia in the middle of the Ionian Sea.

How best to describe Maki? Picture the wild-eyed passion of Anthony Quinn's Zorba, in a body made strong and solid by decades working his farm and tending to his flock: sheep, chickens, goats, rabbits, mules, and his beloved bees! "The bees, Niko! Others are dying—but I know how to keep mine alive!" he would exclaim with a mad gleam in his eye.

While his body was solid and strong, it was far from the chiseled shape of an Olympian's; rather, he had the stoutness of an old and impenetrable stone wall. And big, wide strong hands made hard by years of working in soil, dry brush, and ancient rocks.

His black, curly hair was just beginning to show wisps of gray now that he was in his sixties. He tended to wear the same clothes: an open short-sleeved shirt, with several buttons undone to give his broad shoulders and chest room to move and breathe. As a traditional Greek, he shunned shorts; even on the hottest of days, he would wear his trousers and black leather belt with strong work shoes made for the fields.

I always knew him as "crazy Maki," the mad cousin who produced his own cheese, olive oil, wine, honey, vegetables, and bread. He even made his own windmill with his bare hands, and the kiln that would bake the most amazing bread was also made by his own hand from clay that he dug out from his rocky property.

He was fiercely proud that he needed no outside support to survive. And he loathed the local corrupt government, which was endlessly trying to tax his land and, at one point, forced him to trade some of his beloved sheep to keep the tax collector at bay. He was green and sustainable before those words existed in common usage. It's fair to say that Maki lived in a similar fashion to the way that my father had lived in his remote village back in the 1930s and '40s.

Kefalonia is a breathtaking combination of ocean, sky, and mountains; a beautiful island with a notorious fiercely independent population. Having survived the Moors, Turks, French, British, Italians, and Nazi occupations—not to mention a devastating earthquake in 1953 that killed thousands and destroyed the entire island except for the northern port village of Fiskardo—well, all those things engender a sense of resilience, strength, and independence.

Not to mention the fact that Kefalonians consider themselves the direct descendants of Odysseus. This has led to a semi-friendly feud with the neighboring island of Ithaca, the land that Homer had said in the Iliad was Odysseus's home. But not so fast, say the Kefalonians. Not only is there some archaeological evidence that seems to suggest that Kefalonia was where Odysseus called home; more significantly, the geological evidence strongly suggests that Kefalonia and Ithaca were one island before a catastrophic earthquake cleaved them into two islands.

Even though the sun may have set on the glory that was ancient Greece, something of that rich culture of those mythical warriors and philosophers still twinkles in the psyche and DNA of modern Greeks: a certain quality of independence, resilience, curiosity, and ingenuity.

No wonder that Kefalonians are fierce, independent—and a bit off-the-grid crazy—like the proverbial fox. And so my cousin Maki has spent his entire life on the island, in the village of Dorizata, next to my mother's village of Pessada, the scenic port town where the ferry for neighboring Zakynthos departs daily. While Maki dug in his heels and created his compound in Kefalonia, his brother felt wanderlust and became a sailor; first the captain of that small Zakynthos ferry, then later, larger freighters that would travel to Russia and other Baltic ports.

But Maki stayed.

While I was a boy in the U.S., he was always referred to by my parents as crazy cousin Maki, whom my mother had feuded with for over thirty years because she had dared to call him a communist. He wasn't a communist. He wasn't anything. He just didn't want to play the game and was living off his land.

I had tended to avoid him during my frequent visits to Kefalonia because he could be rather . . . intense. Strong of opinion, loud in voice, but always loving. But when my organic and quite progressive New York wife heard that I had a cousin who had honeybees, baked his own bread . . . pressed his own olive oil . . . made his own cheese!

This was beyond her wildest dreams! She had been researching on the internet for sustainable adventure tours—so not only was she thrilled to hear that I had such a creature in my family tree right on the island of my heritage—she absolutely insisted that we go and that the kids should bring baking aprons.

But this was crazy cousin Maki! I protested. I'd been successfully avoiding these visits with this tornado of a human being for many years. Not this time. After we arrived on Kefalonia, my wife made the call, and Maki wanted everyone to be at his place ready to bake bread by 6:00 A.M. sharp! Quite conveniently, I was on deadline writing my last book and recused myself from that early-morning start time, agreeing to circle by there for lunch.

And I was the fool who'd missed out. When I got there, my twin sons, Ari and Alexi, all of nine years old, had smiles from ear to ear and twenty-one freshly baked loaves of the sweetest-smelling bread stacked up in wicker baskets in front of Maki's primordial-looking kiln.

Maki's wife set the table for lunch, and as he slapped his big hand behind my neck, he pulled my face close to his and said, "Now you are going to eat real food. Food that you can't find in that America of yours. All of it is grown right here. All of it is more full of taste and nutrients than you can ever find over there. Taste and tell me if there is food like that in America."

He was right. There was something special about that meal, and about his place. Mind you, this was no manicured Shangri-la; this was a working compound, where there were several structures that were unique inventions of his own design. So there was a quirky, unfinished, mad-scientist quality to his home—but something quite special nonetheless.

My kids and I helped him gather brush to feed the animals and looked at his olive oil press. As a psychologist, I had worked with many neurotic, sometimes quite insane people back home in the States, so I like to think that I know something about insanity. As I sat there with the sun setting at Maki's compound, he wasn't looking so crazy to me anymore.

He kept looking at me with a wide smile and used his razor-sharp sense of humor to playfully poke fun at me, his American cousin. And I poked back as everyone laughed. It was a peaceful and satisfying evening, on a level that I rarely, if ever, had experienced in my native New York.

As I sat there on his veranda, I looked at a man—hard and grizzled—who was happy and content. His happiness was not the silly smile and fool's gold of the ignorant; as an autodidact, he knew more about politics, engineering, philosophy, and human dynamics than most college professors. Yet he had been able to embrace a joyous way of living in spite of the physical hardships of his life—or maybe because of them—that was at once fully present and appreciative of the moment, while also allowing his mind to reflect on matters both mundane and profound.

I thought about my wealthy, successful—and quite miserable—clients back in my private practice in the Hamptons, and began to ask myself: Who's really crazy? A content Maki who will live a healthy and long life well into his nineties (like all of our relatives in Greece)—or those of us who chose the rat race, who are like Sisyphus, chasing our unattainable tails as we go to a variety of specialists to address a host of modern-living ailments?

In addition to Maki, I had my own natural Blue Zones experiment within my family: I had three uncles who moved to New York when they were in their thirties back in the 1960s to chase the American dream. All three worked seven days a week in difficult manual labor jobs. Two of them died at the age of fifty-two (heart disease, cancer) before they could even enjoy the fruits of all their hard work. But my third uncle, Dionysius, who had originally come with them and had been their business partner, decided he had had enough of the so-called American dream and moved back to Kefalonia forty years ago.

Today, he's the healthiest, happiest eighty-five-year-old in his village. He's physically fit, has many friends, takes daily long walks, and is involved in the local politics of the village and couldn't be happier. When I ask him if he misses New York, he looks at me and smiles in the same way that an adult smiles at a naive child when asked a foolish question. He smiles as his eyes glint at me as if to say, "Silly boy!"

There was something restorative and healing for Uncle Dionysius when he moved back to the island of his birth and decided to live a simpler, more natural life.

I'm reminded of one more Maki story that can help illustrate how he embodies certain important traits. The summer before COVID, my family and I were in Greece and stopped by to visit him, when something quite amazing happened. The Ionian Islands get very, very hot and dry by mid-August. So, like California, sudden and aggressive wildfires are fairly common. As we were sitting on his veranda one crystal-clear yet breezy night, a large plume of fire about sixty feet high erupted about two hundred yards from his house.

As my wife and I began to rustle our kids together and make sense of the situation, we looked up and saw that the fire had already raced another one hundred feet toward us—the breezy evening was making this fire move faster than any of us had anticipated.

Before I could call, "Maki!," I heard a roar come up from behind me. It was Maki on his ancient motorcycle, with all of its Steve McQueen circa *The Great Escape* glory. Exhaust fumes belched. Dirt kicked up and rocks flew as he came zooming up the road like some misfit Greek island superhero, roared past us, and disappeared straight into the heart of the thickets where the fire was raging, only about one hundred yards away.

Was he mad? Who would drive into that situation? We gathered the kids and shuttled everyone farther up the road away from the spreading fire; a few minutes later, a soot-faced Maki came roaring back: he had untied his animals and moved them all up to safety to higher ground. Duty. Honor. Reason.

"Crazy" Maki knew exactly what he was doing after all—and had the life force to quickly jump into action and act on that plan. He remains a happy man, albeit with several fewer acres—but with his animals and his sanity intact.

Maki lives an organic and healthy life, intuitively incorporating certain ancient—and now scientifically proven—lifestyle elements in his daily routine. Below I've listed some wellness tips inspired by both the ancients that can help us all live a more natural and grounded life—while also nurturing the traits of the Philosopher-Warrior.

OLD-SCHOOL WISDOM: ANCIENT WELLNESS TIPS INSPIRED BY PLATO AND PYTHAGORAS

Start each day with a quiet reflective or contemplative walk.

Pythagoras believed that people needed to take some time each morning to center themselves before engaging with other people: "It was essential to not meet anyone until their own soul was in order and they were composed in their intellect."

Take several minutes each evening to look up at the night sky and just . . . wonder.

Plato is quoted as saying that "all philosophy begins in wonder." Indeed, the ancient Greeks were obsessed with cosmology—the study of the nature of the universe. When we search the heavens with contemplative awe, an amazing shift can happen inside us.

To paraphrase Spike Lee: "Do the right thing."

The Greeks believed that character mattered. It was essential to live an honest and esteemable life of integrity and virtue. They believed that to achieve our highest potential, we need to live correctly. We all know in most instances what the "right thing" is; Pythagoras and Plato believed that we must act on that knowledge and then *do* the right thing.

Make it a point to do a dialectic each day where you challenge your own assumptions about a subject—anything really, politics, science, the arts—and reexamine what your values and beliefs are about that subject.

As NYU Professor Jonathon Haidt has done with his Heterodoxy Academy, spend time with people with differing perspectives and allow them to question you as you as you also question your own beliefs. In this question-and-answer *elenchus*, you may find a deeper truth than you had realized. Just as in the Hegelian dialectic, the coming together of two opposing ideas (*thesis* and *anti-thesis*) can come together to form a new more integrated *synthesis* closest to the truth.

Do a five-minute music meditation each day where you listen to stringed, nonvocal music; attempt to "experience" the music in a nonrational way. In fact, try to become the music.

Pythagoras believed that the entire universe was vibrational and that we, as humans, could be "tuned" to be in sync with that larger rhythm. For that reason, his disciples would listen to the music/vibration of the lyre as a means to retune themselves.

Do thirty to forty-five minutes of physical exercise every day.

Since the Pythagoreans viewed the body as being analogous to a musical instrument that needed to be properly tuned via the mind/body "purification" of philosophy, they included daily physical exercise like running, wrestling, and so on as part of their holistic practice.

Make it a point to have one lively and engaged in-person discussion every day with at least one (preferably more) people about any topic that you're passionate about.

The Greeks were big on spontaneous conversations in the town square about things that interested them. Socrates would wander Athens and engage with almost anyone, as other groups would gather around lunch or outdoors.

Value moderation in everything.

Again, since the metaphysical philosophers felt that the mind/body is our purest instrument, Plato and Pythagoras felt that we needed to treat it accordingly.

Do something creative every day.

Pythagoras and his followers played the lyre daily. But creativity, which nourishes the psyche, can be in almost any form. Just allow your mind some time each day to break free from the structure of routine as it wanders and creates something—perhaps even inspired from somewhere outside of yourself.

Be a mentor or be mentored—and honor that relationship.

Mentoring was and is the name of the game. Socrates mentored Plato, who mentored Aristotle. In those relationships, there is a mutually beneficial symbiosis that can allow you to achieve the highest human value—helping another human being.

So where does all of this leave us?

Resistance Is *Not* Futile

I freely concede that we have achieved wondrous advancements in the sciences and in our technological abilities. But our *species* is deteriorating; we're getting weaker, both physically and mentally. Sure, science can extend our life spans; but we have become so technology-dependent that our own capabilities, health, and development have eroded. Thinner screens, unhealthier people. More information, less wisdom. Tech-precocious kids who have "seen it all," yet grow into thirty-five-year-old quasi-men still living in their mom's basements, stuck in perpetual adolescence.

The question that will be answered in the near future is what will happen after a collision between two forces: the collision of humanity with an evolving and intelligent technology—a technology that's been made by our own hand.

How we survive that collision—if we survive it—and what action we take to reclaim our control over what we have created will determine our future.

It's not too late. Using the ancient tools that are our legacy, we can dim our screens, escape our digital cages, and recover our physical, emotional, and mental health.

I hope this book will help others to do so, as others have helped me.

ACKNOWLEDGMENTS

This book was not easy for me to write. The world was falling apart as I wrote it, my parents had died, and the topics covered were sometimes very depressing. But if this book is about the turbulence of the modern age and the need for resilience, honor, grit, and passion to do the meaningful work that's needed, then it's been a wonderful yet difficult process.

This book has also been a very personal experience because I deeply felt my mother and father as I wrote it and was reminded again and again about the importance of honoring those who came before us, loved us, and showed us the way. Of course, all my gratitude and love go to my wife, Luz, the woman who inspires me and who has a warmth and strength that I so admire. And my two growing sons, soon to be men—they are growing up in surreal and difficult times—I can only hope that I can be there to lend my love and support along their journey.

My eternal gratitude to my extremely bright and dedicated agent, Adam Chromy—he took my vision and helped bring it to life. And to my extremely patient, kind, and insightful editor—George Witte. His understanding and cooperation were invaluable. Also a sincere thanks to my friends and coworkers along the way—hopefully, we helped each other through this life as well as this extraordinary period of time.

And my sincere wish for a better, healthier, more reflective, and more cooperative era ahead. Thank you all.

NOTES

CHAPTER 1: ADDICTED TO THE MATRIX

1. Matt Bailey, "What Mark Zuckerberg Really Means When He Talks About the Metaverse," *Slate,* October 28, 2021.
2. James Barrat, *Our Final Invention* (New York: St. Martin's Press, 2019), pp. 151–160.
3. Thor Benson, "If This Era of Automations Mirrors the Past, We're in Trouble," *Inverse,* January 29, 2020.
4. Sascha Brodsky, "How Self-Driving Cars Can Be Hacked," *Lifewire,* February 26, 2021.
5. Reza Zafarini, Mohammed Al Abassi, Huan Liu, *Social Media Mining* (Boston: Cambridge University Press, 2014).
6. Kate O'Flaherty, "Amazon, Apple, Google Eavesdropping: Should You Ditch Your Smart Speaker?," *Forbes,* February 26, 2020.
7. Amber Dance, "The Shifting Sands of 'Gain of Function' Research," *Nature,* October 27, 2021.
8. Adrianna Rodriguez, "Screen Time Among Teenagers During Covid More Than Doubled Outside of Virtual School, Study Finds," *USA Today,* November 1, 2021.
9. Matthias Pierce et al., "Mental Health Before and During Covid-19 Pandemic: A Longitudinal Probability Sample Survey of the U.K. Population," *Lancet* 7, no. 10 (July 21, 2020): 883–892.
10. Meilan Solly, "Humans May Have Been Crafting Stone Tools for 2.6 Million Years," *Smithsonian,* June 4, 2019.

11. Francesco Berna et al., "Microstratiagraphic Evidence of In Situ Fire in the Acheulean Strata of Wonderwerk Cave, Northern Cape Province, South Africa," *Proceedings of the National Academy of Sciences of the United States of America* 109, no. 20 (May 15, 2012): 1215–1220.
12. Shoshana Zuboff, *The Age of Surveillance Capitalism* (New York: PublicAffairs, 2019).
13. David Meyer, "Facebook Is 'Ripping Apart' Society, Former Executive Warns," *Fortune,* December 12, 2017.
14. *The Social Dilemma,* directed by Jeff Orlowski (Boulder, CO: Exposure Labs, 2020).
15. Ibid.
16. Olivia Solon, "Ex-Facebook President Sean Parker: Site Made to Exploit Human 'Vulnerability,'" *Guardian,* November 9, 2017.
17. Georgia Wells et al., "Facebook Knows Instagram Is Toxic for Teen Girls, Company Shows," *Wall Street Journal,* September 14, 2021.
18. Rana Foroohar, *Don't Be Evil* (Redfern, NSW, Australia: Currency, 2019).
19. Kate Conger, "Google Removes 'Don't Be Evil' Clause from Its Code of Conduct," *Gizmodo,* May 18, 2018.
20. Nicholas Kardaras, "Our Digital Addictions Are Killing Our Kids," *New York Post,* May 19, 2018.
21. Kent C. Berridge et al., "Pleasure Systems in the Brain," *Neuron* 86, no. 3 (May 6, 2015): 646–664.
22. Rita Goldstein and Nora Volkow, "Dysfunction of the Prefrontal Cortex in Addiction: Neuroimaging Findings and Clinical Implications," *Nature Reviews Neuroscience* 12, no. 11 (October 20, 2011): 652–669.
23. Anna Lembke, *Dopamine Nation* (New York: Dutton, 2021).
24. M. J. Koepp et al., "Evidence for Striatal Dopamine Release During a Video Game," *Nature,* 393 (May 21, 1998): 266–268.
25. S. H. Gage et al., "Rat Park: How a Rat Paradise Changed the Narrative of Addiction," *Addiction* 114, no. 5 (May 2019): 917–922.
26. Bruce Alexander, "Addiction: The View from Rat Park," Bruce K. Alexander, 2010, https://www.brucekalexander.com/articles-speeches/rat-park/148-addiction-the-view-from-rat-park.

27. Salvador Rodriguez, "Facebook Teaming Up with Ray Ban Maker for First Smart Glasses in 2021," NBCNews.com, September 16, 2020.
28. Hannah Towey, "Mark Zuckerberg Said He Wanted to Transform Facebook from a Social Media Company into a 'Metaverse Company,'" *Business Insider,* July 22, 2021.

CHAPTER 2: A WORLD GONE MAD

1. Matthias Pierce et al., "Mental Health Before and During Covid-19 Pandemic: A Longitudinal Probability Sample Survey of the U.K. Population," *Lancet* 7, no. 10 (July 21, 2020): 883–892.
2. Stacy Simon, "Obesity Rates Continue to Rise Among Adults in the U.S.," American Cancer Society, April 6, 2018.
3. William Haseltine, "Cancer Rates Are on the Rise in Adolescents and Young Adults New Study Shows," *Forbes,* December 9, 2020.
4. "Physical Inactivity a Leading Cause of Disease and Disability Warns WHO," World Health Organization, April 4, 2002.
5. "U.S. Obesity Rates Reach Historic Highs—Racial, Ethnic and Geographic Disparities Continue to Persist," Trust for America's Health, 2019.
6. "Rates of New Diagnosed Cases of Type 1 and Type 2 Diabetes Continue to Rise Among Children, Teens," Centers for Disease Control and Prevention, 2020.
7. Adrianna Rodriguez, "Screen Time Among Teenagers During Covid More Than Doubled Outside of Virtual School, Study Finds," *USA Today,* November 1, 2021.
8. Robert Preidt, "Heart Disease Is World's No. 1 Killer," WebMD, December 10, 2020.
9. "Morbidity and Mortality Report," Center for Disease Control and Prevention, 2020.
10. "Why 'Deaths of Despair' Are Rising in the U.S.," Harvard School of Public Health, November 26, 2019.
11. Jamie Ballard, "Millennials Are the Loneliest Generation," YouGovAmerica, July 30, 2019.
12. Michelle Guerrero et al., "24-Hour Movement Behaviors and Impulsivity," *Pediatrics* 144, no. 3 (September 2019).
13. American Foundation for Suicide Prevention Fact Sheet, 2019.

14. Bill Mory, "TLC Can Help with Depression," *Herald Democrat,* October 17, 2019.
15. George Brown et al., "Social Class and Psychiatric Distress Among Women in an Urban Population," *Sociology,* May 1, 1975.
16. Johann Hari, *Lost Connections: Why You're Depressed and How to Find Hope* (New York: Bloomsbury, 2019).
17. Dan Buettner, *The Blue Zones* (Washington, D.C.: National Geographic, 2008).
18. Stephen Ilardi, *The Depression Cure* (Boston: Da Capo, 2010).
19. Peter Wehrwein, "Astounding Increase in Antidepressant Use by Americans," Harvard Health Publishing, October 20, 2011.
20. "Depression Fact Sheet," World Health Organization, 2020.
21. Christina Sagioglou and Tobias Greitemeyer, "Facebook's Emotional Consequences: Why Facebook Causes a Decrease in Mood and Why People Still Use it," *Computers in Human Behavior* 35 (June 2014): 359–363.
22. Edward O. Wilson, *Biophilia* (Boston: Harvard University Press, 1984).
23. Richard Louv, *Last Child in the Woods* (Chapel Hill, NC: Algonquin Books, 2008).
24. Donald Rakow and Greg Eells, *Nature Rx: Improving College Student Mental Health* (Ithaca, NY: Comstock, 2019).

CHAPTER 3: THE SOCIAL CONTAGION EFFECT

1. Paige Leskin, "American Kids Want to Be Famous on YouTube, and Kids in China Want to go to Space: Survey," *Business Insider,* July 17, 2019.
2. Danny Moloshok, "Kylie Jenner Is Not a Billionaire, Forbes Magazine Now Says," Reuters, May 29, 2020.
3. Andrew Martin, "The Puma Clyde: The Story of the First NBA Player Shoe Endorsement Deal," *Medium,* May 7, 2020.
4. Rick Telander, "Senseless," *Sports Illustrated,* May 14, 1990.
5. Nicholas Kardaras, "Digital Heroin," *New York Post,* 2016.
6. Lisa Cannon, "Nobody Is Lonelier Than Generation Z," *Lifeway Research,* May 4, 2018.

7. Jeff Horwitz, "The Facebook Files," *Wall Street Journal,* October 1, 2021.
8. Nicole Goodkind, "Whistleblower to Senate: Facebook Is 'Morally Bankrupt' and 'Disastrous' for Democracy," *Fortune,* October 5, 2021.
9. Simon Freeman, "Web Summit 2021: Facebook Whistleblower Frances Haugen Calls for Mark Zuckerberg to Step Down," *Evening Standard (UK),* November 2, 2021.
10. Brett Molina, "Facebook's Controversial Study: What You Need to Know," *USA Today,* June 30, 2014.
11. Tawnell Hobbs et al., "The Corpse Bride Diet: How TikTok Inundates Teens with Eating Disorder Videos," *Wall Street Journal,* December 17, 2021.
12. "Excessive Screen Time Linked to Suicide Risk," *Science Daily,* November 30, 2017.
13. Holly Shakya and Nicholas Christakis, "Association of Facebook Use with Compromised Well-Being: A Longitudinal Study," *American Journal of Epidemiology* 185, no. 3 (February 1, 2017): 203–211.
14. "Hyper-Texting and Hyper-Networking Pose New Health Risks for Teens," Case Western Reserve School of Medicine, November 9, 2010.
15. Mai-Ly Steers et al., "Seeing Everyone Else's Highlight Reels: How Facebook Usage Is Linked to Depressive Symptoms," *Journal of Social and Clinical Psychology* 33, no. 8 (October 2014): 701–731.
16. Julie Jargon, "Teen Girls Are Developing Tics. Doctors Say TikTok Could Be a Factor," *Wall Street Journal,* October 19, 2021.
17. Harvey Singer et al., "Elevated Intrasynaptic Dopamine Release in Tourette's Syndrome Measured by PET," *American Journal of Psychiatry* 159, no. 8 (August 1, 2002).
18. Andy Pulman and Jacqui Taylor. "Munchausen by Internet: Current Research and Future Direction," *Journal of Medical Internet Research* vol. 14,4 e115. 22 Aug. 2012.
19. Christopher Bass and Peter Halligan, "Factitious disorders and malingering: challenges for clinical assessment and management," *Lancet,* 383, 9926 (April 19, 2014): 1422–1432.
20. Mariam Hull et al., "Tics and TikTok: Functional Tics Spread Through Social Media," *Movement Disorder Clinical Practice* 8, no. 8 (November 2021): 1248–1252.

21. Evan Andrews, "What Was the Dancing Plague of 1518?," History.com, March 25, 2020.

CHAPTER 4: VIRAL VIOLENCE

1. Alex Shoumatoff, "The Mystery Suicides of Bridgend County," *Vanity Fair,* February 27, 2009.
2. Erica Goode, "Chemical Suicides, Popular in Japan, Are Increasing in the U.S.," *New York Times,* June 18, 2011.
3. Loren Coleman, *Suicide Clusters* (London: Faber & Faber, 1987).
4. Justin Moyer, "'Cannibal Cop' Wins in Court Again," *Washington Post,* December 4, 2015.
5. Zack Beauchamp, "Our Incel Problem," *Vox,* April 23, 2019.
6. Ashifa Kassam, "Woman Behind 'Incel' Says Angry Men Hijacked Her Word 'As Weapon of War,'" *Guardian,* April 25, 2018.
7. Adam Nagourney et al., "Before Deadly Spree, Troubled Since Age 8," *New York Times,* June 1, 2014.
8. "Elliot Rodger: How Misogynist Killer Became 'Incel Hero,'" BBC News, April 26, 2018.
9. Zack Beauchamp, "Our Incel Problem," *Vox,* April 23, 2019.
10. Robert Foyle Hunwick, "Why Does China Have So Many School Stabbings," *New Republic,* November 2, 2018.
11. "Gunfire on School Grounds in the United States," Everytown Research, 2021.
12. "The UT Tower Shooting," *TexasMonthly.com*
13. "Columbine Shooting," History.com, March 4, 2021.
14. Ned Potter et al., "Killer's Note: 'You Caused Me to Do This,'" ABC News, May 22, 2008.
15. Dave Cullen, *Columbine* (New York: Twelve, 2010).
16. Eric Horng and Kate Klonick, "'Columbine Massacre' Game Puts Players in Killers' Shoes," ABC News, September 15, 2006.
17. Susan Arendt, "V-Tech Rampage Creator Will Take Game Down for a Price," *Wired,* May 15, 2007.
18. Vinny Vella and Chris Palmer, "What We Know and Don't Know About the SEPTA Rape Case," *Philadelphia Inquirer,* November 1, 2021.

19. Michael Smerconish, "A Brother's Search for the Real Kitty Genovese," *Philadelphia Inquirer,* June 19, 2006.
20. Jane Musgrave, "Corey Johnson's Longtime Best Friend Tells Jury of Fatal Stabbing, Attacks at 2018 Sleepover," *Palm Beach Post,* October 28, 2021.

CHAPTER 5: SOCIAL MEDIA AND THE BINARY TRAP

1. Randy Sansone and Lori Sansone, "Borderline Personality and the Pain Paradox," *Psychiatry* 4, no. 4 (April 2007): 40–46.
2. Kristalyn Salters-Pedneault, "History of the Term 'Borderline' in Borderline Personality Disorder," *Verywell Mind,* April 10, 2020.
3. *Diagnostic and Statistical Manual of Mental Disorders,* 5th ed. (Washington, D.C.: American Psychiatric Association, 2013).
4. Kristalyn Salters-Pedneault, "Suicidality in Borderline Personality Disorder," *Verywell Mind,* March 26, 2020.
5. Anthony Bateman and Peter Fonagy, "Mentalization Based Treatment for BPD," *Journal of Personality Disorders* 18, no. 1 (June 2005).
6. Marsha Linehan, *Building a Life Worth Living* (New York: Random House, 2021).
7. Patrick Hahn, "The Real Myth of the Schizophrenogenic Mother," *Mad in America: Science, Psychiatry and Social Justice*, January 10, 2020.
8. Phil Reed, "Munchausen by Internet: What is Digital Factitious Disorder?," *Psychology Today*, November 30, 2021.
9. Taoufik Alsaadi et al., "Psychogenic Nonepileptic Seizures," *American Family Physician* 72, no. 5 (September 1, 2005): 849–856.
10. J. A. Lucy, "Sapir-Whorf Hypothesis," *International Encyclopedia of the Behavioral & Social Sciences,* 2001.
11. Lisa Littman, "Parent Reports of Adolescents and Young Adults Perceived to Show Signs of a Rapid Onset of Gender Dysphoria," *PLOS ONE,* 2018.
12. Lisa Märcz, "Feral Children: Questioning the Human-Animal Boundary from an Anthropological Perspective," BA thesis (September 2018).
13. Ibid.

14. Paroma Mitra and Ankit Jain, *Dissociative Identity Disorder* (Treasure Island, FL: StatPearls Publishing, 2022).

CHAPTER 6: THE NEW TECHNOCRACY

1. Margaret O'Mara, *The Code: Silicon Valley and the Remaking of America* (New York: Penguin Random House, 2019).
2. Adrienne LaFrance, "The Largest Autocracy on Earth," *Atlantic,* November 2021.
3. Paige Leskin, "A Facebook Cofounder Says That Zuckerberg's Master Plan Always Boiled Down to One Word: 'Domination,'" *Business Insider,* May 9, 2019.
4. Aaron Mak, "Mark Zuckerberg Wrote a Program to Beat a High Schooler at Scrabble," *Slate,* September 10, 2018.
5. Margaret O'Mara, *The Code: Silicon Valley and the Remaking of America* (New York: Penguin Random House, 2019).
6. *Ibid.*
7. Forbes Staff, "Bill Gates Honors Paul Allen, Recipient of the 2019 Forbes 400 Lifetime Achievement Award for Philanthropy, at Eighth Annual Summit on Philanthropy," *Forbes,* June 28, 2019.
8. Alvin Toffler, *Future Shock* (New York: Bantam, 1980).
9. Margaret O'Mara, *The Code: Silicon Valley and the Remaking of America* (New York: Penguin Random House, 2019).
10. Shoshana Zuboff, *The Age of Surveillance Capitalism* (New York: Public Affairs, 2019).
11. Halle Kiefer, "HBO Must 'Change Direction' So It Can Get More of That Sweet, Sweet Viewer Engagement," *Vulture,* July 8, 2018.
12. Nicholas Confessore, "Cambridge Analytica and Facebook: The Scandal and the Fallout So Far," *New York Times,* April 4, 2018.

CHAPTER 7: MAINTAINING THE DYSTOPIA

1. Olivia Solon, "Ex-Facebook President Sean Parker: Site Made to Exploit Human 'Vulnerability,'" *Guardian,* November 9, 2017.
2. Lina Khan, "The Amazon Antitrust Paradox," *Yale Law Journal,* January 2017.

3. Keach Hagey et al., "Facebook's Pushback: Stem the Leaks, Spin the Politics, Don't Say Sorry," *Wall Street Journal,* December 29, 2021.
4. Miranda Devine, *Laptop from Hell* (Franklin, TN: Post Hill Press, 2021).
5. Colin Lecher, "Facebook Executive: We Got Trump Elected, and We Shouldn't Stop Him in 2020," *Verge,* January 7, 2020.
6. David Leonhardt, "The Lab-Leak Theory," *New York Times*, May 27, 2021.
7. Josh Hawley, *The Tyranny of Big Tech* (Washington, D.C.: Regnery Publishing, 2021).
8. Brian Merchant, "Life and Death in Apple's Forbidden City," *Guardian,* June 18, 2017.
9. "Apple Boss Defends Conditions at iPhone Factory," BBC News, June 2, 2010.
10. Ciara Torres-Spelliscy, "Blood on Your Handset," *Slate,* September 20, 2013.
11. Glenn Leibowitz, "Apple CEO Tim Cook: This Is the No. 1 Reason We Make iPhones in China (It's Not What You Think)," *Inc.,* 2017.
12. "iPhone Would Cost $30,000 to Produce in the U.S.," *Medium,* September 23, 2019.
13. Cade Metz, "A.I. Is Learning from Humans. Many Humans," *New York Times Magazine,* August 16, 2019.

CHAPTER 8: GOD COMPLEXES AND IMMORTALITY

1. Ray Kurzweil, *The Singularity Is Near* (New York: Penguin Books, 2005).
2. Ernest Becker, *Denial of Death* (New York: Free Press, 1973).
3. Paul Ham, *Hiroshima Nagasaki* (New York: Thomas Dunne Books, 2014).
4. Plato, *The Republic,* trans. R. E. Allen (New Haven, CT: Yale University Press, 2006).
5. Jaden Urbi, "The Complicated Truth About Sophia the Robot—An Almost Human Robot or PR Stunt," CNBC, June 5, 2018.

6. Adrian Cho, "Tiny Black Holes Could Trigger Collapse of the Universe—Except That They Don't," *Science,* August 3, 2015.
7. "Stephen Hawking Warned Artificial Intelligence Could End Human Race," *Economic Times,* March 14, 2018.
8. *Hyper Evolution: Rise of the Robots, directed and produced by Matt Cottingham* (London: Windfall Films, 2018).

CHAPTER 9: MY PERSONAL ODYSSEY

1. I also describe my near-death, coma, and rebirth in my earlier book *How Plato and Pythagoras Can Save Your Life* (San Francisco: Conari Press, 2011).
2. Iamblichus, *On the Pythagorean Life* (Liverpool: Liverpool University Press, 1998).
3. Michael Murphy and James Redfield, *God and the Evolving Universe* (New York: TarcherPerigee, 2003)
4. Porphyry, *Life of Pythagoras,* English edition (1920).

CHAPTER 10: BEYOND THERAPY

1. "The Great Halifax Explosion," History.com.
2. Jerome Groopman, "The Grief Industry," *New Yorker,* 2004.
3. Thomas Szasz, *The Manufacture of Madness* (New York: Syracuse University Press, 1970).
4. James Hillman, *The Soul's Code* (New York: Ballantine Books, 1996).
5. Kelly McGonigal, "How To Make Stress Your Friend," TED Global, 2013.
6. Roy Baumeister et al., "Exploding the Self-Esteem Myth," *Scientific American,* January 2005.
7. Walter Mischel, *The Marshmallow Test* (New York: Little, Brown, 2014).
8. Jennifer Clopton, "ADHD Rates Are Rising in the U.S., but Why?," WebMD, November 26, 2018.
9. Perri Klass, "Fixated by Screens, but Seemingly Nothing Else," *New York Times,* May 9, 2011.

10. Jonathon Haidt and Greg Lukianoff, *The Coddling of the American Mind* (New York: Penguin Press, 2018).
11. Nassim Taleb, *Antifragile: Things That Gain from Disorder* (New York: Random House, 2011).
12. Bessel van der Kolk, *The Body Keeps the Score* (New York: Penguin, 2014).
13. Lawrence Patihis et al., "Reports of Recovered Memories of Abuse in Therapy in a Large Age-Representative U.S. National Sample: Therapy Type and Decade Comparisons," *Clinical Psychological Science*, May 31, 2018.
14. Will Self, "A Posthumous Shock: How Everything Became Trauma," *Harper's,* December 2021.
15. E. Van Teijlingen, *Midwifery and the Medicalization of Childbirth* (Hauppauge, NY: Nova Science Publishers, 2000).
16. S. K. Tamana et al., "Screen-time Is Associated with Inattention Problems in Preschoolers: Results from the CHILD Birth Cohort Study," *PLOS ONE* 14, no. 4, e0213995 (2019).
17. Angela Duckworth, *Grit: The Power of Passion and Perseverance* (New York: Scribner, 2016).
18. Viktor Frankl, *Man's Search for Meaning* (Boston: Beacon Press, 1946).
19. Nicholas Kulish, "Homeless in Poland, Preparing an Odyssey at Sea," *New York Times,* August 1, 2009.

CHAPTER 11: THE PHILOSOPHER-WARRIOR

1. Benvenuto Cellini, *The Autobiography of Benvenuto Cellini* (New York: Modern Library, 1910).
2. C. G. Jung, *Archetypes and the Collective Unconscious* (Princeton, NJ: Princeton University Press, 1959).
3. Joseph Campbell, *The Hero with a Thousand Faces* (Novato, CA: New World Library, 1949).
4. Karl Jaspers, *The Future of Mankind* (Chicago, IL: University of Chicago, 1961).
5. Bertrand Russell, *A History of Western Philosophy* (New York: Simon & Shuster, 1945).

6. Plato, *The Republic,* trans. R. E. Allen (New Haven, CT: Yale University Press, 2006).
7. Richard Matheson, "The Enemy Within," *Star Trek*, Season 1, Episode 5. Directed by Leo Penn. Aired October 6, 1966 on NBC.
8. Nikos Kazantzakis, *Zorba the Greek* (New York: Simon & Schuster, 1946).